Also by FRANCES TOWNER GIEDT,
BONNIE SANDERS POLIN, PH.D.,
and NUTRITION SERVICES STAFF of JOSLIN DIABETES CENTER

The Joslin Diabetes Gourmet Cookbook:
  Heart-Healthy, Everyday Recipes for Family and Friends

The Joslin Diabetes Quick and Easy Cookbook:
  200 Recipes for 1 to 4 People

The Joslin Diabetes Healthy Carbohydrate Cookbook

The Joslin Diabetes Great Chefs Cook Healthy Cookbook

Frances Towner Giedt AND *Bonnie Sanders Polin*, PH.D.,
WITH THE NUTRITION SERVICES STAFF
OF JOSLIN DIABETES CENTER

SIMON & SCHUSTER
NEW YORK, LONDON,
TORONTO, SYDNEY, SINGAPORE

Simon & Schuster
Rockefeller Center
1230 Avenue of the Americas
New York, NY 10020

First Simon & Schuster trade paperback edition 2003

Simon & Schuster and colophon are registered trademarks of Simon & Schuster, Inc.

For information regarding special discounts for bulk purchases, please contact
Simon & Schuster Special Sales at 1-800-456-6798 or business@simonandschuster.com

DESIGNED BY DEBORAH KERNER/DANCING BEARS DESIGN

Manufactured in the United States of America

10 9 8 7 6 5 4 3 2 1

The Library of Congress has cataloged the hardcover edition as follows:
Giedt, Frances Towner.
    The Joslin diabetes great chefs cook healthy cookbook / Frances Towner Giedt and Bonnie Sanders Polin,
  Ph.D., with the nutrition services staff at Joslin Diabetes Center; foreword by Alan C. Moses, M.D.
       p.   cm.
    Includes index.
    1. Diabetes—Diet therapy—Recipes.   I. Title: Great chefs cook healthy cookbook. II. Polin,
Bonnie Sanders.   III. Joslin Diabetes Center.   IV. Title.

RC662 .G538 2002
641.5'6314—dc21   2002070745

ISBN 0-7432-1586-9
0-7432-1588-5 (Pbk)

GREAT CHEFS® is a trademark of G.C.I., Inc.

Acknowledgments

Our expertise with recipes suitable for people who have diabetes has grown through the years of living with and writing about the disease. That know-how is still expanding with knowledge and inspiration springing from many sources. We are indebted to many individuals, both intimates and total strangers, who have, in their own unique ways, contributed to this cookbook of which we are very proud.

To the 100 chefs without whom this cookbook could not have happened, we extend our heartfelt thanks and appreciation. From our first contact through the final submission of their recipes, we have been impressed by their knowledge of food. Many were acquainted with cooking for people with diabetes; others were eager to learn. All were enthusiastic about the project and their fantastic recipes will inspire us all to be even more inventive with our cooking.

To our colleagues at the Joslin Diabetes Center: Joan Hill, R.D., C.D.E., L.D., Director of Education; Karen Chalmers, M.S., R.D., C.D.E., L.D., Director of Nutrition; Judy Giusti, M.S., R.D., C.D.E., L.D.; Amy Campbell, M.S., R.D., C.D.E., L.D.; Diana Hanson, M.S., R.D., L.D.; Laurie Higgins, R.D., C.D.E., L.D.; Patty Rais-Keeley, R.D., C.D.E., L.D.; Melinda Maryniuk, M. Ed., R.D., C.D.E., L.D., F.A.D.A.; JoAnne Rizzotto, R.D., C.D.E., L.D.; Emmy Suhl, M.S., R.D., C.D.E., L.D.; and Susan Sjostrom, J.D., Director of Publications. Your nutritional data for the recipes has helped us to create yet another invaluable cookbook for people with diabetes and anyone who wants to cook and eat marvelous, healthy food. We also wish to thank Alan C. Moses, M.D., Chief Medical Officer at Joslin Diabetes Center for his insightful Foreword.

To our editor Sydny Miner, who performed her difficult job superbly and diplomatically, we extend our special thanks. We also wish to acknowledge the whole production team at Simon & Schuster: Estelle Laurence, copy editor; Deborah Kerner, designer; Toni Rachiele, copy editor; Linda Evans, production manager; and Laura Holmes, editorial assistant. A special recognition goes to Ann Stratton, for her stunning food photography; Rory Trovato, for his superb food styling; Bette Blau, for her terrific propping; and Jackie Seow, for her arresting cover design. All of you put your hearts and talents into this book and our gratitude is beyond words.

To our agent Loretta Fidel, who has been a deep well of sound advice, encouragement, and good nature. Thank you for helping us along the way from concept to publication.

To our husbands, David Giedt and Gerry Polin, M.D., for their constant support, love, and unending patience during the many months that our lives were consumed by the writing of this cookbook. They have happily eaten virtually all of the recipes and enthusiastically encouraged us to recruit more and more chefs. Without them our joy in cooking and writing cookbooks would be greatly diminished.

To those who contributed ideas on chefs to bring into the book—from food editors, restaurant critics, friends, and colleagues to faceless names from around the world who answered our e-mails for assistance in identifying those chefs who should be approached. You number far too many to individually thank.

To you, the reader, for yearning to expand your knowledge about food and cooking for people with diabetes, for yourself, your family, and your friends. Our heartfelt thanks.

—FRANCES TOWNER GIEDT AND
BONNIE SANDERS POLIN, PH.D.

We want to thank those who worked tirelessly for reimbursement for medical nutrition therapy. It is now a reality for those with diabetes. Since education is the framework of diabetes self-management and behavior change, it is important for each patient to learn everything he or she needs to know about diabetes and the challenge of choosing healthy foods for meals and snacks.

The Joslin philosophy still continues to echo the thoughts of Elliott P. Joslin, expressed more than fifty years ago: "Diabetes is a serious disease and deserves the best effort of doctor and patient from start to finish."

—JUDY GIUSTI, M.S., R.D., C.D.E., L.D.

JOAN HILL, R.D., C.D.E., L.D., DIRECTOR OF EDUCATION

Contents

Foreword

$\mathcal{F}$ood is often the focal point of our social interactions. Snacks while watching the ballgame, friends sharing a dinner at your home, an evening out on the town at a restaurant . . . these are some of the events that have become a central part of the entertainment process. For individuals with diabetes, these occasions may create a sense of uncertainty or apprehension. What can I eat? How will it affect my blood glucose levels? How much insulin should I take?

People with diabetes are taught that what they eat can affect their glucose control and may impact their long-term quality of life. Emphasis often is placed on weight loss for adolescents or adults with type 2 diabetes and on consistency of food intake for patients with type 1 (insulin dependent) diabetes. However, over the last decade, there is increasing recognition that there is a much greater number of food options for patients with diabetes. We now focus on "healthy" eating for *all* people including individuals with diabetes. The Joslin Diabetes Center has been proud to contribute to the health and improved quality of life of patients with diabetes by creating a series of cookbooks that include practical, fun, and healthy ideas for "good eating." The current book is no exception.

In the pages that follow, you will see that people with diabetes can eat every bit as well as people who do not have diabetes. Here you will share with some of the great chefs an approach to food preparation and eating that ranges from *haute cuisine* to the simple "throw together" meal. Be the master chef yourself! Experiment with new ingredients while at the same time keeping track of the amount of fat, protein, and carbohydrate that goes into that special meal. These chefs all share a desire to make their creations part of the daily lives of people who previously may have felt restricted in their approach both to eating out and to eating in. Now we *all* can share and enjoy these culinary delights while eating healthier meals—the same wonderful dishes to be enjoyed by those who have diabetes and those who don't. Enjoy!

—ALAN C. MOSES, M.D., CHIEF MEDICAL OFFICER,
JOSLIN DIABETES CENTER AND JOSLIN CLINIC

Introduction

This book is a second of its kind. Our first book, *The Joslin Diabetes Gourmet Cookbook*, originally published nine years ago, allowed people with diabetes to enjoy gourmet foods with their families for the first time. After its publication and becoming the winner of the coveted James Beard Foundation Cookbook Award and a Julia Child Cookbook Award nomination, we received hundreds of letters thanking us for making a person with diabetes feel more like the rest of the world, and for bringing families back to the dinner table where everyone could, and would, share the same meal. We also received countless letters from physicians, diabetes educators, and dietitians who thanked us for helping their patients adhere to regimes that before had been burdensome. Our second and third books are written specifically for those who cook primarily for only one or two people and for those who wish to eat a more plant-based diet. These cookbooks are also proof that healthy food need not be boring or bland.

Now, we are proud to offer a cookbook of recipes from some of the premier chefs of the world who have agreed to share their talents and expertise. Month after month, world-class chefs publish cookbooks for the general population with recipes that cannot be used by those of us with diabetes, because specific nutritional data is not included and the recipes are usually too high in fat and calories. *The Joslin Diabetes Great Chefs Cook Healthy Cookbook* is a resource for anyone who has felt alienated from other gourmet chef cookbooks because they want or need to cook healthfully yet wish to have beautiful, incredibly flavorful meals.

The Joslin Diabetes Great Chefs Cook Healthy Cookbook includes recipes that will allow you to count the carbohydrates, exchanges, or calories of your daily diet while enjoying diverse, elegant meals from soups to desserts. It's like having a four-star restaurant in your own home, and is a book to read and reread as you travel around the world of great chefs and their restaurants.

In this new book, you'll find everything from the "super elegant" to the "What's for dinner? I just walked in the door." The chefs, who share these recipes with you for your benefit, have no desire to inhibit your own flair. Read the recipes and you'll see that in many cases, the recipe is for a whole meal—entrée, supporting starches and vegetables, as well as the tongue-tingling sauces and pretty garnishes that make a dish look like one from a four-star restaurant (which, in most cases, they are). That doesn't mean you have to prepare the entire recipe. You might just wish to make the entrée, adding a steamed vegetable and salad of your own. Another time you might only wish to prepare the supporting starches and vegetables to add to broiled fish or chicken seasoned your own way. Other times you'll want to "dog-ear" a recipe to go back to for a particular sauce or a fancy garnish, to put a crowning touch on a dish of your own. Try a new technique or a different cuisine. Buy a food you've never tried or make an old friend in a new way. In some recipes we have separated out exchanges for various parts of these recipes so you can do just that. You will learn new ways to make old standbys more exciting by adding new sauces and condiments that can be used in your kitchen with many other meals.

The Joslin Diabetes Great Chefs Cook Healthy Cookbook is a book to read and reread. It is a series of cooking classes for anyone interested in learning to cook incredible food that is good for you. It is full of tips to make you a better home cook. We, too, have learned from the generous chefs who shared their cooking secrets. You will note that there is a preponderance of fish and shellfish recipes, but that's actually quite indicative of how the rest of the world and we are now eating—more fish and less meat.

This has not been an easy book to write. Those of us with diabetes, whether type 1 or type 2, know what we must do to control blood glucose levels on a daily and sometimes hourly basis. Writing our own recipes and being in total control of what we write, is difficult, but routine. Trying to set guidelines for our prospective chefs brought back to us, in the most graphic terms, just how daunting it can be for someone with diabetes or other health issues with dietary considerations to eat in a healthy way. Each recipe is as the chef planned with only some changes in the portion size (no doggy-bagging is allowed or needed with these recipes) plus some minor changes in the amount of fats by only using a limited amount of the sauce or dressing instead of the whole recipe. (This makes for some great leftovers of su-perb sauces and dressings for other meals.) Guidelines are important, and making the nutri-tion profile of a glorious recipe conform to healthy amounts of fat, carbohydrates, and protein sometimes led to a recipe being slightly altered, with the chef's approval, or if the recipe could not be changed, regrettably not included. The recipes appearing in the book are always as the chef intended, a personal expression of his or her ingenuity and style of cooking.

Why did we persevere? Food is the central part of all of our lives. As people with dia-betes we may feel we have had to give up some of our favorite foods. We know that we must eat in a healthy balanced way, and at the same time we want to enjoy the best that is avail-able in terms of recipes and menus. In many cases, the chefs already had an awareness of di-abetes by having a loved one or a friend with diabetes, or, in some cases, having it themselves. In other instances, the chefs asked a lot of questions and, on their own, researched diabetes and its dietary requirements before they wrote down their recipes. Some chefs have re-ported back that they are now cooking healthier and that their customers are responding very positively to the changes.

These chefs believe, as do we, that ingredients are everything in cooking. In most cases the chefs use only organic foods—ones free of pesticides and growth hormones and all of the other things used by growers and producers to increase productivity but not necessarily guard your health. Whenever you have a choice, consider buying organic. You'll cook and eat better. Nowadays organic foods are offered in local supermarkets as well as in natural foods stores, and in many cases, are only a click of your mouse away via the Internet. See Sources (page 296).

We are very proud to present *The Joslin Diabetes Great Chefs Cook Healthy Cookbook*, an opus dedicated to our chefs and to you our readers, who we know will relish these recipes for years to come. We feel this is the most unique and delectable collection of healthy recipes ever assembled, all written so you can duplicate them in your home kitchen. Enjoy!

—FRANCES TOWNER GIEDT AND
BONNIE SANDERS POLIN, PH.D.

A NOTE FROM JOSLIN DIABETES CENTER

People with diabetes come from all walks of life. Rich or poor, the disease does not discriminate. Those who have had diabetes for 20 or 30 years or longer may remember restrictive meal plans. Perhaps the most restrictive aspect of these meal plans was the ban on sugar. Of course, times have changed. Today, we know that people with diabetes can eat healthily and still enjoy deliciously prepared cuisine. Carbohydrate counting provides a tool for improved blood glucose control. Whether it is used to adjust insulin based on the amount of carbohydrate eaten or to allow people to make consistent carbohydrate choices, people with diabetes have more flexibility than they did 20 years ago. The Nutrition Services Staff at Joslin Diabetes Center believes that everyone in the family, including people with diabetes, can enjoy healthy eating and dining out. General recommendations for healthy eating are the same for everyone in the family: Eat whole grains, fruit, vegetables, and legumes; limit protein portions; decrease saturated fat; and drink plenty of water to keep well hydrated.

Dining out should be a positive experience, not boring or restrictive. People with diabetes can dine at their favorite restaurants and enjoy eating healthful meals. With the ability to check blood glucose frequently, give multiple daily injections of insulin or wear an insulin pump, diabetes no longer means following restrictive meal plans. If on a special occasion you eat more than you had planned, go for a walk. This will help to burn those extra calories for those of you who are watching your weight. It will also help to keep blood glucose under control.

For those who like to take extra time to prepare delicious food, this book will provide you with the epicurean pleasures of fine dining in the comfort of your own home.

Joslin Choices and nutritional information are listed for each recipe using the latest data available from ESHA (The Food Processor, Version 7.7), the United States Department of Agriculture, and, when necessary, manufacturers' food labels. If the ingredient called for is listed with alternative ingredients, the calculations were made with the first ingredients listed. Optional ingredients were not included in the nutritional analysis. Recipes for stock are based on the stock recipes given in this book. To obtain similar sodium counts, use a salt-free, fat-free broth, canned or homemade.

Nutrition is one of the keys to diabetes self-management in addition to exercise and medication. Use this cookbook as a tool to live a healthier lifestyle. Take advantage of the wide variety of delicious recipes and sample menus; make meal planning and dining a creative, enjoyable experience. *Bon appétit!*

—JUDY GIUSTI, M.S., R.D., C.D.E., L.D.
DIABETES NUTRITION EDUCATOR
JOSLIN DIABETES CENTER

Judy Giusti, M.S., R.D., C.D.E., L.D., a nutrition educator in Nutrition Services at Joslin Diabetes Center, provided nutrition expertise and analysis for our recipes. Judy is a certified diabetes educator and provides nutrition and diabetes education at Joslin Diabetes Center to adults, adolescents, and young children. She also works in the Joslin Diabetes and Pregnancy Program providing nutrition counseling to pregnant women with type 1, type 2, and gestational diabetes. She is a team member of the Diabetes Outpatient Intensive Treatment Program. Judy has lectured nationally and locally and has written articles for both health professionals and patients.

Starters, Soups, and Salads

Starters

Spiced Beef and Rice-Stuffed Grape Leaves with T'zatziki Sauce

Maha Jeha Arnondin, MEZZA
ARLINGTON, TEXAS

Until now the recipe for these savory stuffed grape leaves has been written only in Chef Maha's native language, safeguarded by successive generations of her Lebanese family. At her restaurant, Maha uses only fresh grape leaves to make these spicy appetizers. She grows her own vines to assure her supply and freezes each leaf between small squares of parchment paper for use throughout the year. Once baked, the stuffed grape leaves can be frozen to enjoy later. If you must use brined leaves, be sure to rinse them well and drain on paper towels before using.

1½ cups uncooked white rice
6 ounces butter, melted and clarified
2 teaspoons salt
1¼ teaspoons white pepper
½ teaspoon ground cinnamon
1¼ teaspoons ground nutmeg

1 pound extra-lean ground beef
about 90 fresh grape leaves
3 cups Chicken Stock (page 31)
juice of 1 or 2 large lemons
T'zatziki Sauce (recipe follows)

Rinse the rice with hot water, drain, and place in a large mixing bowl. Add the clarified butter, salt, white pepper, cinnamon, and nutmeg. Mix well. Add the ground beef and mix well.

Blanch the grape leaves in batches in boiling water for 10 seconds. Remove the grape leaves and plunge into a bowl of ice water to stop the cooking. Carefully lay out several grape leaves on a work surface. Fill each leaf with about 1 teaspoon of the rice-beef mixture, depending on size of the leaf. Fold the sides in and roll tightly, enclosing the rice-beef mixture. Lay the filled grape leaves side by side in a heavy shallow roasting pan. Continue filling the grape leaves until all the filling has been used.

Preheat the oven to 250°F. Cover the filled grape leaves with the Chicken Stock. Tightly cover the pan with plastic wrap, then aluminum foil. Bake for 1 hour. Check to see if the rice is tender; bake longer if needed, until the liquid is absorbed.

Remove from the oven and sprinkle the baked grape leaves with the fresh lemon juice. Arrange 6 grape leaves on each serving plate with 2 tablespoons of the T'zatziki Sauce. Freeze any remaining stuffed grape leaves. Once frozen, transfer to a self-sealing plastic freezer bag.

MAKES ABOUT 90 STUFFED GRAPE LEAVES

Joslin Choices (6 stuffed grape leaves): 1½ medium-fat protein, 1½ carbohydrate (bread/starch), ½ fat

Per Serving: 268 calories (41% calories from fat), 13 g total fat (7 g saturated fat), 14 g protein, 27 g carbohydrate, 3 g dietary fiber, 38 mg cholesterol, 517 mg sodium, 236 mg potassium

T'zatziki Sauce

1 large cucumber
1½ cups plain nonfat yogurt
½ tablespoon Worcestershire sauce

¼ cup finely chopped fresh mint
salt (optional)

Peel the cucumber and cut in half lengthwise. Using a small spoon, scoop out and discard the seeds. Finely mince half the cucumber. Puree the remaining half in a food processor or blender.

In a bowl, combine the minced and pureed cucumber, yogurt, Worcestershire, and mint. Season with salt (if using) to taste. Chill until ready to serve. Use within 3 days.

MAKES ABOUT 2 CUPS

Joslin Choices: free food

Per 2-Tablespoon Serving: 12 calories (0 calories from fat), 0 total fat (0 saturated fat), 1 g protein, 2 g carbohydrate, 0 dietary fiber, 1 mg cholesterol, 16 mg sodium, 11 mg potassium

Carpaccio Vegetariano (Vegetarian Carpaccio)

Maristella Innocenti, I COPPI
NEW YORK CITY

Whether dining in the warm interior or the lush garden, you might think you're actually eating in Tuscany. Maristella Innocenti came from Florence to cook for her sister Lorella and her husband John Brennan, owners of this delightful East Village restaurant, using their family recipes. This carpaccio is very simple, relying on the freshest of ingredients and a drizzle of good extra-virgin Tuscan olive oil for its superb intermingling of earthy flavors.

2 medium zucchini, very thinly sliced
8 large button mushrooms, very thinly sliced
salt (optional)
freshly ground pepper
4 teaspoons pine nuts

1 8-ounce piece Grana Padano cheese or
  Parmigiano, thinly shaved
4 teaspoons extra-virgin olive oil
4 teaspoons finely chopped parsley

Arrange the zucchini on a large serving plate and top with the mushrooms.

Season with a little salt (if using) and pepper to taste. Sprinkle with the pine nuts and cheese shavings.

Drizzle with the olive oil, sprinkle with the parsley, and serve.

MAKES 4 SERVINGS

Joslin Choices: 2 medium-fat protein, 1 vegetable, 1 fat

Per Serving: 212 calories (61% calories from fat), 15 g total fat (6 g saturated fat), 15 g protein, 6 g carbohydrate, 2 g dietary fiber, 22 mg cholesterol, 533 mg sodium, 467 mg potassium

Dungeness Crab Martini with Pickled Cucumbers

Tim Richards, BOEDEAN SEAFOOD
TULSA, OKLAHOMA

If you live in Green Country, the northeast section of Oklahoma that contains Tulsa and its surrounding towns, you can purchase fresh fish as well as gourmet catering at Boedean Seafood. At their restaurant, Boedean, seafood is presented in as beautiful a fashion as it is at any restaurant in the country. Chef Richards is a graduate of the culinary program at Oklahoma State University and has been a chef in Tulsa for the last 15 years. His recipes marry the freshest of ingredients with his talent for combining diverse items. This is always a pleasant surprise to those of us who hail from the Coast and have moved to Tulsa. Salute Chef Richards: The starter he shares is the healthiest martini we know.

PICKLED CUCUMBERS:
1 medium cucumber
¼ cup rice wine vinegar
1 tablespoon sugar
pinch salt (optional)

1 teaspoon celery salt
1 teaspoon ground white pepper
2 dashes Tabasco sauce
kosher salt (optional)
freshly ground pepper

CRAB MARTINI:
¼ cup tomato juice
¼ cup ketchup
⅛ cup rice wine vinegar
⅛ cup prepared horseradish

¾ pound Dungeness crabmeat (see Note below)

⅛ cup shredded fresh horseradish for garnish
chopped fresh chives for garnish

Peel the cucumber and remove the seeds. Thinly slice crosswise and combine with the vinegar, sugar, and salt (if using). Cover and refrigerate for 2 hours.

In a bowl, combine the tomato juice, ketchup, vinegar, prepared horseradish, celery salt, white pepper, Tabasco, kosher salt (if using), and freshly ground pepper to taste. Toss with the crabmeat.

TO SERVE: Fill 4 martini glasses with the cucumber mixture. Place the crab mixture on top and garnish with the fresh horseradish and chives. Serve cold.

MAKES 4 SERVINGS

Joslin Choices: 2 very-low-fat protein, 1 carbohydrate (bread/starch)

Per Serving: 129 calories (9% calories from fat), 1 g total fat (0 saturated fat), 19 g protein, 12 g carbohydrate, 1 g dietary fiber, 60 mg cholesterol, 1,004 mg sodium, 250 mg potassium

Note: This recipe is not recommended for low-sodium diets. If your market doesn't sell Dungeness crabmeat, you can also use king, snow, stone, blue, or back-fin crab.

Smoked Duck, Radish, and Almond Rolls
with Grilled Watermelon, Frisée, and Herb Salad

Tim Pak Poy, CLAUDE'S
SYDNEY

When chef-owner Tim Pak Poy took over Claude's, he brought this already popular Sydney restaurant to new culinary heights. Situated on Oxford Street, Woollahra, in the heart of the city's gallery and antique district, Claude's is regarded as one of Australia's finest restaurants by critics and patrons of superbly crafted food. His recipe here shows Tim Pak Poy's expertise with duck. You can buy duck breast already smoked, see Sources (page 296), or, if you're feeling ambitious, smoke it yourself.

Fresh lychees, the Chinese fruit with a creamy flesh in a hard bright red shell, are available in many markets from May to about mid-July. They are also available canned but we've never seen them made without sugar, so we made the Lychee Puree a separate part of the recipe as an optional garnish.

2 smoked duck breasts, about 1 pound total

5 sheets nori (dried seaweed)

6 red radishes, cleaned

¼ cup sliced almonds, toasted

3 scallions, white part only, thinly sliced
  on diagonal

2 teaspoons balsamic vinegar

1 tablespoon extra-virgin olive oil

salt (optional)

freshly ground pepper

1 10-inch round seedless watermelon, sliced 1 inch
  thick, about 1 pound total with rind

1 small head frisée, washed, dried, and torn into
  bite-size pieces

½ cup fresh French tarragon, leaves picked, rinsed,
  and dried

½ cup fresh chervil, leaves picked, rinsed, and
  dried

¾ cup flat-leaf parsley, rinsed and dried

¼ cup purchased plum sauce

Lychee Puree (optional, recipe follows)

Preheat the oven to 350°F. Line a baking sheet with parchment paper.

Using a very sharp knife, carefully slice the duck breasts lengthwise into very thin slices, discarding any fat. Set the slices aside. Finely shred any duck scraps and set aside.

Cut the nori sheets into 1-cm (about ⅓-inch) strips and lightly toast in the oven. If done ahead, store for up to 2 days in an airtight container until ready to use.

Shred the radishes. Set aside 1 tablespoon of the almonds. Combine the remaining almonds with the radishes and scallions. Combine 1 teaspoon of the balsamic vinegar with 1 teaspoon of the olive oil. Add to the almond-radish mixture. Toss to evenly coat. Season with salt (if using) and pepper to taste.

TO ASSEMBLE: Lay 2 slices of duck diametrically opposed on a flat work surface, overlapping slightly. Repeat until you have 12 sets of overlapped slices. Divide the almond-radish mixture between the sets, spreading evenly on the duck slices. Working from one end, roll up each set, jelly-roll style. Secure with a toothpick and set upright on a tray. (At this point, the duck rolls can be assembled ahead and refrigerated for up to 2 hours with a light bread board resting on top to firm the rolls.)

When almost ready to serve, light a grill and lightly oil the grid. When the coals are hot, place the watermelon slice on the grill about 4 to 6 inches above medium coals. Grill for 1½ to 2 minutes per side, turning once, until lightly streaked with grill marks. Remove from the grill and cut into 12 wedges.

In a bowl, toss together the frisée, tarragon, chervil, and parsley. Combine the remaining 1 teaspoon balsamic vinegar and 2 teaspoons olive oil. Drizzle over the frisée mixture and toss again to evenly coat.

TO FINISH: Wrap the duck rolls in the nori strips, brushing one end of the strip with a little water to form a seal. Arrange the duck rolls upright on individual plates. Top each roll with a teaspoon of the plum sauce and scatter the reserved almonds decoratively on the top. Arrange a wedge of the grilled watermelon and a portion of the frisée salad on each plate. If using, place the Lychee Puree in a squeeze bottle and pipe a pattern around the duck roll. Serve at once.

MAKES 12 SERVINGS

Joslin Choices (without Lychee Puree): 1 medium-fat protein, 1 vegetable

Per Serving: 92 calories (37% calories from fat), 4 g total fat (1 g saturated fat), 9 g protein, 6 g carbohydrate, 1 g dietary fiber, 29 mg cholesterol, 53 mg sodium, 230 mg potassium

Lychee Puree

½ pound fresh lychees, peeled and seeded
1 tablespoon fresh lime juice

1 tablespoon confectioners' sugar

Place all the ingredients in a food processor or blender. Puree until smooth.

MAKES ENOUGH FOR 12 SERVINGS

Joslin Choices (Lychee Puree only): free food

Per Serving: 15 calories (5% calories from fat), 0 total fat (0 saturated fat), 0 protein, 4 g carbohydrate, 0 dietary fiber, 0 cholesterol, 0 sodium, 34 mg potassium

Dinner Buffet Menu

Smoked Duck, Radish, and Almond Rolls with Grilled Watermelon,
Frisée, and Herb Salad (page 10)

Spiced Beef and Rice-Stuffed Grape Leaves with Tzatziki Sauce (page 5)

Haricots Verts, Couscous, and Mint Salad (page 139)

Herbed Shrimp Wrapped in Prosciutto (page 14)

Joslin Choices: 3½ medium-fat protein, 2½ carbohydrate (bread/starch), 1 vegetable,
1½ fat, 602 calories (44% calories from fat)

Olive Oil

This wonderful oil is used by virtually all of the chefs—they love it as much as we do for cooking—from light forms to the very first cold-pressed. When olives ripen they change colors from green to violet and then to black and can be pressed for their oil at any stage of the ripening process. This is why olive oils have differences in flavor, viscosity, and color.

Virgin olive oil is the most sought after and the most expensive. Some people say virgin olive oil (extra-virgin means that the acidity is naturally less then 1%) is wasted for cooking. Many of these chefs disagree. They call for it in cooking. We formerly used extra-virgin oil only in uncooked foods, such as salads. No more; we're using this wonderful oil in cooking and seeing a difference in the end result.

If the olive oil says "olive oil" without mention of "virgin" or "extra-virgin," you can be assured that it has been heated or changed with chemical influence or both. These oils are still fine to use, but they are a bit dull in taste.

The last category, "light olive oil," means the oil has been filtered, removing the color and some of what makes olive oils taste so good. If you're cooking with it, that won't matter so much; but if you're dressing a salad, mix it with some extra-virgin olive oil to give it back some of its integrity.

Whether you choose a domestic olive oil or one imported from Spain, Greece, France, or Italy is a matter of taste. Picking an olive oil is much like choosing a cheese—some are strong, others are mild, some are peppery in taste, others are buttery and sweet, some are grassy and citrusy while yet others are fruity. Some are just exquisite. Choose the one that is to your taste.

Herbed Shrimp Wrapped in Prosciutto

Peter Assue, CITY LIMITS DINER

WHITE PLAINS, NEW YORK

At this bright and whimsical diner with two locations in Westchester County, Chef Assue delights his guests with simple, artfully prepared dishes such as this scrumptious appetizer where the flavor of the herb-infused shrimp plays with the highly seasoned taste of the prosciutto wrapping.

¼ cup extra-virgin olive oil

zest of 2 lemons

4 sprigs fresh rosemary

4 sprigs fresh thyme

4 cloves garlic, minced

1 teaspoon fennel seeds, toasted and crushed

24 large raw shrimp (16 to 20 count), peeled and deveined

12 very thin slices prosciutto, cut in half lengthwise, about 2 ounces total

fresh rosemary and thyme leaves for garnish (optional)

In a nonreactive bowl, combine 3 tablespoons of the olive oil, the lemon zest, rosemary, thyme, garlic, and fennel seed. Toss with the shrimp, cover, and refrigerate for 30 minutes. Drain.

Lay 1 slice of the prosciutto vertically on a clean work surface. Place 1 shrimp at the bottom and roll the shrimp in the prosciutto. Transfer to a baking sheet that has been lined with waxed paper. Repeat until all the shrimp are wrapped.

Place a sauté pan over medium heat. Swirl in the remaining 1 tablespoon olive oil. When the oil is hot, carefully add the shrimp a few at a time. Do not overcrowd the pan. Sauté for 1½ to 2 minutes on each side, transferring the cooked shrimp to a baking sheet that has been lined with paper towels to drain. Continue until all the shrimp are cooked.

Arrange 3 shrimp on each of 8 small plates. If using, garnish each serving with a scattering of rosemary and thyme leaves. Serve warm.

MAKES 8 SERVINGS

Joslin Choices: 1 medium-fat protein

Per Serving: 92 calories (70% calories from fat), 7 g total fat (1 g saturated fat), 6 g protein, 1 g carbohydrate, 0 dietary fiber, 35 mg cholesterol, 120 mg sodium, 73 mg potassium

Baked Goat Cheese Parcels with Sweet-and-Sour Leeks

Peter Gorton, THE HORN OF PLENTY
TAVISTOCK, ENGLAND

Situated in an elegant country home turned into a hotel, The Horn of Plenty in Devon beckons guests to relax over a meal of layered textures and tastes. Chef Gorton's early training took him to Melbourne, Bangkok, London, and Paris; one only has to read his changing menus to see nuances of these cuisines. Peter has written a cookbook, owns a renowned cooking school, and writes regular articles in national and local culinary publications. He also has television shows in Great Britain and participates in charity events, giving his time to fight hunger and to aid the ill.

GOAT CHEESE PARCELS:
5 ounces low-fat goat cheese
freshly ground pepper
4 filo dough sheets
refrigerated butter-flavored cooking spray
2 tablespoons finely chopped hazelnuts

BEET DRESSING:
2 teaspoons Dijon mustard
3 tablespoons water
1 clove garlic, peeled and quartered
2 tablespoons olive oil
2 tablespoons red wine vinegar
1 teaspoon freshly ground pepper, or to taste
6 ounces diced canned beets

$\frac{1}{3}$ cup chopped fresh herbs—mixture of basil, thyme, chives, chervil, etc.

TOMATO GARNISH:
1 medium tomato, seeded and finely chopped
2 teaspoons reserved mixed fresh herbs

SWEET-AND-SOUR LEEKS:
2 pounds fresh leeks, tough green leaves removed and well washed
2 large cloves garlic, minced
1 tablespoon granulated sugar
2 tablespoons olive oil
juice of large lemon
1 tablespoon reduced-sodium soy sauce (optional)

Preheat the oven to 400°F.

TO MAKE THE GOAT CHEESE PARCELS: Mix the goat cheese with pepper to taste. Shape the cheese into 12 small balls and set aside. Place 1 sheet of filo on a flat surface and coat with the cooking spray. Sprinkle with half the chopped hazelnuts. Top with another filo sheet and coat with cooking spray. Cut the dough into 6 3-inch circles, discarding the scraps. Place a cheese ball in the center of each circle, and using your fingers, shape each circle into a little money bag around the cheese ball, leaving the top open. Repeat the process, using the remaining 2 sheets of filo dough, the remaining hazelnuts, and the remaining cheese balls.

Place on a nonstick baking sheet and chill until firm, about 5 minutes. Bake until golden, about 8 to 10 minutes.

TO MAKE THE DRESSING: In a blender combine the mustard, water, garlic, olive oil, vinegar, and pepper. Process until blended and stir in the beets. Reserve 2 teaspoons of the fresh herb mixture, stirring the remaining herb mixture into the beet dressing. Set aside.

TO MAKE THE TOMATO GARNISH: Combine the tomato and reserved herb mixture. Set aside.

TO MAKE THE SWEET-AND-SOUR LEEKS: Cut the leeks into julienne strips. In a large nonstick skillet, sauté the garlic and sugar in the olive oil until the mixture begins to color. Add the leeks and stir over medium heat to coat with the garlic and sugar. Sprinkle with the lemon juice and soy sauce (if using). Cover and simmer gently over low heat until tender. Serve hot or cold.

TO ASSEMBLE: Spoon some of the dressing into the center of each of 6 large plates. Place a small round of leeks in the middle of the dressing and top with 2 Goat Cheese Parcels. Decorate the plate with the Tomato Garnish. Serve at once.

MAKES 6 SERVINGS

Joslin Choices: 2 carbohydrate (bread/starch), 3 fat

Per Serving: 295 calories (43% calories from fat), 15 g total fat (3 g saturated fat), 6 g protein, 39 g carbohydrate, 4 g dietary fiber, 4 mg cholesterol, 402 mg sodium, 417 mg potassium

Leek Terrine with Vinaigrette and Truffles

Didier Montarou, LA CUPOLA AT THE WESTIN PALACE

MADRID

Considered by restaurant critics to be the finest hotel restaurant in Madrid, La Cupola offers Mediterranean specialties inspired by the fruits of the sea and bounty of the earth in an elegant dining room that combines turn-of-the-century grandeur with new refurbishments. Chef Montarou's leek terrine uses fresh truffles, available only in the late fall to midwinter here in the United States, and then only in very few specialty markets. We made this with imported canned truffles and still found it to be divine.

30 medium leeks, washed, trimmed, and cut into
   10-inch lengths
salt (optional)
fresh ground white pepper
2 truffles

TRUFFLE VINAIGRETTE:
Reserved truffle peels
juice of 1 large lemon
salt (optional)
freshly ground white pepper
3 tablespoons extra-virgin olive oil

TO PREPARE THE TERRINE: Divide the leeks into 5 bunches of 6 each and tie each bunch with kitchen string. In a large stainless-steel pot, bring lightly salted water to a boil. Add the leeks and return to a boil. Cook for 10 to 15 minutes. Transfer the leeks to a large bowl of ice water to cool. Then drain, squeeze out any excess water, and untie the bunches.

Line a 10 x 4 x 3-inch terrine mold with aluminum foil, leaving a 1-inch overhang on all sides. Place a layer of about 4 to 5 leeks in the bottom of the mold, with the white parts at one end. Lightly season with salt (if using) and white pepper. Layer more leeks on top; this time the white end on top of the green tops of the first layer. Repeat alternate layering, seasoning each layer with salt (if using) and pepper, until the mold is full.

Place a board the size of the interior of the mold on top of the leeks. Place a weight on top of the mold. Refrigerate for at least 6 hours. This will compress the leeks and extract the excess water. Invert the mold, with the board in place, to drain off the liquid. Then remove the board and unmold onto a dish.

TO PREPARE THE TRUFFLES: Using a small paring knife, peel the truffles and reserve the peel for the Truffle Vinaigrette. Finely slice the truffles, then cut into thin julienne strips.

TO PREPARE THE VINAIGRETTE: In a blender, process the truffle peels, lemon juice, salt (if using), and white pepper. Add the olive oil and process for 1 second longer.

TO SERVE: Unmold the terrine, inverting onto a cutting board, and discard the foil. With a large, sharp knife, slice the terrine. Transfer the slices to serving plates and spoon the Truffle Vinaigrette over each slice. Garnish with the julienne of truffles. Serve cold.

MAKES 6 SERVINGS

Joslin Choices: 3 carbohydrate (bread/starch), 1 fat

Per Serving: 260 calories (26% calories from fat), 8 g total fat (1 g saturated fat), 5 g protein, 48 g carbohydrate, 6 g dietary fiber, 0 cholesterol, 62 mg sodium, 580 mg potassium

Sizzling Fajita Mushrooms

Bruce Auden, BIGA ON THE BANKS

SAN ANTONIO, TEXAS

Biga on the Banks continues to bring raves and culinary awards to Chef Auden, a chef who adds the exotic flavors of Mexico and Asia to French cooking techniques. The new elegant space, housed in the old main library, overlooks a lush section of San Antonio's famed River Walk. Appetizers here are scene setters. If you love mushrooms as we do, you'll particularly enjoy this one. And it's so easy to prepare!
You'll need a sizzle pan with a wooden base (fajita pan) to prepare this recipe.

5 ounces cremini mushrooms, sliced

5 ounces shiitake mushrooms, stemmed and sliced

5 ounces portobello mushrooms, stemmed and roughly chopped

6 ounces chanterelle mushrooms, whole

½ medium red onion, julienned

½ teaspoon chopped garlic

2 tablespoons olive oil

1 tablespoon balsamic vinegar

2 tablespoons dry white wine

1½ tablespoons chopped fresh aromatic herbs, such as oregano, basil, mint, or cilantro

4 1-inch-thick slices crusty bread, grilled

Place the sizzle pan on a hot grill or on the stove over high heat. In a bowl, combine the mushrooms, red onion, garlic, olive oil, and balsamic vinegar. Empty the ingredients into the hot sizzle pan and cover.

Cook until the mushrooms are tender, about 5 to 7 minutes. Remove from the heat. Splash with the white wine to make the pan sizzle. Sprinkle with the herbs and set the sizzle pan on its wooden base. Serve with the grilled bread while still sizzling.

MAKES 4 SERVINGS

Joslin Choices: 1 medium-fat protein, 2 carbohydrate (bread/starch)

Per Serving: 266 calories (27% calories from fat), 8 g total fat (1 g saturated fat), 11 g protein, 34 g carbohydrate, 8 g dietary fiber, 0 cholesterol, 197 mg sodium, 251 mg potassium

Chef's Choice of Mushrooms

Here in the United States we are only starting to tap the mushroom market, which has over 8,000 edible and delicious species worldwide. One only has to visit an open-air market in another country to see what we're missing here in the States, but now we're getting more varieties, both flown in from distant lands and grown locally.

When selecting fresh mushrooms, inspect them carefully. They should be dry to the touch and not the least bit slimy. Look for firm, tight mushrooms that are solid in color (no blotches). Since they are very perishable, refrigerate as soon as you get home, in a paper bag or covered loosely with a damp paper towel. Use within 2 days.

Don't wash mushrooms; they are like sponges and will soak up the water, becoming soggy and losing flavor. Gently wipe them off with your fingers or a damp paper towel. If that doesn't release the dirt, brush them gently with a mushroom brush, then wipe the dirt off with a damp paper towel, and dry gently with additional paper towels. Trim the stems and handle the caps carefully. Discard any part of the stem that's tough. Unless you really know what you're doing, find your mushrooms at the store, not in the woods. Sure, foraging for mushrooms is fun (and we've done it when living in the East), but inexperienced mushroomers, beware. Along with edible mushrooms, a forest can also have mushrooms that range from mildly toxic to lethal. Don't take chances with your own or someone else's health and life.

Here is a glossary of the many kinds of mushrooms that our chefs call for in their recipes. If you don't find the variety you want, ask your produce man if he can order it for you, or order it from a specialty produce purveyor (see Sources, page 296).

Chanterelle: Trumpet-shaped with a mild, very delicate flavor. Can be either brownish-black or bright golden in color. The black variety is highly fragrant and often called a "false truffle." The golden variety has an apricot-like flavor. Wild/Cultivated

Cremini: A close relative of the common supermarket button mushroom with a similar shape, cocoa-colored, with a more intense flavor. It has a creamy texture when eaten raw; cooked, it produces a lot of flavorful liquid. Cultivated.

Champignon or Button: Most common variety that is either white or cream-colored, with a very mild flavor. Cultivated.

Morel: The darling of Boyne City, Michigan, the self-proclaimed "mushroom capital of the world." Each spring these cone-shaped morels with a spongy yellow to dark brown cap appear in the aspen groves and near mixed stands of other trees, in orchards, and around town. Morels are highly prized for their earthy, nutty taste, and hunting for them is as important for the locals as Mardi Gras is to New Orleans. Morels also grow in other parts of Michigan, Massachusetts, Connecticut, and in parts of the Pacific Northwest. Dried morels reconstitute easily and produce a very savory soaking liquid that can be used in the cooking. The yellow variety has been domesticated. Wild/Cultivated.

Oyster: A fan-shaped wood mushroom that grows in clusters. Oyster mushrooms have a mild flavor and a silky texture. Although widely available dried, they have little flavor. Wild/Cultivated.

Porcini (cèpe): Taupe to brown in color with parasol-shaped caps that can grow as wide as 10 inches and with thick stems. It has a smoky, robust flavor that makes it a favorite of many mushroom lovers. Often used dried in soups. Wild.

Portobello: Taupe to brown in color with saucer-shaped caps that look like a thatched roof, portobello mushrooms, like cremini, are closely related to the common button mushrooms. However, their meatiness and woodsy, pungent flavor reminds us of good filet mignon. Wild/Cultivated.

Shiitake: Large, tawny-colored mushrooms with parasol-shaped caps with a cream-colored inside. We love these smoky, meaty-flavored imports from Japan and consider them to have the most intense flavor of the many kinds of mushrooms available here in the States. Dried shiitakes give off a rich broth when reconstituted. Wild/Cultivated.

Truffle: Black truffles, also known as black diamonds, come from France's Périgord and Quercy regions and the Umbria region of Italy. They are intensely pungent and the most popular variety of truffle. The white (actually off-white or beige) truffles come from Italy's Piedmont region and have an earthy, garlicky aroma and flavor. Although undeniably best fresh, here in the States we often have to resort to using canned truffles or truffle paste (in a tube). Considered to be one of the rarest and most expensive foods in the world, truffles are found by specially trained pigs and dogs (the latter not as apt to eat its prized find), growing underground near the roots of oak, chestnut, hazel, or beech trees. They're rather unappealing in appearance, but once you've tasted the paper-thin shavings of a fresh truffle, you'll never forget the experience. Wild.

Roasted Red Pepper, Chipotle Chile, and Sun-Dried Tomato Spread with Toasted Crostini

Phillip R. Bouza, BARTON CREEK RESORT
AUSTIN, TEXAS

Chef Bouza shares this savory appetizer recipe that is sure to be a hit at any party. We liked this spread so much the first time we made it that we spooned some of it into a baked potato for lunch. Can you just imagine it with grilled chicken breasts or fish? Once you've tried it, you'll find many other uses for this Texas creation.

1 large red bell pepper, roasted
1 tablespoon minced shallots
2 ounces sun-dried tomatoes, packed in oil and garlic, well drained
1½ ounces canned chipotle chiles in adobo (page 78)
¼ cup Chicken Stock (page 31) or canned low-fat, low-salt chicken broth

1 tablespoon sour cream
1 tablespoon chopped fresh cilantro, plus extra sprigs for garnish
salt (optional)
freshly ground pepper
16 toasted Crostini (page 23)

Peel the roasted pepper, seed, and coarsely chop.

In a hot sauté pan, combine the shallots, roasted pepper, sun-dried tomatoes, and the chipotle chiles. Sauté for 4 minutes, stirring occasionally. Add the Chicken Stock and simmer until the vegetables are tender and the liquid has reduced, about 10 to 15 minutes. Let cool, then place in a food processor and pulse until finely chopped. Stir in the sour cream and process until smooth.

Add the chopped cilantro. Adjust for seasoning, adding salt (if using) and pepper to taste. Transfer to a small serving dish and surround with Crostini. Garnish with sprigs of cilantro.

MAKES ABOUT 1 CUP OR 8 SERVINGS

Joslin Choices: 2 carbohydrate (bread/starch)

Per 2-Piece Serving: 160 calories (11% calories from fat), 2 g total fat (1 g saturated fat), 6 g protein, 30 g carbohydrate, 3 g dietary fiber, 2 mg cholesterol, 300 mg sodium, 112 mg potassium

Crostini

You can buy packages of these "little toasts" in specialty food stores, but they are much cheaper when made at home and so easy to do. Once made, store them in an airtight container at room temperature and use within 2 days.

1 narrow loaf Italian or French bread, about 1 pound

2 cloves garlic, peeled and cut in half

Preheat the oven to 350°F, or preheat the toasting element of a toaster oven.

Slice the bread into 20 ¼-inch-thick slices. Lay on a baking sheet and toast until bread begins to color, 10 to 15 minutes, turning once. Remove from the oven and rub while still hot with a cut clove of garlic. Set aside.

MAKES 20 PIECES

Joslin Choices: 1 carbohydrate (bread/starch)

Per 1-Piece Serving: 62 calories (0% calories from fat), 1 g total fat (0 saturated fat), 2 g protein, 12 g carbohydrate, 1 g dietary fiber, 0 cholesterol, 137 mg sodium, 27 mg potassium

Tomato Galette

Tony Howorth, CAFÉ DU JARDIN AT COVENT GARDEN
LONDON

When we first asked the president of the London Restaurant Association for a chef recommendation for this book, we were immediately put in touch with Tony Howorth, the culinary talent of Café du Jardin. Located in Covent Garden in the heart of London's theater district, the restaurant makes use of the freshest of vegetables—each dish made special with a European flair.

GALETTES:

unbleached all-purpose flour for rolling dough

1 sheet from a 17¼-ounce package frozen puff pastry, thawed

3½ ounces sun-dried tomatoes (dry-packed)

6 ripe plum (Roma) tomatoes, about ¾ pound total, sliced

1⅔-ounce package fresh basil

1 large egg, beaten with 1 tablespoon water

BASIL OIL:

1⅔-ounce package fresh basil, leaves picked

1 clove garlic

⅛ teaspoon salt (optional)

freshly ground pepper

⅓ cup extra-virgin olive oil

1 teaspoon coarse sea salt (optional)

TO MAKE THE GALETTES: Lightly flour a work surface. Unfold the puff pastry and roll out until very thin, forming a 15 x 10-inch rectangle. Cut out 6 4-inch circles and discard the scraps. Using the tines of a fork, prick the entire surface of each circle. Place on a nonstick baking sheet lined with parchment paper and let rest in the refrigerator for 30 minutes.

Meanwhile, soak the sun-dried tomatoes in warm water for 5 minutes. Blanch the plum tomatoes in boiling water for 1 minute; drain, peel, and thinly slice. Set aside. Puree the plumped sun-dried tomatoes in a food processor, adding 1 or 2 drops of water, until the mixture forms a soft paste. Set aside. Chop the basil. Set aside.

Preheat the oven to 400°F. Remove the puff pastry from the refrigerator and brush evenly with the beaten egg mixture. Bake for 10 to 15 minutes until puffed and golden brown. Cool on a rack. Lower the oven temperature to 200°F.

When the pastry is cool, spread the tomato puree over the top of each pastry circle and return to the baking sheet. Arrange overlapping layers of sliced tomato on top of the puree. Sprinkle the tomato slices with the chopped basil. Return the pan to the oven to heat.

Meanwhile, make the Basil Oil: In a food processor or blender, combine the basil leaves, garlic, salt (if using), pepper, and olive oil. Process until smooth.

When the galettes are hot, transfer to individual serving plates and drizzle each galette with 1 teaspoon of the Basil Oil. If using, sprinkle with sea salt. Serve hot. Cover and refrigerate any remaining Basil Oil to use within 3 days.

MAKES 6 SERVINGS

Joslin Choices: 2 carbohydrate (bread/starch), 3 fat

Per Serving: 337 calories (56% calories from fat), 18 g total fat (3 g saturated fat), 7 g protein, 32 g carbohydrate, 4 g dietary fiber, 18 mg cholesterol, 461 mg sodium, 755 mg potassium

Infusing Oils

Oils can be infused with the flavors of fresh herbs, spices, and fruits to make a refreshing and more healthful alternative to butter and other fats. You can make these flavored oils with any light oil—olive, grapeseed, or canola. The result will not only add flavor but will also give moisture to your recipes. The easiest way to prepare flavored oils is to heat the spice or herb with the oil and then remove it from the heat. Cover and allow to sit for 4 hours. Strain the mixture through a coffee filter and pour the infused oil into a clean jar or bottle, discarding the solids. To make citrus oil, combine the zest of citrus fruit with oil and steep in the refrigerator for 4 days. Strain and refrigerate again. All infused oils must be refrigerated and will keep for a month, except those made with fruit, which should be used within 2 weeks. For the best taste, return the amount of oil the recipe calls for back to room temperature before using. Discard any warmed-over oil made with fresh ingredients.

Tian de Tomates Confit

Guillaume Lubard, ALCAZAR
PARIS

Sir Terence Conran of interior design fame has come to Paris from London to open his brasserie Alcazar on the Left Bank, where Chef Lubard holds forth in the open kitchen, a large modern design that delights the eye. This is a perfect restaurant for those of us who want to limit the amount of food we eat: The wait staff will be happy to serve you two appetizers instead of a five-course meal. *Bon Appétit* calls the restaurant "... modern and marvelous."

Two suggestions when making this dish: Use sun-dried tomatoes packed in a bag, not oil. They rehydrate beautifully in warm water. Since the recipe only calls for 1 tablespoon balsamic vinegar, use the very best you can afford. Many varieties in supermarkets are watered down and very light in flavor, compared to the real aged vinegar.

1 shallot, peeled and minced	16 slices mozzarella cheese, using 4 ounces from
3 whole pimentos	a ball of mozzarella
2 small avocados	4 ounces sun-dried tomatoes, rehydrated
juice of 1 large lemon	2 teaspoons sesame seeds
Tabasco sauce	2 tablespoons olive oil
salt (optional)	1 tablespoon balsamic vinegar
freshly ground pepper	

Place the minced shallot in a bowl. Drain the pimentos of all the oil and dice small. Add to the shallots. Cut the avocados in half, remove the stone, and mash the flesh with a fork. Add the avocados to the pimento mixture and stir in the lemon juice and a few drops of Tabasco. Season to taste with salt (if using) and pepper.

Line 4 ramekins with plastic wrap. Lay 2 slices of the mozzarella cheese in the bottom of each ramekin. Place a layer of sun-dried tomatoes on top and press down firmly. Top with remaining mozzarella slices. Fill each ramekin with the avocado mixture and chill in the refrigerator for 2 hours.

TO SERVE: Place a serving plate over each ramekin and turn it upside down onto a plate. Pull away the plastic wrap and sprinkle with the sesame seeds. Drizzle the plates with the olive oil and balsamic vinegar in decorative patterns.

MAKES 4 SERVINGS

Joslin Choices: 1 high-fat protein, 1½ carbohydrate (bread/starch), 3 fat

Per Serving: 385 calories (56% calories from fat), 24 g total fat (7 g saturated fat), 12 g protein, 32 g carbohydrate, 10 g dietary fiber, 22 mg cholesterol, 154 mg sodium, 596 mg potassium

Soups

Chicken and Corn Soup

Paul Ramsey, PINEHURST

PINEHURST VILLAGE, NORTH CAROLINA

When Chef Ramsey speaks of his goals, he says he wants the "quality of our food service to equal that of the infamous golf," at Pinehurst. This Chicken and Corn Soup shows Chef Ramsey's ability to combine the best chicken soup ever with roasted corn, giving us the New American Cuisine for which he is famous.

1 whole chicken, about 3 pounds, cut into 6 pieces
4½ quarts Chicken Stock (page 31) or low-fat, low-salt canned chicken broth
4 strips lemon zest
2 sprigs fresh thyme
2 fresh sage leaves
1 shallot, minced

1 clove garlic, minced
pinch saffron
2 cups fresh corn kernels
1 medium onion, finely diced
2 small leeks, well washed, thinly sliced
2 medium ribs celery, finely diced
½ teaspoon salt (optional)

Rinse the chicken pieces and pat dry with paper towels. Remove and discard any fat. Simmer the chicken in the Chicken Stock until fully cooked, about 1 hour. Twenty minutes before removing the chicken, add the lemon zest, thyme, sage, shallot, garlic, and saffron. Remove the chicken and cut off 6 ounces of boneless breast meat. Remove the remaining chicken from the bones and refrigerate for another use. Discard the bones, skin, and other solids.

Strain the stock, removing all the fat. Return the defatted stock to the stove and add the corn, onion, leek, celery, and salt (if using). Simmer until the vegetables are tender, about 10 minutes. Finely chop the reserved breast meat and add to the soup. Heat through and ladle into 8 heated soup bowls. Serve hot.

MAKES 8 SERVINGS

Joslin Choices: 2½ very-low-fat protein, 1 carbohydrate (bread/starch)

Per Serving: 172 calories (12% calories from fat), 2 g total fat (1 g saturated fat), 21 g protein, 15 g carbohydrate, 2 g dietary fiber, 16 mg cholesterol, 415 mg sodium, 565 mg potassium

Pheasant-Lentil Soup

Todd Slossberg, THE CENTURY ROOM AT HOTEL JEROME
ASPEN, COLORADO

Twice nominated by the James Beard Foundation as "Best Chef in the Southwest," Chef Slossberg was called to his culinary career at the age of 15. An honors graduate of the Culinary Institute of America in Hyde Park, New York, he refined his kitchen skills at this 100-year-old hotel in the heart of Aspen using locally grown vegetables, elk, lamb, and organically raised poultry and game. His pheasant soup is a fine example of his philosophy of serving beautiful food, simply prepared.

1 cup diced carrots

1 cup thinly sliced leek, white part only

⅔ cup diced white onion

⅔ cup diced celery

1 tablespoon minced garlic

1 tablespoon olive oil

1 cup French lentils, sorted and rinsed
  (see page 30)

6½ cups Chicken Stock (page 31)

1 cup diced/peeled fresh tomato

5 tablespoons Madeira wine

5 tablespoons chopped flat-leaf parsley

1¼ teaspoons chopped fresh thyme leaves

salt (optional)

freshly ground pepper

12 ounces skinless and boneless cooked pheasant,
  warmed (see Note below)

Place the carrots, leek, onion, celery, garlic, and olive oil in a pot. Sauté over medium-low heat until the vegetables are limp but not browned, about 5 minutes. Add the lentils, stock, and ⅔ cup of the tomato. Simmer the soup until the lentils are tender but still a little firm, about 25 minutes.

Transfer half the soup to a food processor or blender. Puree and mix back into the pot. Adjust the consistency as desired by either pureeing more of the soup or thinning with more stock. Add the Madeira, 3 tablespoons of the chopped parsley, and the thyme. Taste and add salt (if using) and pepper to taste.

To serve, distribute the cooked, warm pheasant meat among 8 heated soup plates or bowls. Sprinkle with the remaining ⅓ cup diced tomato and 2 tablespoons chopped parsley. Ladle the hot soup over and serve.

MAKES 8 SERVINGS

Joslin Choices: 3 very-low-fat protein, 1 carbohydrate (bread/starch)

Per Serving: 206 calories (15% calories from fat), 3 g total fat (1 g saturated fat), 22 g protein, 20 g carbohydrate, 5 g dietary fiber, 25 mg cholesterol, 181 mg sodium, 600 mg potassium

Note: You may substitute skinless and boneless cooked chicken thighs or the breast of other wild birds for 1 pheasant.

Lentils

Lentils have been popular in Europe, the Middle East, and India for generations as a meat substitute. Lentils are never used fresh; rather, they are dried as soon as they are ripe. Lentils are used in stews, salads, sandwiches, and soups. We find them pureed, whole, and combined in recipes with rice, vegetables, and other forms of protein.

Lentils are legumes, packed with protein, fiber, and carbohydrate. Unlike other legumes, however, lentils don't need presoaking. They come in a multitude of colors: red, green, brown, yellow, pink, or black. There are many more lentil varieties in the world than we're likely to see here in the States. The most common varieties are German (shades of brown and green) and the smaller, darker green French lentils from Le Puy. There are also the ordinary brown lentils that you'll find in every supermarket. The other varieties, along with more than 50 kinds of colorful Egyptian and Indian lentils, are available at some specialty food stores, natural foods stores, Mediterranean markets, or by mail order (see Sources, page 296). Store lentils in an airtight container and they will keep for a year. Read the label when cooking lentils. Some are done in as little as 10 to 12 minutes, while others can take as long as 25 to 30 minutes.

Chicken Stock

We depend on this flavorful stock for cooking. Developed for our first book, it freezes well. We make it when we're working on a project that will keep us home, as it does take a couple of hours to slowly cook. Whenever you buy a whole chicken and are cutting it up for breasts, thighs, and legs, freeze the rest. It doesn't take long to accumulate the needed 3 pounds.

3 pounds chicken with bones such as wings, backs, and necks
2 onions, peeled and stuck with 1 whole clove
1 clove garlic, peeled
1 carrot, peeled and sliced
1 rib celery with leaves, cut into large pieces
4 quarts water

6 peppercorns
1 large bay leaf
4 sprigs flat-leaf parsley
1 sprig fresh thyme or ¼ teaspoon crushed dried
¼ teaspoon salt (optional)

Place the chicken, onions, garlic, carrot, celery, and water in a large stockpot.

Bring to a boil; skim and discard the foam that rises to the surface. Add the remaining ingredients. Reduce the heat to a simmer, cover, and gently cook for 2½ hours, skimming occasionally to remove any foam.

Strain through a sieve or colander lined with cheesecloth. Discard the solids. Set aside to cool, uncovered, to room temperature. Remove all the fat that rises to the surface. Store in sealed containers in the refrigerator for as long as 3 days or freeze for up to 6 months.

MAKES 4 QUARTS

Joslin Choices: free food

Per 1-Cup Serving: 9 calories (33% calories from fat), trace total fat (trace saturated fat), 1 g protein, 0 carbohydrate, 0 dietary fiber, 3 mg cholesterol, 11 mg sodium, 16 mg potassium

Rhode Island Clear Clam Chowder

Jasper White, SUMMER SHACK
CAMBRIDGE, MASSACHUSETTS

On every visit to the Boston area, we always dine at one of Jasper White's restaurants. His newest venture is, for us, the best. We love seafood and Jasper excels at preparing all kinds. Recognized by the James Beard Foundation as one of the best new restaurants in the country, Summer Shack (open year round, despite the name) is designed to look like a clam shack and serves some of the best clams, oysters, and lobster in New England.

Like some of our chefs, Chef White's first recipe submission included raw seafood (or fish), something that we as people with diabetes are urged to avoid (see Joslin's statement on page 90). He graciously suggested we adapt this recipe that first appeared in his *50 Chowders* by Jasper White (Simon & Schuster, 2000). We've had the chowder and it's marvelous.

8 pounds small quahogs or large cherrystone clams

4 ounces Canadian bacon, cut into 1/3-inch dice

1 tablespoon olive oil

2 medium onions, cut into 1/2-inch dice

3 medium ribs celery, cut into 1/3-inch dice

1 tablespoon chopped fresh thyme

2 bay leaves

1/8 teaspoon fennel seeds, crushed

1/2 to 1 teaspoon crushed red pepper flakes (optional)

2 pounds Yukon Gold or other all-purpose potatoes, peeled and cut into 1/2-inch dice

2 cups Fish Stock (page 93), bottled clam juice, or Chicken Stock (page 31)

freshly ground black pepper

1 tablespoon fresh lemon juice

kosher or sea salt (optional)

2 tablespoons chopped flat-leaf parsley

2 tablespoons snipped chives

2 tablespoons chopped fresh chervil (optional)

2 cups 1% low-fat milk

Scrub the clams and rinse clean. Steam them open (see page 34). Discard any that don't open. Strain the broth and remove the clams from their shells; you should have 4 cups of broth and 1 pound of clams. Cover the clams with plastic wrap and keep refrigerated. Reserve the clam broth. After the clams have cooled a bit, dice them into 1/2-inch pieces. Cover again and keep refrigerated until ready to use.

Place a 4- to 6-quart heavy pot over low heat and add the bacon. Once it has rendered a bit of fat, increase the heat to medium and cook until the bacon is a crisp golden brown. Pour off all the fat, leaving the bacon in the pot.

Add the olive oil, onions, celery, thyme, bay leaves, fennel seeds, and red pepper flakes (if using), and sauté over low heat, stirring occasionally with a wooden spoon, for 10 to 12 minutes, until the onions are softened but not browned.

Add the potatoes, the reserved clam broth, and the Fish Stock. Continue to cook over medium heat until the chowder begins to simmer. If it begins to boil, turn down the heat slightly so that it maintains a steady simmer. Cook for about 15 minutes longer, until the potatoes are very tender. Remove the pot from the heat, stir in the diced clams, and season to taste with black pepper and the lemon juice. (It is unlikely that you will need to add any salt; the clams usually provide enough.) Discard the bay leaves.

If you are not serving the chowder within the hour, let it cool a bit, then refrigerate; cover the chowder after it has chilled completely.

When ready to serve, reheat the chowder over low heat; do not let it boil. Stir in the parsley, chives, and chervil. At the same time, heat the milk over low heat; do not let it boil.

Ladle the chowder into cups or bowls, making sure that the clams, potatoes, onions, and bacon are evenly divided; do not fill the cups or bowls more than three-quarters full. As is customary in Rhode Island, serve the hot milk in a small pitcher so each person can add some to their chowder.

MAKES 12 SERVINGS

Joslin Choices: 2 very-low-fat protein, 1½ carbohydrate (bread/starch)

Per Serving: 176 calories (16% calories from fat), 3 g total fat (1 g saturated fat), 16 g protein, 21 g carbohydrate, 2 g dietary fiber, 33 mg cholesterol, 235 mg sodium, 875 mg potassium

Cleaning and Steaming Clams

Clams are either hard-shell (such as quahog, littleneck, cherrystone, cockle) or soft-shell (steamer, geoduck, razor clam). Never store clams in sealed plastic or under water. To keep clams alive until you're ready to cook, place them in a bowl in the refrigerator and use them within a day or two, the sooner, the better.

Hard-shell clams require little more than scrubbing under running water with a stiff brush. Soft-shell clams usually contain a lot of sand and you'll need to purge them before steaming them. Once scrubbed with a stiff brush under running cold water, place the clams in a large bowl and cover with fresh water. Add 2 tablespoons of cornmeal and let stand for 1 hour. Drain and rinse the clams again.

Place the clams in a pot large enough to hold them in a single layer. Add water or desired cooking liquid to cover the bottom of the pot. Cover the pot and steam over medium heat until the clams open, shaking the pot occasionally, a few minutes for small clams or up to 10 minutes for the very large ones. Remove from the heat and discard any clams that didn't open. Use as directed in the recipe.

Spicy Lobster Gazpacho with Avocado Crème Fraîche

David Paul Johnson, DAVID PAUL'S LAHAINA GRILL
LAHAINA, MAUI, HAWAII

There's gazpacho and then there's David Paul Johnson's gazpacho, a favorite of the thousands of diners who frequent this culinary mecca for superb Hawaiian food. A lively play of spicy heat with the fresh flavors of locally grown vegetables, this elixir is smoothed out with a finish of cream flecked with buttery avocado. Most markets will steam your lobster at no charge.

GAZPACHO:

1 cup quartered husked tomatillos, washed

4 large cloves garlic, peeled

1 large green bell pepper, seeded and finely diced

1 large red bell pepper, seeded and finely diced

1 large yellow bell pepper, seeded and finely diced

¼ cup finely chopped red onion

¼ cup finely chopped scallions (white part and
   2 inches green)

¼ cup finely chopped white onion

1 green jalapeño chile pepper, seeded and finely
   diced (see page 78)

1 red jalapeño chile pepper, seeded and finely
   diced (see page 78)

2 cups diced and peeled ripe tomatoes

juice of 1 large lemon

juice of 1 large lime

1 teaspoon ground cumin

1½ tablespoons kosher salt (optional)

1 teaspoon black peppercorns, freshly ground

1 24-ounce can V8 juice (see Note below)

1 cup peeled, seeded, and diced cucumber

2 tablespoons extra-virgin olive oil

2 tablespoons finely chopped cilantro

AVOCADO CRÈME FRAÎCHE:

1 small Hass avocado

1 cup Crème Fraîche (page 37) or low-fat
   sour cream

1 teaspoon finely minced garlic

1 tablespoon lemon juice

salt (optional)

1 1¼-pound Maine lobster, steamed, shelled,
   diced, and chilled

kosher salt (optional)

8 lime wedges

TO MAKE THE GAZPACHO: In a high-speed blender or food processor, place the tomatillos, garlic cloves, and half of the bell peppers, onions, scallions, chiles, and tomatoes. While blending, add the lemon and lime juices, cumin, kosher salt (if using), ground pepper, and the V8 juice. Blend for 2 to 3 minutes, until all the solids are liquefied.

Pour into a large mixing bowl and add the remaining bell peppers, onions, scallions, chiles, and tomatoes. Stir in the cucumber. Blend in the olive oil and cilantro. Cover the soup and refrigerate for at least 1 hour before serving. Taste for final seasoning and adjust, if necessary. If the soup appears to be thick, thin it out with the addition of a little more V8 juice.

TO MAKE THE AVOCADO CRÈME FRAÎCHE: Cut the avocado in half and discard the pit. Using a spoon, scoop out the avocado pulp and place it in a small bowl. With a fork, mash the avocado until there are no visible lumps. Add the crème fraîche, minced garlic, lemon juice, and salt (if using). Blend well. Cover and refrigerate for at least 1 hour or until the thickness has been regained.

TO SERVE: Place some of the lobster meat in the bottom of 8 soup plates or soup bowls. Pour about 1 cup of the gazpacho over each lobster serving. Spoon a tablespoon-size dollop of the prepared crème fraîche in the center of each serving. Garnish with a lime wedge.

MAKES 8 SERVINGS

Joslin Choices: 1 carbohydrate (bread/starch), 2 fat

Per Serving: 196 calories (56% calories from fat), 13 g total fat (4 g saturated fat), 5 g protein, 18 g carbohydrate, 5 g dietary fiber, 19 mg cholesterol, 299 mg sodium, 490 mg potassium

Note: If you're on a low-sodium diet, use low-sodium V8 juice. It will lower the sodium content per serving to 199 mg.

Crème Fraîche

We developed this low-fat recipe for our first book, *The Joslin Diabetes Gourmet Cookbook*. Since then, we almost always have this tangy concoction in our refrigerators to garnish fresh fruit, mix with flavored vinegar for a quick salad dressing, stir into sauces, or top desserts, soups, and vegetables.

2 tablespoons 1% cultured buttermilk   2 cups plain low-fat yogurt

In a heavy saucepan, combine the buttermilk and yogurt. Heat until just luke-warm (do not overheat). Remove from the heat, cover, and let stand at room temperature for 24 hours. Refrigerate until needed.

MAKES ABOUT 2 CUPS

Joslin Choices: ½ carbohydrate (½ nonfat milk)

Per ¼-Cup Serving: 35 calories (25% calories from fat), 1 g total fat (trace saturated fat), 3 g protein, 4 g carbohydrate, 0 dietary fiber, 4 mg cholesterol, 42 mg sodium, 130 mg potassium

Gulf Coast Shrimp Gazpacho

Todd Phillips, REATA

ALPINE AND FORT WORTH, TEXAS

Praised by everyone from *Texas Monthly* to *Martha Stewart Living,* this popular Texas restaurant with Todd Phillips at the kitchen helm combines cowboy cooking with uptown flavors. The Alpine restaurant, named for the mythical ranch in the legendary 1956 movie *Giant,* starring Elizabeth Taylor and James Dean, still thrives, but the Fort Worth location on the thirty-second floor overlooking downtown Fort Worth was badly damaged in the 1998 tornado that devastated much of the surrounding area. Re-opening just six weeks later after millions spent on repairs and redecorating, the restaurant was again shut down in late 2000, when the building was closed to the public by the city. That last weekend thousands of devoted patrons waited for up to five hours to get inside to eat a final meal. We were one of them and now eagerly wait for their opening in a new location. In the meantime, we have settled for Reata on the Road, catering to parties, street fairs, and festivals.

SHRIMP:

16 large raw shrimp, about 1 pound total

1 tablespoon paprika

1 tablespoon ground cumin

1 tablespoon garlic powder

1 tablespoon crushed dried thyme

2 large cloves garlic, minced

2 tablespoons kosher salt (optional)

¼ cup olive oil, plus extra for brushing grill grid

GAZPACHO:

4 medium cucumbers, peeled

4 ribs celery, cut into quarters

1 large red bell pepper, seeded

1 medium red onion

2 cups loosely packed cilantro leaves

2½ cups tomato juice (see Note, page 39)

juice of 1 large lime

1 tablespoon Worcestershire sauce

1 teaspoon Tabasco sauce

1 teaspoon salt (optional)

1 teaspoon freshly ground pepper, plus extra
     for garnish

2 tablespoons extra-virgin olive oil

Peel and devein the shrimp. Using a spice grinder or a mortar and pestle, grind the paprika, cumin, garlic powder, and thyme together until very fine. In a mixing bowl, toss the shrimp with the paprika mixture, the garlic, the salt (if using), and the ¼ cup olive oil. Cover and marinate for at least 12 hours or overnight.

TO MAKE THE GAZPACHO: Cut the cucumbers in half lengthwise and, using a small spoon or melon baller, scoop out and discard the seeds. Thinly slice the cucumbers on the diagonal. Chop the celery, bell pepper, and onion. Place the vegetables in a mixing bowl. Add the cilantro leaves, tomato juice, lime juice, Worcestershire sauce, Tabasco, salt (if using), and pepper. Cover and refrigerate for at least 12 hours or overnight.

Preheat the grill to high and brush the grid with olive oil. Remove the shrimp from the marinade and thread onto skewers. Grill for 2 to 3 minutes per side, turning once, until the shrimp are bright pink and firm to the touch. Remove the shrimp from the skewers and set aside.

TO SERVE: Place 1 cup of the chilled gazpacho into each of 4 chilled soup plates. Drizzle ½ tablespoon of the olive oil on each plate of the gazpacho. Place 4 grilled shrimp in the middle of each serving. Freshly grind some pepper over the shrimp and serve at once.

MAKES 4 SERVINGS

Joslin Choices: 1 medium-fat protein, 1 carbohydrate (bread/starch), 2 fat

Per Serving: 249 calories (50% calories from fat), 15 g total fat (2 g saturated fat), 10 g protein, 24 g carbohydrate, 6 g dietary fiber, 47 mg cholesterol, 721 mg sodium, 1,164 mg potassium

Note: If you're on a low-sodium diet, use low-sodium tomato juice. It will lower the sodium content per serving to 188 mg.

La Crème d'Artichaut à la Citronelle
(Cream of Artichoke Soup with Lemongrass)

Michel Guérard, LES PRÉS D'EUGÉNIE

EUGÉNIE-LES-BAINS, FRANCE

Chef Michel Guérard has been practicing his craft since 1947; during that time, he has received some of France's highest culinary honors and written several books, on subjects ranging from the classic French cuisine to *La Cuisine à Vivre*.

Les Prés d'Eugénie is a hotel and the passion of Chef Guérard and his wife Christine. Winning its third Michelin star in 1977, the hotel continues to delight its patrons with selections ranging from classic gourmet to *cuisine minceur*. We are honored to share his recipe with you.

INFUSION:
9 fluid ounces chicken bouillon
1½ ounces chopped lemongrass
20 lemon verbena leaves

SOUP:
1 heaping cup chopped onion
1¼ teaspoons coriander seeds
1 small clove garlic, minced
2 tablespoons olive oil
pinch salt, plus more salt (optional)

¼ teaspoon turmeric
17 fluid ounces chicken bouillon
1 teaspoon grated orange zest
1 peeled medium orange, quartered
1 18¼-ounce can artichoke hearts, drained
    and quartered
1 small sprig fresh thyme
1 small bay leaf
2 cups whole milk
freshly ground pepper
fresh coriander (cilantro) leaves

TO MAKE THE INFUSION: In a pot, bring the bouillon to a boil. Add the chopped lemongrass and lemon verbena leaves. Remove from the heat and let sit, covered, to infuse for 15 minutes, then pass through a fine sieve, discarding the solids. Set the infusion aside.

In a second pot, gently combine the onion with the coriander seeds, garlic, olive oil, and salt. Add the turmeric, chicken bouillon, orange zest, orange, and the artichoke hearts. Add the thyme sprig and bay leaf. Cook slowly, partially covered, for 35 minutes. Add the milk and season with additional salt (if using) and pepper. Discard the thyme sprig and bay leaf.

Working in batches, puree the soup in a food processor, then pass the soup through a fine sieve into a large bowl. Whisk in the reserved infusion. Cool the soup quickly in an ice bath. Serve the soup from a soup tureen, garnished with coriander leaves. Serve warm or cold.

MAKES 8 SERVINGS

Joslin Choices: 1 carbohydrate (bread/starch), 1 fat

Per Serving: 125 calories (42% calories from fat), 6 g total fat (2 g saturated fat), 5 g protein, 14 g carbohydrate, 2 g dietary fiber, 8 mg cholesterol, 859 mg sodium, 213 mg potassium

Lemon Verbena

This is one of the many herbs that we grow in our garden. It thrives in the hot sun, and in the South, the plant can reach its full height of 10 feet, producing pale green, pear-shaped leaves with a powerful citrus aroma and a delightful lemon flavor. In a short but hot summer, lemon verbena will still reach 4 to 5 feet in height. If you plan to bring the plant indoors for the winter, plant the lemon verbena in a 6- or 8-inch clay pot and bury the pot in the ground, otherwise, digging the plant up in the fall will be difficult as it produces a deep taproot. In a container, you can still expect plenty of leaves for cooking use, as well as delicate spires of tiny pale lavender lemon-scented blossoms. Place the plant in a sunny window indoors and don't be alarmed if it loses its leaves sometime during the winter months. Don't let the pot dry out, and come March it will begin putting forth new leaves. In cooking, lemon verbena takes the place of lemon zest.

Corn Chowder

Jimmy Schmidt, RATTLESNAKE
DETROIT, MICHIGAN

When Jimmy Schmidt takes to the kitchen your meal will be as glorious as the view of the river at this Detroit restaurant. *Gourmet* describes the restaurant as the "best city dining" in Detroit, where "power brokers hunker down over Jimmy Schmidt's down-to-earth American food." This chowder is a fine example.

The chowder can also be served chilled; adjust the texture as necessary by adding a little water and season with extra Tabasco to taste.

30 ears just-picked sweet corn
2 tablespoons sugar
2 to 4 tablespoons unsalted butter
3 medium yellow onions
3 large cloves garlic, finely minced
4 cups water
¼ cup yellow cornmeal or as necessary

sea salt (optional)
freshly ground pepper
Tabasco sauce to taste (optional)
½ cup low-fat sour cream
¼ cup chopped cilantro leaves, plus sprigs for
    garnish
¼ cup fresh chives, washed, dried, and chopped

Husk the corn and remove the silks. Place the husked corn in batches in a large pot of cold water with the sugar. Bring the pot to a boil over high heat and cook for exactly 1 minute after the boil is detected. Drain immediately. Once the corn has cooled enough to handle, cut the corn kernels from the cob. Scrape the cobs with the back of a knife to help release all of the corn milk. Reserve one-third of the best kernels for garnish. Process the remaining corn kernels through a juicer to extract all their liquids and flavor.

Meanwhile, place another large soup pot over medium heat. Add sufficient butter to just barely coat the bottom of the pot. Add the onions and garlic, cooking until tender and opaque and with a slight golden color appearing on their edges. Add the corn puree, 4 cups water, and half the cobs to the pot. Cook the soup at a simmer until the flavor is developed, about 1 hour. Add the yellow cornmeal, as necessary, to thicken slightly to chowder consistency, cooking about 5 minutes over medium heat to allow the cornmeal to thicken fully. Remove from the heat. Remove and discard the corn cobs.

Transfer the chowder in batches to a blender or food processor. Puree until smooth. Strain though a medium sieve. Season with salt (if using), pepper, and Tabasco (if using) to taste.

TO MAKE THE GARNISH: In a small bowl combine the sour cream, chopped cilantro, chives, and additional Tabasco to your taste. Chill until ready to serve.

TO SERVE: Ladle the hot chowder into rimmed soup bowls. Spoon a dollop of the sour cream mixture into the center of the soup. Place a sprig of cilantro on top and sprinkle with some of the reserved corn kernels. Serve at once.

MAKES 18 SERVINGS

Joslin Choices: 2 carbohydrate (bread/starch)

Per Serving: 180 calories (15% calories from fat), 3 g total fat (1 g saturated fat), 5 g protein, 38 g carbohydrate, 4 g dietary fiber, 6 mg cholesterol, 31 mg sodium, 368 mg potassium

Fennel and Tarragon Soup

Jerry Traunfeld, THE HERBFARM
WOODINVILLE, WASHINGTON

This silky soup has a creamy texture but it gets its body from finely pureed fennel bulbs. Fresh tarragon, blended in at the last instant, intensifies the anise flavor. Though tables are booked several months ahead at this extremely popular restaurant, you can enjoy Jerry's nationally acclaimed culinary expertise at home anytime.

1 tablespoon extra-virgin olive oil

1 large leek, white only, washed and
   coarsely chopped

2 large fennel bulbs, stalks removed, coarsely
   chopped

4 cups Chicken Stock (page 31)

¾ teaspoon salt (optional)

¼ cup lightly packed fresh tarragon leaves
   or more if the tarragon has mild flavor

freshly ground black pepper

additional tarragon leaves for garnish

Heat the olive oil in a large saucepan over medium heat. Add the leek and cook, stirring often, until it is translucent and softened, but not browned, about 4 minutes. Add the fennel, stock, and salt (if using). Bring the soup to a boil, reduce the heat to low, cover, and simmer until the fennel is very soft, about 30 minutes.

Stir in the tarragon leaves. Puree the soup in batches in a food processor or blender until very smooth. Return the soup to the saucepan, bring it back to a simmer. Season with pepper.

Serve in heated soup bowls, floating a few tarragon leaves in each bowl.

MAKES 6 SERVINGS

Joslin Choices: 1 vegetable, ½ fat

Per Serving: 75 calories (31% calories from fat), 3 g total fat (0 saturated fat), 5 g protein, 8 g carbohydrate, 3 g dietary fiber, 0 cholesterol, 156 mg sodium, 461 mg potassium

Portobello Mushroom Chili

Tim Creehan, BEACH WALK CAFÉ
DESTIN, FLORIDA

When Tim first applied to work in the kitchen of one of Louisiana's finest restaurants at age 15, he was politely but firmly turned down. He did get a job there as a busboy, however, and spent every free moment at work studying the chef's movements and techniques. Later allowed in the kitchen to cook, he perfected his craft until 1988 when he opened his first restaurant in the Florida panhandle. For eight years he experimented with the healthy cooking style that would become his trademark. Now chef-owner of the popular Beach Walk Café in Miami Beach, he's high on the list of rising culinary stars that know that light and healthy food can, and should, taste great.

5 cups chopped portobello mushroom caps
1 cup diced yellow onion
2 teaspoons minced garlic
2 cups low-sodium tomato sauce
3 cups water
1 teaspoon salt (optional)

1 teaspoon ground cumin
2 tablespoons good-quality chili powder
cayenne pepper to taste
½ cup shredded white Cheddar cheese
½ cup diced red onion

In a large pot, combine the mushrooms, onion, garlic, tomato sauce, water, salt (if using), cumin, chili powder, and cayenne pepper. Bring to a boil; reduce the heat to a simmer and cook to desired thickness, 20 to 25 minutes, stirring occasionally.

TO SERVE: Ladle into 8 soup bowls, topping each serving with a tablespoon of white Cheddar cheese and a tablespoon of red onion. Serve at once.

MAKES 8 SERVINGS

Joslin Choices: 1 vegetable, ½ fat

Per Serving: 82 calories (32% calories from fat), 3 g total fat (2 g saturated fat), 4 g protein, 10 g carbohydrate, 3 g dietary fiber, 7 mg cholesterol, 76 mg sodium, 466 mg potassium

Potage of Diced Vegetables in Saffron Broth

Jean-Louis Gerin, JEAN-LOUIS
GREENWICH, CONNECTICUT

Fran can still remember her first dining experience at this distinguished Connecticut restaurant, shortly after Jean-Louis and his wife Linda opened the restaurant in 1985. Since that time, the Gerins have always been one step ahead of the times, constantly updating the restaurant in terms of its food selections and its decor. Known for his full-flavored cuisine, based on an extraordinary talent for achieving complex flavors through reductions and uncompromising quality in ingredients, Chef Jean-Louis was recently awarded the medal of *Chevalier du Mérite Agricole* from the French government, honoring him for his work in promoting French culinary arts in the U.S.A. When he sent us the recipe for this soup, he described it as having a "playful" mix of flavors. We agree!

2 tablespoons olive oil
1 cup sliced leek (equal amounts pale green and white)
1 tablespoon minced garlic
1 cup diced carrot
1 cup diced onion
1 sprig fresh thyme
1 bay leaf
2 pinches saffron threads

1 8-ounce bottle unsalted clam juice
2 cups water
½ cup diced tomato
2 tablespoons sliced scallion
¼ cup heavy cream (if serving the soup warm) or
   1 cup fresh orange juice (if serving the soup cold)
4 cooked and peeled large shrimp for garnish

In a soup pot, heat the olive oil over medium heat. Add the leek and garlic. Cook, stirring, for 2 minutes. Add the carrot, onion, thyme, bay leaf, and saffron. Cook for 2 minutes. Add the clam juice and water. Bring to a boil, reduce the heat, and simmer for 5 minutes. (At this point, you can cover the soup and refrigerate it overnight to enhance the flavor and the color of the saffron.)

Bring the soup back to a full boil. If serving the soup hot, add the tomato and scallion. Stir in the heavy cream and heat the soup but do not let it boil. Discard the bay leaf. Cut each shrimp into thirds lengthwise, making sure not to cut through the tail.

When ready to serve, ladle the soup into heated soup plates and float the shrimp on top, spreading the shrimp out into a fan. Serve hot.

If serving the soup cold, blend the tomato, scallion, and orange juice into the hot soup. Remove from the heat and refrigerate, covered, for at least 2 hours. Ladle the soup into chilled soup plates and garnish with the shrimp, spread into a fan. Serve cold.

MAKES 4 SERVINGS

Joslin Choices (hot version): 1 carbohydrate (bread/starch), 2 fat

Per Serving: 185 calories (64% calories from fat), 13 g total fat (5 g saturated fat), 5 g protein, 13 g carbohydrate, 2 g dietary fiber, 32 mg cholesterol, 130 mg sodium, 387 mg potassium

Joslin Choices (cold version): 1 carbohydrate (bread/starch), 1½ fat

Per Serving: 161 calories (44% calories from fat), 8 g total fat (1 g saturated fat), 5 g protein, 19 g carbohydrate, 3 g dietary fiber, 11 mg cholesterol, 125 mg sodium, 499 mg potassium

Sunchoke Soup with Mushroom-Filled Buckwheat Crêpes

Yochen Voss, THE MANOR
WEST ORANGE, NEW JERSEY

The Oranges in New Jersey are known for many luxuries but none more deserved than The Manor, which truly is a stately manor house with formal gardens and was voted one of "America's Top Tables" by the readers of *Gourmet*. Chef Voss came to The Manor via the Steirereck in Vienna, Austria, and the Residence in Essen-Kettwig, Germany. His food is American-French with hints of Italian and Asian, bringing elegance and perfection of taste to northern New Jersey.

CRÊPES:
7 ounces skim milk
2 large eggs
5 ounces buckwheat flour
pinch salt

SOUP:
2 large shallots, chopped
1 tablespoon olive oil
1 pound sunchokes (Jerusalem artichokes), peeled and sliced ½ inch thick
3 cups Vegetable Stock (page 115)
juice of ½ lime

salt (optional)
freshly ground pepper

MUSHROOM FILLING:
1 teaspoon olive oil
1 small shallot, chopped
½ clove garlic, chopped
2¼ pounds mixed seasonal mushrooms, cleaned and diced

½ leek, cleaned, blanched, and sliced into long strips

TO MAKE THE CRÊPES: In a medium bowl, whisk all the ingredients into a firm lump-free batter and let rest for at least 1 hour. Use a 10-inch Teflon pan to cook the crêpes, swirling a scant ¼ cup of the batter to evenly coat the bottom of the pan. Cook the crêpe for about 45 seconds, until the top begins to bubble and the edges start to pull away from the sides of the pan. Turn the crêpe over and cook another 30 seconds. Turn the crêpe out onto a plate and continue making crêpes until 4 perfect crêpes are made.

Meanwhile, in a large pot, sauté the shallots in olive oil. Add the whole sunchokes and sauté until they lightly brown. Add the Vegetable Stock and simmer until the sunchokes are soft, about 30 minutes. Transfer to a food processor or blender and process until smooth. Add the lime juice, salt (if using), and pepper to taste. Pulse again to blend. Return the soup to the pot and keep warm.

Heat the olive oil in a large nonstick skillet. Add the chopped shallot and garlic. Sauté until transparent. Add the diced mushrooms and sauté another 3 to 4 minutes.

Place 1 crêpe on a flat surface. Add one quarter of the mushroom filling to the center of the crêpe. Fold up the crêpe to form a little money bag. Tie the top of the bag with one of the long strips of leek. Place the filled bag in each of 4 shallow soup bowls and add the hot soup. Serve at once.

MAKES 4 SERVINGS

Joslin Choices: 1½ low-fat protein, 4 carbohydrate (bread/starch)

Per Serving: 412 calories (21% calories from fat), 11 g total fat (2 g saturated fat), 22 g protein, 65 g carbohydrate, 9 g dietary fiber, 110 mg cholesterol, 304 mg sodium, 1,843 mg potassium

Sunchokes

Sunchokes are also known as Jerusalem artichokes, but are not related to the common globe artichoke nor do they come from Jerusalem. Sunchokes are actually a variety of sunflower and the name comes from the Italian word for sunflower, *girasole.* Its lumpy, brown-skinned tubers often resemble fresh ginger. When eaten raw, they are crisp, reminding one of jicama or water chestnuts, the white flesh nutty, sweet, and crunchy.

Sunchokes can be purchased fresh in season from late fall through the spring. Select the smoothest tubers with firm, tight skin with no mold or discoloration. Refrigerate the sunchokes in a plastic bag with holes poked in the bag for up to 1 week. Sunchokes can be used raw and are also excellent steamed, stir-fried, braised, roasted, and sautéed. Watch carefully when cooking as they will overcook quickly and become very mushy. One way that sunchokes are like artichokes is that they must be placed in acidulated water (water with a small amount of lemon juice, lime juice, or vinegar) after being cut so they do not discolor.

Winter Soup Dinner

Sunchoke Soup with Mushroom-Filled Buckwheat Crêpes (page 48)

Spiced Caramel Pears (page 268)

Joslin Choices: 1½ low-fat protein, 5 carbohydrate (4 bread/starch, 1 fruit), 507 calories (18% calories from fat)

Clear Tomato Soup with Crab and Avocado

Laurent Tourondel, CELLO

NEW YORK CITY

Chef Tourondel sent us this recipe calling for Taylor Bay Scallops, which are sometimes difficult to find in many parts of the country. He suggested substituting cooked crab or shrimp. When we tried the recipe with back-fin crabmeat, the result was a testament to this chef's ability to take simple ingredients and present a dish that is much more than the sum of its parts. This is perfection in a bowl.

If crabmeat is not available, use an equal amount of small scallops or cooked shrimp.

10 large vine-ripened tomatoes, about 5 pounds total, whole

1/8 teaspoon salt (optional)

freshly ground pepper

1/8 teaspoon sugar, plus pinch more if needed

1/2 pound fresh crabmeat, back-fin, Dungeness, king, snow, stone, or blue (see Headnote above)

1 small ripe but still firm avocado

2 medium vine-ripened tomatoes, peeled, seeded, and diced

1 tablespoon extra-virgin olive oil

6 sprigs fresh basil

Coarsely chop the 10 whole tomatoes. Place in a large pot. Add the salt (if using), pepper, and sugar. Bring to a medium boil, stirring constantly. Reduce the heat and simmer until the tomatoes have released all of their liquid, about 10 minutes. Pour the contents of the pot into a cheesecloth-lined colander over a large bowl to catch the liquid. Place a heavy object on top in order to extract all the liquid. Allow to drain overnight in the refrigerator.

The next day, place the drained liquid in a pot. Reduce until the desired sweetness is attained. Another pinch of sugar may be added, if needed. Strain through a fine sieve or colander lined with cheesecloth. Season with additional salt (if using) and pepper. Transfer the soup to a decorative pitcher, cover, and chill.

Pick through the crab meat to remove any cartilage, being careful not to break up the clumps of crab. Refrigerate until ready to serve.

TO ASSEMBLE: Slice the avocado in half; remove the pit and peel. With the cut side down on a chopping board, slice the avocado width-wise into paper-thin slices. Arrange some of the slices in a circular pattern in the bottom of each of 6 shallow soup plates. Season the crabmeat with pepper. Pile the crabmeat in the center of each avocado circle. Season the diced tomato with pepper. Place some of the diced tomato on top of the crab mounds and drizzle each with ½ teaspoon olive oil. Garnish each plate with a basil sprig. At the table, pour the soup in equal amounts into each soup plate.

MAKES 6 SERVINGS

Joslin Choices: 1 low-fat protein, 1 carbohydrate (bread/starch)

Per Serving: 132 calories (27% calories from fat), 4 g total fat (1 g saturated fat), 11 g protein, 16 g carbohydrate, 4 g dietary fiber, 27 mg cholesterol, 167 mg sodium, 742 mg potassium

Avocados

Native to the tropics, avocados are a fruit with a buttery texture and a mild nutlike flavor. The two most widely sold avocados are the small pear-shaped Hass (often called "California avocado") and Fuerte. A Hass is ready to use when its pebbly skin is purplish black and yields slightly to the touch. A Fuerte avocado is large and can weigh as much as 4 pounds; it has a thin, smooth skin that stays green when ripe. When ripe, a Fuerte avocado will also yield to gentle pressure. Its flesh is more watery and has less flavor than the Hass, so you'll need to add more seasonings to get the same results as you would when using the Hass variety.

You can ripen avocados in a brown paper bag at room temperature in 2 to 4 days at home. Once opened, exposure to air will dull the flavor of an avocado and brown its flesh. Cut the avocado just before you're ready to serve it, discarding the pit and the peel. A sprinkling of lemon or lime juice will help keep your avocado from discoloring somewhat. Avocados are high in fat, but it's unsaturated fat, and so they can be a part of a healthy diet.

Cold Tomato Soup with Basil Cream in Ice Bowls

Waldy Malouf, BEACON

NEW YORK CITY AND STAMFORD, CONNECTICUT

Chef Malouf wrote, "This is a soup to make when tomatoes are at the peak of flavor and you have so many you don't know what to do with them. Basil and tomatoes grow happily together. When the basil plants are fragrant and bushy and the tomato vines are laden with fruit—some of it less than perfect— it's time to make big batches of this delicious soup. Freeze some so you'll be able to bring back summer in the winter. For a special presentation, serve the soup in ice bowls, following the directions at the end of the recipe."

We both have several containers of this marvelous soup in our freezers, waiting for the first really cold winter evening, at which time we'll again enjoy the flavors of summer. For best results, freeze the soup in meal-size batches before seasoning it. Freeze the basil puree separately. Add the basil to the soup after it has thawed; season with salt and freshly ground pepper and serve hot or cold.

BASIL PUREE:
1 bunch fresh basil, washed and dried
⅓ cup extra-virgin olive oil

SOUP:
1 tablespoon extra-virgin olive oil
1 large onion, chopped
1 medium leek, white part only, carefully cleaned
  and chopped
1 large rib celery, chopped
3 or 4 sprigs fresh thyme
4 or 5 sprigs parsley
3 cloves garlic, split
2 bay leaves
1 tablespoon black peppercorns
1 whole clove

6 reserved basil stems (see basil puree above)
6 large very ripe tomatoes, peeled and seeded
5 cups Chicken Stock (page 31)
1½ cups tomato juice
⅓ cup basil puree (see above)
coarse salt (optional)
freshly ground pepper

GARNISH:
1 heaping tablespoon reserved basil puree
  for garnish
½ cup heavy cream
salt (optional)
freshly ground pepper
12 reserved basil leaves (see basil puree above)

TO MAKE THE BASIL PUREE: Pick off the basil leaves until you have 2 cups. Reserve 6 of the stems for the herb sachet and 12 additional perfect leaves for the garnish. In a food processor, puree the 2 cups basil leaves with the olive oil. Put the puree in a small covered container and refrigerate.

In a heavy-bottomed soup pot, over medium heat, warm the olive oil and sauté the onion, leek, and celery, stirring frequently, until soft, about 15 minutes. Tie the thyme and parsley sprigs, garlic, bay leaves, peppercorns, the whole clove, and the basil stems in a square of cheesecloth to form an herb sachet. Add to the soup pot, along with the tomatoes, stock, and tomato juice. Bring to a boil and simmer the soup, uncovered, for 30 minutes. Reserve a heaping tablespoon of the ⅓ cup basil puree for the garnish; add the remainder to the soup. Simmer for 5 minutes more. Let the soup cool slightly, then remove the herb sachet. Using a food processor, puree the mixture in batches until smooth. Season to taste with salt (if using) and freshly ground pepper. Refrigerate for 4 hours or overnight.

Whip the heavy cream until soft peaks form. Add the reserved basil puree and season with a little salt (if using) and pepper. Whip until stiff and refrigerate.

At serving time, taste the cold soup and reseason it if necessary. Ladle the soup into cold soup bowls and garnish with a spoonful of basil-flavored whipped cream and a basil leaf.

MAKES 12 SERVINGS

Joslin Choices: ½ carbohydrate (bread/starch), 2 fat

Per Serving: 151 calories (67% calories from fat), 11 g total fat (3 g saturated fat), 4 g protein, 8 g carbohydrate, 2 g dietary fiber, 14 mg cholesterol, 195 mg sodium, 345 mg potassium

To Make the Ice Bowls: Fill 8-inch round foil cake pans (1 per person) half full of water and drop in 4 or 5 leaves of basil. Set a soup bowl in each one and stack the pans in the freezer overnight. Just before serving, place a folded linen napkin on each of 8 large plates. Remove the ice with the soup bowls in place and set on the prepared plates. Ladle the cold soup into the bowls and garnish as above. Serve immediately.

The First Warm Evening Dinner

Cold Tomato Soup with Basil Cream in Ice Bowls (page 53)

Potato-Crusted Sea Bass with Grilled Eggplant, Tomato, and Mint Salad
(page 105)

Iced Espresso

Joslin Choices: 2½ low-fat protein, 3 carbohydrate (bread/starch), 3 fat,
544 calories (47% calories from fat)

Note: Items not referring to a specific recipe are not included in the nutritional analysis. Consult the Joslin Food Choices (page 287) for that information.

Yellow Tomato Soup with Avocado, Red Onion, and Mint

Todd Gray, EQUINOX
WASHINGTON, D.C.

Chef Todd Gray and his wife, Ellen, opened Equinox to rave reviews from magazines as diverse as *Travel + Leisure* to *Esquire* and the *Washingtonian* to *Gourmet.* Chef Gray, a graduate of the Culinary Institute of America, has many awards to his name, including the James Beard Award, for Galileo, where he was executive chef. In its first year Equinox won the Restaurant Association of Metropolitan Washington's Best New Restaurant of the Year 2000, *Condé Nast Traveler's* "60 Hot Tables," *Bon Appétit's* 100 Very Best Restaurants, *Gourmet's* American Top Tables, and too many more to mention.

Just look at the combinations in this yellow tomato soup—it showcases his spirited American style well.

1 tablespoon grapeseed oil	1 medium ripe avocado, pitted, peeled,
2 Vidalia onions, peeled and sliced	and chopped
6 large cloves garlic, crushed	1 tablespoon fresh lime juice
10 medium yellow tomatoes, quartered	2 ⅓-inch-thick slices red onion, minced
⅛ teaspoon salt (optional)	1 small clove garlic, minced
freshly ground pepper	3 to 4 tablespoons chopped fresh mint
5½ cups canned low-sodium vegetable broth	3 tablespoons olive oil

In a large saucepan, heat the grapeseed oil over medium-high heat. Add the onions and garlic. Sauté for 3 minutes. Add the yellow tomatoes and cook for 5 minutes. Add salt (if using), pepper, and vegetable broth. Simmer for 30 minutes.

Meanwhile, in a small bowl, combine the avocado, lime juice, red onion, garlic, and mint. Cover and chill.

Remove the soup from the heat and puree in a food processor or blender. With the motor running, slowly drizzle in the olive oil through the feed tube. Process until the mixture is smooth. Transfer to a bowl, cover, and chill thoroughly.

Chill 6 large soup bowls in your refrigerator. Ladle in the soup and place a spoonful of the avocado mixture in the center. Serve immediately.

MAKES 6 SERVINGS

Joslin Choices: 1 carbohydrate (bread/starch), 2 fat

Per Serving: 200 calories (49% calories from fat), 12 g total fat (2 g saturated fat), 6 g protein, 22 g carbohydrate, 7 g dietary fiber, 0 cholesterol, 121 mg sodium, 1,325 mg potassium

Salads

Asparagus and Gingered Grapefruit Salad

Ris Lacoste, 1789

WASHINGTON, D.C.

Bonnie was first introduced to this D.C. landmark when her best friend had his wedding reception at this elegant Georgetown Federal-style town house. It's hard not to fall in love with the setting, and even harder not to be enthralled by Chef Ris Lacoste's cuisine. This accomplished and award-winning chef earned the *grand diplôme* from the Parisian school La Varenne. After returning to the United States from cooking in Europe, she began her collaboration with Chef Bob Kinkead and opened several restaurants in New England. When these two talented people came to Washington and opened 1789, they were named "Restaurateurs of the Year" in 1992 and the awards have continued, including being named guest chef at La Varenne at the Greenbrier and having 1789 named Restaurant of the Year 2000. Chef Lacoste writes articles for *Fine Cooking Magazine* and teaches students from L'Académie de Cuisine. Her seasonal cooking is represented in this recipe, in which the freshest of spring asparagus is layered with the citrus of grapefruit. The melding of the taste and textures make for a salad that shines.

2 cups Miso Vinaigrette (recipe follows)
2 cups Ginger Lime Glaze (recipe follows)
42 spears large asparagus
salt (optional)

4 to 5 pink grapefruit
2 scallions, cut thinly at an angle
¼ cup mixed black and white sesame seeds

Make the Miso Vinaigrette and Ginger Lime Glaze ahead of time and keep in the refrigerator. If desired, peel each stem of asparagus just to the tip. Blanch in a large pot of boiling salted water until the stems bend, 1 to 2 minutes. Remove immediately and place in ice water to stop the cooking and preserve the green color. Remove from the water as soon as the asparagus is chilled, and drain. Keep at room temperature if just before serving. If made ahead, refrigerate until 10 to 15 minutes before ready to use.

Working over a large bowl to catch any juice, cut and discard the peel and white pith from the grapefruit. Cut between the membranes of the fruit to release the segments into the bowl. Squeeze the juice from the membranes into the bowl and discard them. Continue until you have 36 perfect sections. Place the sections in a separate bowl and cover with the Ginger Lime Glaze. Reserve the fresh-squeezed juice for another use.

TO ARRANGE THE SALAD: Cover the asparagus with 1 cup of the Miso Vinaigrette, saving enough of the dressing that remains to drizzle onto the bottom of each salad plate. Let the asparagus soak in the dressing for a couple of minutes. Cover the bottom of each salad plate with a drizzle of the Miso Vinaigrette. Arrange a log pile of 7 asparagus spears in the center of each plate. Arrange 3 grapefruit sections fanned out on each side of the asparagus. Sprinkle with the scallions and sesame seeds.

Miso Vinaigrette

1 3-inch piece fresh ginger, peeled and finely diced
1 tablespoon minced garlic
1 tablespoon miso
1½ tablespoons chile paste with garlic
½ bunch cilantro, cleaned, dried, and chopped
3 fluid ounces dry sherry
½ cup rice vinegar

5 ounces fish sauce (nuoc nam) (see Note below)
¼ cup fresh lime juice
1 tablespoon honey
2 tablespoons dark sesame oil
½ cup peanut oil

Combine all the ingredients in a bowl except for the sesame oil and peanut oil. Whisk in each oil one at a time. This dressing will last indefinitely, covered in the refrigerator.

Ginger Lime Glaze

1 8-inch piece fresh ginger, peeled and cut into
   very fine threads
grated zest of 4 large limes

1½ cups tarragon vinegar
¾ cup sugar

Combine all the ingredients in a nonreactive pot. Bring to a boil. Remove from the heat and let sit for 5 minutes to infuse the flavors. Bring back to a boil and repeat the process. Bring back to a boil for a third time. Set aside until cool enough to cover and refrigerate. The glaze will last indefinitely and makes a great base for iced or hot tea.

MAKES 6 SERVINGS

Joslin Choices: 1 very-low-fat protein, 1½ carbohydrate (fruit), 3 fat

Per Serving: 290 calories (54% calories from fat), 18 g total fat (3 g saturated fat), 6 g protein, 27 g carbohydrate, 5 g dietary fiber, 0 cholesterol, 1,356 mg sodium*, 625 mg potassium

Note: Available at Asian markets or see Sources (page 296).

*This recipe is not recommended for low-sodium diets.

Asparagus and Red Grape Tomato Salad with Citrus Vinaigrette

Cindy Wolf, CHARLESTON
BALTIMORE, MARYLAND

Chef Cindy Wolf is known for her celebration of fresh foods. Here she uses spring asparagus at its peak for a salad with a dressing that you want to use with seasonal harvests. Grape tomatoes are sweet baby plum (Roma) tomatoes. They add visual beauty and a beautiful taste to this wonderful salad.

1 pound fresh asparagus
1 pint red grape tomatoes, cut in half lengthwise
2 tablespoons extra-virgin olive oil

zest and juice of 1 large lemon
pinch salt
freshly ground pepper

In a large pot of lightly salted boiling water, blanch the asparagus until just tender, 1 to 2 minutes for very thin spears, 4 to 5 minutes for thick spears. Drain and place in an ice water bath until completely chilled. Drain well. Cut the asparagus into 1-inch pieces.

Toss the asparagus with the remaining ingredients. Divide among 4 chilled salad plates and serve.

MAKES 4 SERVINGS

Joslin Choices: 2 vegetable, 1 fat

Per Serving: 104 calories (56% calories from fat), 7 g total fat (1 g saturated fat), 4 g protein, 9 g carbohydrate, 2 g dietary fiber, 0 cholesterol, 154 mg sodium, 524 mg potassium

Asparagus and Sweet Onion Salad

Paul Liebrandt, ATLAS

NEW YORK CITY

Atlas, on Central Park South, and Chef Liebrandt were named "... the new taste leader" in New York City by *New York* magazine in 2001. This young chef who came to the United States from England has transformed this restaurant with his globally influenced American cuisine and a surprise around every corner. The play of sweet and tart along with the mixing of textures make for a salad that you will want to enjoy often.

5 medium sweet onions

2 teaspoons peanut oil

20 spears fresh green asparagus, about ¾ pound total, trimmed

salt (optional)

freshly ground pepper

juice of 1 large lemon

2 teaspoons pistachio oil

¼ cup plain nonfat yogurt

1½ tablespoons blanched slivered almonds

1 small Granny Smith apple with peel, cored and cut into thin julienne strips

1½ tablespoons chopped pistachios

Slice the onions very thinly. In a heavy nonstick skillet, cook the onions in peanut oil over low heat for about 2 hours, covered, until the onion has reduced to jam consistency. Keep warm and set aside.

Cook the asparagus in lightly salted, rapidly boiling water until al dente or just tender, about 2 minutes. Remove and place in an ice water bath to cool for 2 minutes. Drain and pat dry. Season with salt (if using), pepper, lemon juice, and pistachio oil.

Attractively spread the onion in a rectangle that can accommodate a stack of the asparagus spears on a serving platter. Stack the asparagus on top. Put the yogurt into a squeeze bottle and pipe about 1 tablespoon in a decorative pattern onto the platter around the asparagus. Refrigerate the remaining yogurt for another use. Sprinkle the almonds, julienned apples, and pistachio nuts over the dish. Serve at once.

MAKES 4 SERVINGS

Joslin Choices: 1½ carbohydrate (bread/starch), 1 fat

Per Serving: 200 calories (32% calories from fat), 7 g total fat (1 g saturated fat), 7 g protein, 29 g carbohydrate, 7 g dietary fiber, 0 cholesterol, 15 mg sodium, 622 mg potassium

Baby Beet and Sweet Onion Salad over Spinach with Ricotta Salata

Robert Patchen, PACI

SOUTHPORT, CONNECTICUT

Paci is owned and operated by Chef Patchen and his wife Donna. It is nestled on the eastbound side of the Southport train station in a mid-1800s freight depot that has been renovated to combine New England architecture with a modern European style. The unique design won the 1997 James Beard Restaurant Design Award. Self-taught, Chef Patchen first worked as an apprentice in his grandparents' Italian restaurant at age eight.

This salad is a fine example of his cuisine—seasonal ingredients exquisitely plated in a fresh and flavorful way.

12 Chioggia or red baby beets and 12 Golden baby beets, about 1¼ pounds total

2 tablespoons extra-virgin olive oil

salt (optional)

freshly ground pepper to taste

1½ teaspoons fennel seeds

1 medium sweet onion, such as Vidalia, Maui, Walla Walla, or 1015, thinly sliced

3 tablespoons balsamic vinegar

2 tablespoons fresh lemon juice

12 ounces organic baby spinach, washed and dried

1 ounce Ricotta Salata

Preheat the oven to 350°F.

Clean the beets, scrubbing under running cold water with a stiff brush; cut off beet tops. Place in a roasting pan and drizzle with 1 tablespoon of the olive oil. Turn the beets to coat all the sides. Sprinkle with salt (if using), pepper, and fennel seeds. Roast, uncovered, for 45 minutes, until the beets are tender. Remove from the oven and cool. When cool enough to handle, slip off the skins, and chill.

When ready to serve, cut the beets in half and place in a bowl with the sliced onion, ½ tablespoon of the olive oil, salt (if using), and pepper to taste. Toss. Add 1½ tablespoons of the balsamic vinegar and 1 tablespoon of the lemon juice. Mix well.

Dress the baby spinach with the remaining ½ tablespoon olive oil, the remaining 1½ tablespoons balsamic vinegar, and the remaining 1 tablespoon lemon juice. Toss. Arrange the spinach in a shallow serving dish and pile the beet mixture in the center. Grate the Ricotta Salata over all and serve.

MAKES 4 SERVINGS

Joslin Choices: 1 carbohydrate (bread/starch), 2 fat

Per Serving: 192 calories (42% calories from fat), 9 g total fat (2 g saturated fat), 6 g protein, 22 g carbohydrate, 4 g dietary fiber, 2 mg cholesterol, 185 mg sodium, 1,008 mg potassium

Ricotta Salata

Despite its name, this is not the soft ricotta cheese that we all know and use in lasagna and other Italian cooking. This is a hard Italian cheese in which the sheep's-milk curds and whey are pressed and dried before the cheese is aged, giving this pure white cheese a dense but slightly spongy texture and a salty (salata means "salted"), milk flavor. We found Ricotta Salata at a local Italian delicatessen that carries a large selection of imported Italian cheeses. It's also available at large cheese shops, some natural food stores, and from mail-order and Internet companies (see Sources, page 296).

Green Pear, Fennel, and Witloof (Endive) Salad

David Hay, THORN PARK COUNTRY HOUSE
SEVENHILL, SOUTH AUSTRALIA

Just 90 miles north of Adelaide, the capital of South Australia, is the tiny township of Sevenhill. Here you will find chef and co-owner David Hay practicing his culinary craft. Thorn Park Country House is an 1850s antique-filled homestead set in English-style gardens with rambling roses and showy hawthorns, from which the property takes its name.

Noted for his brilliant, modern, Australian cuisine, Chef Hay is considered a rising star by travel writers and restaurant critics. He claims one of his secrets is the area's fabulous produce. Here is his recipe for a marvelous salad made with pears, fennel, and witloof—white leaf Belgian endive to those of us who don't live "down under."

3 large heads witloof (white leaf Belgian endive), leaves separated
1 bunch rocket (arugula)
1 bulb fennel, trimmed and sliced into thin strips
2 green pears, halved, cored, and finely sliced
¼ cup pecan halves, toasted and coarsely chopped

½ cup shaved Parmesan cheese
1 tablespoon walnut oil
2 tablespoons extra-virgin olive oil
1 tablespoon champagne vinegar
salt (optional)
freshly ground pepper

Wash and dry the greens. Combine in a large salad bowl with the fennel, pears, pecans, and Parmesan cheese.

Whisk together the oils, vinegar, salt (if using), and pepper to taste. Drizzle over the salad and toss. Serve immediately

MAKES 6 SERVINGS

Joslin Choices: 1 high-fat protein, 1 carbohydrate (fruit), 1 fat

Per Serving: 182 calories (61% calories from fat), 13 g total fat (3 g saturated fat), 5 g protein, 14 g carbohydrate, 4 g dietary fiber, 7 mg cholesterol, 177 mg sodium, 329 mg potassium

Baby Spinach and Arugula Salad with Granny Smith Apples, Chèvre, and Tomatoes with a Balsamic Vinaigrette

Brian Partelow, EMERSON INN BY THE SEA
ROCKPORT, MASSACHUSETTS

Whether you choose to dine in the elegant turn-of-the-century dining room or outside on the ocean-front veranda, looking out over the rock gardens and sweeping view of the Atlantic Ocean, the food lives up to the unparalleled ambience of the restaurant. This salad is a wonderful example of Chef Partelow's uncanny talent to take ordinary ingredients and come up with something very special.

VINAIGRETTE:
6 tablespoons balsamic vinegar
1 teaspoon Dijon mustard
2 teaspoons honey
1 large clove garlic, minced
1 shallot, minced
salt (optional)
freshly ground pepper
¾ cup canola oil

8 ounces baby spinach, washed and dried
8 ounces baby arugula, washed and dried
4 ounces chèvre, diced
2 medium tomatoes, diced
1 large Granny Smith apple, cored and diced

In a blender, combine the vinegar, mustard, honey, garlic, shallot, salt (if using), and pepper to taste. With the motor running on medium speed, slowly add the canola oil through the lid opening until the dressing is emulsified.

In a large salad bowl, combine the spinach and arugula with ¼ cup of the dressing. Top with the chèvre, tomatoes, and apple. Divide among 8 large plates and serve. Refrigerate remaining dressing for another use.

MAKES 8 SERVINGS

Joslin Choices: 1 vegetable, 1 fat

Per Serving: 102 calories (60% calories from fat), 7 g total fat (2 g saturated fat), 5 g protein, 6 g carbohydrate, 2 g dietary fiber, 7 mg cholesterol, 89 mg sodium, 358 mg potassium

Spinach Salad with Peppered Walnuts and Black Truffle Vinaigrette

Tim Richards, BOEDEAN SEAFOOD

TULSA, OKLAHOMA

Tulsans can be proud of their restaurants and most especially Boedean, where every aspect of a meal makes us come back often.

VINAIGRETTE:

1 cup extra-virgin olive oil

¼ cup minced yellow onion

1 tablespoon minced garlic

1 tablespoon minced shallot

⅓ cup rice wine vinegar

⅓ cup balsamic vinegar

¼ cup whole-grain mustard

kosher salt (optional)

freshly ground pepper

⅛ cup minced black truffles

SALAD:

1 tablespoon extra-virgin olive oil

⅓ cup walnut halves

1 teaspoon freshly ground pepper

1 teaspoon ground white pepper

1 teaspoon cayenne pepper

6 ounces fresh spinach leaves, washed and dried

1 medium tomato, cut into 8 wedges

¼ cup shredded red onion

TO MAKE THE VINAIGRETTE: In 1 tablespoon of the olive oil, sauté the onion, garlic, and shallot until limp, about 4 to 5 minutes. Whisk in the remaining ingredients. Set aside. (Makes about 2⅓ cups.)

In a heavy sauté pan, heat the olive oil. Add the walnuts and mix in the peppers. Sauté until the walnuts are browned and evenly coated. Set aside.

When ready to serve, divide the spinach among 4 large plates. Distribute the walnuts around the edge of each plate. Top the spinach with the tomato wedges and shredded onion. Drizzle 1 teaspoon of the vinaigrette over each salad and serve. Refrigerate the remaining dressing for another use.

MAKES 4 SERVINGS

Joslin Choices: 1 vegetable, 2 fat

Per Serving: 132 calories (73% calories from fat), 11 g total fat (1 g saturated fat), 3 g protein, 6 g carbohydrate, 3 g dietary fiber, 0 cholesterol, 46 mg sodium, 370 mg potassium

Joslin Choices (vinaigrette only): free food

Per 1-Teaspoon Serving: 21 calories (92% calories from fat), 2 g total fat (0 saturated fat), 0 protein, 0 carbohydrate, 0 dietary fiber, 0 cholesterol, 9 mg sodium, 3 mg potassium

West Indies–Style Slaw with Avocado, Hearts of Palm, and Orange-Cumin Dressing

Chris Schlesinger, EAST COAST GRILL

CAMBRIDGE, MASSACHUSETTS

Joan Hill, Director of Education at Joslin Diabetes Center, alerted us to this chef and his restaurant. Most sought for its slow-cooked barbecue and grilled seafood, East Coast Grill is where talented Chef Schlesinger hones his fondness for exotic flavors found in his extensive travels. Coauthor of six cookbooks, a regular contributor to *The New York Times* and *Food & Wine,* he is also a contributing editor to *Saveur* magazine. This exceptional slaw displays his culinary talents well.

1 tomato, about 3 inches in diameter, seeded and diced small

2 cups fresh orange juice, simmered until reduced to ½ cup

2 tablespoons cumin seeds

¼ cup olive oil

¼ cup red wine vinegar

¼ cup roughly chopped cilantro

kosher salt (optional)

freshly ground pepper

1 cup julienned red cabbage

1 cup julienned green cabbage

½ cup julienned carrots

1 cup julienned hearts of palm

2 avocados, peeled, pitted, and thinly sliced

In a large bowl, combine the tomato, reduced orange juice, cumin, olive oil, vinegar, cilantro, salt (if using), and pepper to taste. Whisk to combine. Add the cabbages, carrots, hearts of palm, and avocados. Toss to coat thoroughly with the dressing.

Serve immediately or refrigerate.

SERVES 8

Joslin Choices: 1 vegetable, 3 fat

Per Serving: 161 calories (70% calories from fat), 14 g total fat (2 g saturated fat), 3 g protein, 10 g carbohydrate, 5 g dietary fiber, 0 cholesterol, 89 mg sodium 430 mg potassium

Mexican Chopped Salad

Mary Sue Milliken and Susan Feniger, CIUDAD
LOS ANGELES

Ciudad (which means "city" in Spanish), owned and operated by the "Two Hot Tamales" of Food Network fame, has brought life to downtown Los Angeles. It is urban and hip with a jazzy Latin feel and a menu that shows the talents of these two chefs. This easy salad is adapted from a recipe that first appeared in their popular *Mexican Cooking for Dummies* (IDG Books Worldwide) and shows what veteran cooks can do with simple ingredients. Enjoy!

DRESSING:
⅓ cup pine nuts, toasted
1 teaspoon ground cumin
salt (optional)
freshly ground pepper to taste
¼ cup red wine vinegar
½ cup extra-virgin olive oil

2 medium tomatoes, cored, seeded, and diced
1 small red onion, diced
1 medium green apple, peeled, cored, and diced
½ cup fresh corn kernels (cut from 1 ear of corn)
1½ cups crushed baked low-fat tortilla chips
1 small avocado, peeled, seeded, and thinly sliced

1 small or ½ large head romaine lettuce, cut into
   ½-inch wide crosswise strips

TO MAKE THE DRESSING: Toast the pine nuts in a small dry frying pan over medium heat for 2 minutes, shaking frequently. Add the cumin and continue toasting and shaking the pan, 1 minute longer. Remove from the heat. Add the salt (if using), pepper, vinegar, and olive oil to the pan and whisk until blended. Let cool.

In a large bowl, combine the lettuce, tomatoes, onion, apple, corn, and tortilla chips. Toss well. Drizzle with 3 tablespoons dressing. Toss until well coated. Top with avocado slices and serve at once.

MAKES 6 SERVINGS

Joslin Choices: 1 carbohydrate (bread/starch), 2 fat

Per Serving: 163 calories (48% calories from fat), 9 g total fat (2 g saturated fat), 3 g protein, 20 g carbohydrate, 5 g dietary fiber, 0 cholesterol, 61 mg sodium, 498 mg potassium

Do We Dare Eat Nuts?

Have you noticed that our chefs use nuts to garnish and flavor their recipes? Scientific studies currently indicate that eating 1 ounce of nuts rich in monounsaturated fats a day can reduce the risk of heart disease by up to 10%. The nuts that fit this profile are almonds, Brazil nuts, hazelnuts (also known as filberts), macadamia nuts, pecans, pistachios, and walnuts. Nuts are high in calcium, folic acid, magnesium, potassium, vitamin E, and fiber, but 1 ounce of nuts also contains 180 calories and 17 grams of fat. The good news is that 50 to 80% of their fat is monounsaturated, fat that helps to lower cholesterol and increase the "good" cholesterol.

If you are trying to lose weight, nuts should be used sparingly. Talk to your dietitian to see how often and how much of these little gems to include in your meal plan.

Shaved Fennel, Artichoke, and Parmesan Salad

Alice Waters, CHEZ PANISSE
BERKELEY, CALIFORNIA

Some credit chef and owner Alice Waters with starting today's healthy movement, growing the restaurant's vegetables and herbs, and always using fresh, organically grown products. If you are ever in the area, you will be remiss if you do not stop here for a bite to eat. Chef Waters suggested that we adapt this recipe, which appeared in her *Chez Panisse Vegetables* (HarperCollins), so you can enjoy its play of textures and tastes.

2 large artichokes, about 1½ pounds total
2 large fresh lemons
2 medium fennel bulbs, about 1 pound total
2 tablespoons extra-virgin olive oil
1 tablespoon white truffle oil

salt (optional)
freshly ground pepper
1 piece Parmigiano-Reggiano cheese,
    about 3 ounces
½ cup flat-leaf parsley leaves

Pare the artichokes down to their hearts and, using a small spoon, scoop out the chokes. Drop the hearts into water acidulated with the juice of 1 of the lemons.

Cut off the feathery tops of the fennel at the base of their stalks and remove the outer layers of the bulb leaves. Slice the fennel very thin with a sharp knife or mandolin. Remove the artichoke hearts from the water and slice them very thin the same way. Combine the oils.

TO ASSEMBLE THE SALAD: On a large serving platter, first make a layer of the fennel slices. Squeeze one-third of the lemon juice evenly over the fennel and drizzle with 1 tablespoon of the combined oils. Sprinkle with salt (if using) and pepper. Then make a layer of the artichoke heart slices. Sprinkle another third of lemon juice on the artichokes and drizzle evenly with another tablespoon of the mixed oils. Using a cheese slicer or a vegetable peeler, cut thin shavings of the Parmigiano cheese and arrange them on top of the artichoke slices. Scatter the parsley leaves over the cheese and again season with salt (if using) and pepper. Sprinkle the remaining lemon juice over all and drizzle evenly with the remaining tablespoon of mixed oils. Serve immediately.

MAKES 8 SERVINGS

Joslin Choices: 1 medium-fat protein, 1 vegetable, 1 fat

Per Serving: 138 calories (53% calories from fat), 9 g total fat (3 g saturated fat), 7 g protein, 11 g carbohydrate, 4 g dietary fiber, 8 mg cholesterol, 270 mg sodium, 447 mg potassium

Insalata di Finocchio con Rucola (Fennel Salad with Arugula)

Maristella Innocenti, I COPPI
NEW YORK CITY

Fennel is often referred to as Florence fennel, so it makes sense that this talented chef from Florence, now practicing her craft here in the States, would submit a recipe using this favored Italian ingredient. This is a great salad to have when you're serving fish—its light anise flavor complements fish superbly.

2 medium fennel bulbs, trimmed and chopped
2 large Belgian endives, trimmed and chopped
2 small leeks, white part only, well washed and chopped
3 tablespoons extra-virgin olive oil
2 teaspoons grated lemon zest

juice of 1½ large lemons
salt (optional)
freshly ground pepper
1 bunch arugula, about 20 leaves
1 tablespoon chopped parsley

Combine the fennel, endives, and leeks. Whisk together the olive oil, lemon zest, lemon juice, salt (if using), and pepper. Drizzle over the fennel mixture and toss.

Arrange the arugula on a large serving platter and place the fennel mixture in the center. Sprinkle with the parsley and serve.

MAKES 4 SERVINGS

Joslin Choices: 1 carbohydrate (bread/starch), 2 fat

Per Serving: 210 calories (45% calories from fat), 11 g total fat (2 g saturated fat), 6 g protein, 25 g carbohydrate, 13 g dietary fiber, 0 cholesterol, 130 mg sodium, 1,432 mg potassium

Dinner in Minutes

Fish in Its Own Glass (page 190) •

Insalata di Finocchio con Rucola (Fennel Salad with Arugula) (page 70) •

Fresh Raspberries •

Joslin Choices: 3½ very-low-fat protein, 1 carbohydrate (bread/starch), 3 fat,
371 calories (41% calories from fat) •

Note: Items not referring to a specific recipe are not included in the nutritional analysis. Consult the Joslin Food Choices (page 287) for that information. •

Grilled Portobello Mushrooms over Mesclun with Fresh Herb Vinaigrette

Cyrus Marfatia, EXECUTIVE CHEF

CELEBRITY CRUISE LINE

When Fran first ordered this salad while cruising on one of the many Celebrity Cruise Line's ships, she knew she had to get the recipe for this book. Happily the line obliged so you, too, can enjoy its marvelous flavor and meaty texture. It makes a fine starter course or a light lunch with some crusty Italian bread and a piece of fresh fruit.

FRESH HERB VINAIGRETTE:

½ cup olive oil

¼ cup balsamic vinegar

1 tablespoon finely minced red onion

½ tablespoon finely minced fresh basil

½ tablespoon finely minced fresh oregano

½ tablespoon finely minced fresh thyme

½ tablespoon finely minced garlic

salt (optional)

freshly ground pepper

12 cloves garlic

2 teaspoons olive oil, plus extra for brushing
  mushrooms

6 large Portobello mushroom caps, cleaned

8 cups loosely packed mesclun or mixed baby
  greens, washed and dried

1 large red bell pepper, stem, seeds, and white
  inner ribs removed, finely chopped

In a small jar with a tight-fitting lid, combine the olive oil, balsamic vinegar, red onion, basil, oregano, thyme, and minced garlic. Season to taste with salt (if using) and pepper. Shake well; set aside.

Preheat the oven to 375°F. Peel the garlic cloves and cut the garlic into thin slivers. Place the garlic in a small metal roasting pan and drizzle with the 2 teaspoons olive oil. Cover with aluminum foil and roast in the oven until the garlic is tender, about 15 to 20 minutes. Remove from the oven and keep warm.

Meanwhile, light a grill. Brush the mushroom caps with a little olive oil and grill over medium-high heat until the mushrooms are tender, about 4 to 6 minutes total, turning once. Place the mushrooms in a baking dish and pour the vinaigrette over all. Keep warm.

Divide the mesclun among 6 large serving plates. Remove the mushrooms from the vinaigrette, reserving the vinaigrette. Place a mushroom on top of each serving of mesclun. Garnish with the finely chopped bell pepper and garlic slivers. Drizzle each salad with

1 teaspoon of the reserved vinaigrette. Pour any remaining vinaigrette back into the mixing jar and refrigerate to use within 2 days.

MAKES 6 SERVINGS

Joslin Choices: 1 vegetable, 1½ fat

Per Serving: 131 calories (59% calories from fat), 8 g total fat (1 g saturated fat), 3 g protein, 10 g carbohydrate, 3 g dietary fiber, 0 cholesterol, 26 mg sodium, 591 mg potassium

Chopped Red Onion, Horseradish, and Watercress Salad

Waldy Malouf, BEACON

NEW YORK CITY AND STAMFORD, CONNECTICUT

This is a very unusual salad created by Chef Malouf, who earned a coveted 3-star rating from *The New York Times* for Manhattan's beloved Rainbow Room. Before opening Beacon, he also cooked at the Four Seasons, La Côte Basque, the St. Regis Hotel, La Crémaillère (Banksville, New York), and the Hudson River Club.

2 bunches fresh watercress, washed, trimmed of
   thick stems, and roughly chopped to yield 2 cups
1 large ripe tomato, diced into ½-inch cubes
½ cup chopped fresh mint
1 large red onion, thinly sliced
½ cup fresh-grated horseradish or ¼ cup
   prepared horseradish

¼ cup extra-virgin olive oil
juice of ½ large lemon
coarse salt
freshly ground pepper

Combine all the ingredients, mix well, cover, and refrigerate overnight.

Serve on 8 chilled salad plates.

MAKES 8 SERVINGS

Joslin Choices: 1 vegetable, 1 fat

Per Serving: 82 calories (76% calories from fat), 7 g total fat (1 g saturated fat), 1 g protein, 4 g carbohydrate, 1 g dietary fiber, 0 cholesterol, 147 mg sodium, 136 mg potassium

Small Plates—

300 Calories and Under

Asian-Rubbed Chicken Salad

Donald Rini, SPROUTS AT CAMELBACK INN
SCOTTSDALE, ARIZONA

Chef Rini's chicken salad is as delightful to the eye as it is to the palate—a pretty jumble of highly flavored strips of chicken, red onions, red and yellow peppers, and tomatoes, atop of pile of baby greens. This makes a wonderful light supper or special lunch. Another time, use the rub on mild fish fillets or pork tenderloins.

4 4-ounce boneless, skinless chicken breasts

4 teaspoons Asian Rub (recipe follows)

2 small red onions, thinly sliced

2 roasted red bell peppers, cut into julienne strips

2 roasted yellow bell peppers, cut into julienne strips

3 tablespoons balsamic vinegar

4 cups mixed baby greens

4 medium vine-ripened tomatoes, sliced

Rinse the chicken breasts and remove all visible fat. Rub the chicken with the Asian Rub.

Cover, and refrigerate for 30 minutes.

Preheat the oven to 350°F.

Heat a heavy nonstick skillet over high heat. Add the chicken and sear on both sides, turning once, for about 1 to 2 minutes per side, until nicely browned. Transfer the chicken to a baking dish and roast in the oven for 10 minutes.

Meanwhile, add the onions to the skillet and cook, stirring, until the onions are caramelized, about 10 to 12 minutes. Add the roasted peppers and balsamic vinegar. Allow the vinegar to reduce slightly.

Remove the chicken from the oven and carve into thin slices.

In a mixing bowl, toss the baby greens, sliced chicken, and onion-pepper mixture. Arrange the tomatoes on 4 large plates. Top with the chicken salad mixture and serve.

MAKES 4 SERVINGS

Joslin Choices: 3 very-low-fat protein, 1 carbohydrate (bread/starch)

Per Serving: 208 calories (15% calories from fat), 4 g total fat (1 g saturated fat), 26 g protein, 19 g carbohydrate, 5 g dietary fiber, 63 mg cholesterol, 134 mg sodium, 850 mg potassium

Asian Rub

3 tablespoons Dijon mustard

2 tablespoons honey

½ teaspoon ground cinnamon

½ teaspoon ground nutmeg

½ teaspoon ground ginger

2 tablespoons shredded fresh mint leaves

Combine all the ingredients, mixing thoroughly. Use as directed. Cover and refrigerate any leftover mixture for future use.

Joslin Choices: free food

Per 1-Teaspoon Serving: 9 calories (18% calories from fat), 0 total fat (0 saturated fat), 0 protein, 2 g carbohydrate, 0 dietary fiber, 0 cholesterol, 51 mg sodium, 5 mg potassium

Crispy Chicken Flautas

Liz Baron, BLUE MESA GRILL

ADDISON, DALLAS, FORT WORTH, AND PLANO, TEXAS

Liz Baron and her husband Jim are the culinary geniuses behind this very popular Texas restaurant—a favorite of the locals and a "must try" for anyone visiting the Metroplex. We know of people who fly back to both coasts with bags of their sweet potato chips and mason jars filled with Fire-Roasted Salsa (page 263) in their carry-ons. We didn't get their recipe for the chips but these crispy flautas are bold in flavor and perfect for dipping into the salsa.

4 8-ounce bone-in chicken breasts, skin on
salt (optional)
freshly ground pepper
2 tablespoons fat-free, no-salt-added canned
   chicken broth, plus extra for the tortillas
1 large yellow onion, chopped

½ poblano chile pepper, chopped
½ large green bell pepper, seeded and chopped
1 cup canned no-salt-added tomatoes,
   drained and chopped
12 7-inch corn tortillas
vegetable cooking spray

Preheat the oven to 350°F.

Place the chicken breasts in a shallow roasting pan and season the chicken with salt (if using) and pepper. Roast for 30 minutes. Remove from the oven and cool. When cool enough to handle, shred the chicken, discarding the skin and bones.

Heat the broth in a sauté pan over medium heat. Add the onion and peppers, and sauté until the onion is limp, about 4 minutes. Add the tomatoes and chicken. Simmer for 10 minutes. Remove from the heat, cool, and drain off any excess liquid.

Soften the tortillas in a bit of the chicken broth and lay on a work surface. Divide the chicken mixture among the tortillas, placing it in the center. Roll the tortillas up tightly and secure with 2 toothpicks. Lightly spray with cooking spray.

Light a grill or preheat the oven to 375°F. Place the tortillas, seam side down, on the grill over medium heat. Turn while cooking until crispy, about 5 to 7 minutes. If baking the tortillas, arrange on a baking sheet, seam side down, and bake, turning twice, until crispy, about 20 minutes.

Remove from the grill or the oven and discard the toothpicks. Serve with Fire-Roasted Salsa (see Headnote above).

MAKES 6 SERVINGS

Joslin Choices: 3 very-low-fat protein, 2 carbohydrate (bread/starch)

Per Serving: 259 calories (14% calories from fat), 4 g total fat (1 g saturated fat), 26 g protein, 30 g carbohydrate, 4 g dietary fiber, 60 mg cholesterol, 152 mg sodium, 457 mg potassium

Chile Peppers

Members of the Capsicum family, chiles can be used fresh, roasted, dried, or ground in powder. A mainstay of Southwestern cuisine, chiles are also used in other countries, particularly in Southeast Asia, Mexico, South America, India, and Spain. Not all chiles are alike, especially when talking about their heat. Measured on a scale called scoville heat units, the heat of a habanero, the hottest chile pepper ever measured, can be as much as 1,000 times the heat of the jalapeño. Another interesting fact: the hotter the heat, the smaller the size.

It may be advisable to wear rubber gloves or cover your hands with plastic sandwich bags when working with fresh chiles as their natural oils may irritate and burn your skin. Be particularly careful not to touch your eyes or face when working with chiles. If you do find your skin or eyes burning, stop and immediately apply yogurt, milk, or mayonnaise to your skin and flush your eyes with cold water.

To tame the taste of a chile, carefully cut out and discard the seeds and center ribs where most of the heat lies, just using the flesh. Here are the varieties the chefs call for in their recipes. Many are used in fresh, dried, or powdered form—and are called by different names in each form. We have arranged the list from the hottest chiles to the mildest.

Serrano: Bright green or red, this chile is cylindrical with a rounded end. It's about 2 inches long and has a clean, biting heat. Good when roasted.

Jalapeño: Medium to dark green or red, about 1½ inches long and tapering from a 1-inch shoulder to a rounded tip. This is the best known and most widely used of the fresh chiles. May be used fresh or roasted. When a jalapeño chile is dried and smoked it is called a chipotle. Also comes canned as chipotle adobo in a sauce made of onions, tomatoes, vinegar, and spices.

Poblano: A dark green pepper about 4 to 5 inches long, tapering from the shoulder to a point (also called an ancho when it's red in color). This chile is always cooked or roasted, never eaten raw. Roasting adds a smoky flavor.

Anaheim: A mild green chile (you will sometimes see a red one), Anaheim chiles are elongated and cone-shaped with a slight twist. This pepper can be used raw, but its flavor is improved by roasting, leaving odd bits of charred skin for added flavor. They are also available canned.

Pimento: Mildly sweet and slightly hot, this chile is best known in southern Spain, Hungary, in the southern United States, and in California. Red and almost heart-shaped, a fresh pimento has a stronger flavor than the sweet red bell pepper. It is also available canned and in dried form, known as paprika.

Breast of *Pichón* in Consommé with Baby Vegetables

Didier Montarou, LA CUPOLA AT THE WESTIN PALACE
MADRID

Pichón is the Spanish word for "squab," a very young domesticated pigeon that has never flown. Prized for its very tender, delicately flavored dark meat, squab are available fresh or frozen in gourmet markets or by mail order (see Sources, page 296). Boneless chicken thighs could also be used.

8 thin leeks, white part and some pale green
8 baby zucchini
⅓ cup haricots verts or baby green beans
4 *pichón* breasts, 3½ to 4½ ounces each

2 cups Chicken Stock (page 31)
salt (optional)
freshly ground white pepper
fresh chervil, leaves picked for garnish

Trim the vegetables, leaving them all whole. Blanch each vegetable separately in lightly salted boiling water and refresh in ice water. Drain and set to one side.

Bring the stock to a boil in a saucepan large enough to hold the *pichón* breasts. Lightly season each breast with salt (if using) and pepper. Lower into the broth and simmer gently for about 5 minutes. Remove from the pan, cover, and keep warm. Reduce the broth by just over half.

Return the breasts to the reduced broth and allow to warm through. Remove and cut each breast into 6 slices, at a slight angle. Place the vegetables in the broth to reheat while slicing the *pichón*. Arrange the *pichón* slices in a circle in the middle of 4 shallow soup plates. Drain the vegetables and scatter these over and around the *pichón*. Strain the broth through cheesecloth and pour it into the soup plates over the *pichón* and the vegetables. Scatter the fresh chervil over all.

MAKES 4 SERVINGS

Joslin Choices: 3½ very-low-fat protein, 1½ carbohydrate (bread/starch)

Per Serving: 276 calories (17% calories from fat), 5 g total fat (1 g saturated fat), 29 g protein, 30 g carbohydrate, 6 g dietary fiber, 89 mg cholesterol, 255 mg sodium, 1,002 mg potassium

Creole Fish with Grilled and Smoked Tomato Relish

Tanya Holland, VICTORY KITCHEN
BROOKLYN, NEW YORK

Watching the Food Network, Bonnie was charmed by a chef from Brooklyn, and as soon as the show was over she was on the phone. Chef Holland trained in France at La Varenne Ecole de Cuisine as well as in New York. She contributes to *Food & Wine* and has taught at Cambridge Culinary Institute. Most important, she found us on the Web and e-mailed that she wanted to join the project, as diabetes has affected members of her family. Her approach to cooking is multi-ethnic, combining Caribbean, Mediterranean, Asian, and American Southwest with the Southern influences of her family.

This Creole dish is very representative of Chef Holland's cooking and an example of her ability to serve a healthy meal that will wow your taste buds and eyes at the same time.

4 5-ounce fillets of firm-fleshed fish such
 as grouper, flounder, red snapper
 (skin on, optional)
1 cup thinly sliced onion
4 teaspoons minced garlic
4 teaspoons tomato paste
8 dashes Tabasco sauce

8 dashes Worcestershire sauce
4 teaspoons chopped fresh thyme
1 teaspoon chili powder
1 teaspoon freshly ground pepper
1 tablespoon olive oil
Grilled and Smoked Tomato Relish (recipe follows)

Place the fillets in a shallow baking dish. Whisk all the remaining ingredients except the olive oil and relish together and pour half the amount into a small bowl and set aside. Pour the other half over the fish portions and allow to marinate in the refrigerator for at least 4 hours.

Heat the grill and brush lightly with the oil. Remove the fish from the marinade and grill for about 4 minutes on each side, turning once. Warm the reserved marinade and serve over the fish, and spoon the Grilled and Smoked Tomato Relish onto the fillets.

Grilled and Smoked Tomato Relish

mesquite, apple wood, or other smoking chips
4 plum tomatoes, halved
3 tablespoons minced shallots
2 tablespoons capers, well rinsed and drained
1½ tablespoons red wine vinegar

2 tablespoons chopped fresh basil
1 tablespoon olive oil
salt (optional)
freshly ground pepper

Light a grill.

Place the smoking chips in the grill and grill the tomatoes for about 8 minutes, turning occasionally. Chop the tomatoes into small dice and mix in a bowl with the remaining ingredients, including salt (if using) and pepper to taste. Place in a small bowl and pass separately. Makes about 1½ cups.

MAKES 4 SERVINGS

Joslin Choices: 3 very-low-fat protein, ½ carbohydrate (bread/starch), 1 fat

Per Serving: 193 calories (30% calories from fat), 6 g total fat (1 g saturated fat), 25 g protein, 9 g carbohydrate, 2 g dietary fiber, 67 mg cholesterol, 235 mg sodium, 509 mg potassium

Joslin Choices (tomato relish only): free food

Per 2-Tablespoon Serving: 17 calories (58% calories from fat), 1 g total fat (0 saturated fat), 0 protein, 2 g carbohydrate, 0 dietary fiber, 0 cholesterol, 45 mg sodium, 58 mg potassium

Fats

We all know that fat plays an important part of a healthy meal plan, but why is that? Fat is an essential nutrient but is high in calories, having 9 calories per gram versus 4 calories per gram for carbohydrates and protein. Eating excess fat can easily mean many extra calories per day.

Fats are divided into saturated and unsaturated. Saturated fats are usually solid at room temperature and are linked to cardiovascular disease. These are found primarily in animal fats and dairy products, as well as in tropical fats like coconut and palm oils. Saturated fats can raise blood cholesterol levels more than high cholesterol foods, so it's important to limit saturated fats to about 10% of daily caloric intake. This means if you are on a 1,600-calorie-a-day meal plan, you will want to limit your saturated fat intake to 18 grams a day.

Unsaturated fats are divided into 2 groups, polyunsaturated and monounsaturated. Monounsaturated and polyunsaturated fats both lower LDL ("bad" cholesterol) levels. Monounsaturated fats may increase HDL ('good' cholesterol) if the meal plan is low in saturated fat.

You'll note that our chefs call for a wide variety of oils in the recipes presented in this cookbook. All cooking oils are 100 percent fat at about 120 calories per tablespoon and include various amounts of polyunsaturated and monounsaturated fats, as well as saturated fat. Polyunsaturated oils include: sunflower, safflower, soybean, corn, grapeseed, and sesame oils. Monounsaturated oils include olive oil, canola oil, and peanut oil, and the more expensive nut oils, like walnut and macadamia. The following are approximate percentages, as oils vary from brand to brand.

	POLYUNSATURATED (%)	MONOUNSATURATED (%)	SATURATED (%)
Almond	18	73	8
Avocado	13	71	4
Canola	30	59	7
Corn	59	24	13
Grapeseed	69	0	10
Hazelnut	10	78	7
Olive	8	74	13
Peanut	32	46	17
Safflower	13	9	0
Sesame	42	40	14
Sunflower	68	21	11
Vegetable	74	12	9
Walnut	67	24	9

Once opened, store the nut oils in the refrigerator. The others can be sealed airtight in the pantry for up to 2 months. Saturated fats like butter or hydrogenated margarine need to be stored tightly wrapped in the refrigerator for up to 2 weeks, or frozen if kept for longer periods of time.

Although virtually none of the chefs use cooking oil sprays, they are great for reducing the fat content of food. We keep vegetable and olive oil cooking sprays in our pantry, and a butter-flavored spray in the refrigerator. We also have an olive oil mister, available at fine cookware stores, which gives a fine mist of olive oil onto a cooking or baking surface. When one counts "one thousand and one, one thousand and two" and then stops spraying, the amount of fat added is negligible.

Honeyed Alaskan Black Cod over Portobello Mushrooms and Sautéed Spinach

Laurent Tourondel, CELLO
NEW YORK CITY

Cello is located in a beautiful landmark, turn-of-the-century brownstone on the Upper East Side and is presided over by Chef Tournondel. A French-trained chef, he prides himself on creating dishes that meld many flavors with distinct tastes and textures. Others have described this self-effacing chef's entrées as "luxurious refinement." He and Cello have received raves from *Gourmet, Food & Wine, GQ,* and *The New York Times.*

If you are unable to find black cod, substitute fresh sea bass or a piece of New England cod. Black cod is seasonal but, according to our chef, well worth the effort to find.

Use the best honey you can locate if your market does not carry acacia honey.

This is also a superb marinade to use on chicken breasts.

MARINADE:
1 cup acacia honey
1 tablespoon grapeseed oil
½ cup reduced-sodium soy sauce
⅓ cup white wine vinegar

6 4-ounce portions Alaskan black cod

MARINATED PORTOBELLOS:
2 large portobello mushrooms, about 7 ounces
  each, stems removed

2 tablespoons olive oil
1 large clove garlic, minced
2 sprigs fresh thyme

SAUTÉED SPINACH:
2 teaspoons unsalted butter
1 large clove garlic, minced
½ pound fresh spinach
grated nutmeg to taste
⅛ teaspoon salt (optional)
freshly ground pepper

TO PREPARE THE MARINADE: Combine the acacia honey, grapeseed oil, soy sauce, and white wine vinegar. Reserve 1 tablespoon of the mixture for the garnish. Cover the portioned fillets of fish with the marinade, cover, and refrigerate overnight or up to 24 hours.

About 1 hour before cooking time, marinate the portobello mushrooms in the olive oil, garlic, and thyme. When ready to cook, heat a salamander until red-hot or preheat a broiler. Light a grill.

Scrape the marinade off the cod. Caramelize the top of the cod by passing the hot salamander close to the top of the cod or place under the broiler until the top is caramelized and nicely browned. Change the oven setting to 375°F. Finish cooking the cod in the oven for 7 to 8 minutes, or until the fish flakes or tests done. Remove from the oven and keep warm.

Grill the mushrooms until tender, about 2 minutes per side, turning once. Slice into thin strips. Keep warm.

TO PREPARE THE SPINACH: In a hot sauté pan, melt the butter. When the butter begins to brown, add the garlic, then the spinach. Cook until just wilted, about 2 to 3 minutes, tossing frequently. Season with the nutmeg, salt (if using), and pepper. Keep warm.

TO ASSEMBLE THE DISH: In the center of each of 6 large soup plates, arrange the spinach and top with the portobello strips. Place a portion of the fish on top and drizzle each serving with ½ teaspoon of the reserved marinade. Serve immediately.

MAKES 6 SERVINGS

Joslin Choices: 2½ low-fat protein, 1 carbohydrate (bread/starch)

Per Serving: 207 calories (32% calories from fat), 7 g total fat (2 g saturated fat), 20 g protein, 13 g carbohydrate, 1 g dietary fiber, 40 mg cholesterol, 257 mg sodium, 848 mg potassium

Chilled Cod Soup

Normand Laprise, **TOQUÉ**
MONTREAL

Toqué and its owner, Chef Laprise, have been known as Montreal's most exciting restaurant and most creative chef for more than 10 years. Taped to the private stairwell leading to the kitchen is a copy of an article from *Gourmet* declaring Toqué the best restaurant in Montreal and praising this self-effacing chef's fare as "the work of a genius." Chef Laprise, a guest chef at the James Beard Foundation, is considered to be the inspiration for Quebec's "new" cuisine, which is multicultural. *Bon Appétit, Food & Wine, Gourmet,* and *Elle Québec* give the restaurant and chef rave reviews.

Here he shares a recipe from the Toqué menu. At the restaurant it is served with a salad of wild purslane and endive with garlic croutons. Make your own salad and you will feel that Chef Laprise is cooking for you in your kitchen. *Merci,* Chef Laprise.

2 pounds fresh cod fillets
3 tablespoons extra-virgin olive oil
sea salt (optional)
freshly ground pepper
2 sprigs fresh thyme
1¼ pounds onions, thinly sliced
1 clove garlic, lightly crushed but still intact
¾ pound russet potatoes, peeled and
  thinly sliced

LABNEH:
⅔ cup yogurt cheese
1½ tablespoons chopped fresh mint
2 teaspoons paprika

1 cup milk
sea salt (optional)
sliced cherry tomatoes and thyme sprigs for
  garnish (optional)

Preheat the oven to 350°F.

Choose thick cod fillets and cut a ⅔-pound slab from the thickest part. Cut the remaining cod into 2-inch chunks and reserve. Coat the slab with 1 teaspoon olive oil, season with salt (if using) and pepper, and put 1 sprig of thyme on top. Place on a parchment paper–lined thick baking sheet and encircle the cod with an aluminum paper collar. Bake until done, about 20 minutes. Transfer to a plate. Chill thoroughly in the refrigerator.

TO MAKE THE SOUP: In a heavy sauté pan over very low heat, cook the onions and garlic in the remaining oil until soft and translucent but not colored. Add the potatoes, and stir to coat with the oil and onion mixture. Season to taste. Add the remaining sprig of thyme and cold water to cover. Bring to a boil; reduce the heat to a simmer. Cook until the potatoes are done. Add the cod chunks and cook at a simmer until the fish is cooked through and flakes easily. Remove and discard the garlic.

TO MAKE THE LABNEH: In a small bowl, combine the yogurt cheese, mint, and paprika. In small batches, puree the soup in a food processor or blender while the mixture is hot, adding the milk and yogurt cheese mixture. Pass it through a fine sieve and chill thoroughly in the refrigerator.

Remove the collar from the slab of cod and gently separate the fish into large flakes using a small fork or knife. Check the soup for seasoning and adjust if necesary.

Ladle ½ cup of the soup into each bowl. Place a flake of cod in the center of each with a small amount of sea salt (if using) on each flake. If using, garnish with sliced cherry tomatoes and some sprigs of thyme.

MAKES 12 SERVINGS

Joslin Choices: 1 low-fat protein, 1 carbohydrate (bread/starch)

Per Serving: 133 calories (29% calories from fat), 4 g total fat (1 g saturated fat), 11 g protein, 12 g carbohydrate, 2 g dietary fiber, 22 mg cholesterol, 52 mg sodium, 325 mg potassium

Pesce per Quattro

David Pasternack, ESCA

NEW YORK CITY

Esca and its chef David Pasternack are a hit in Manhattan's theater district; Esca was nominated as the best new restaurant by the James Beard Foundation. While all of the chefs in this book were gracious, Chef Pasternack is one of the few who gave us a direct phone number in the kitchen to keep in touch. His food is elemental, presenting the very essence of each piece of seafood. Here, he gives us a lesson on how to prepare fish in a salt crust. The fish is protected from drying out as it bakes, but absorbs very little of the sodium from the throw-away crust. It's a dramatic and fun way to cook a whole fish.

3 cups fine sea salt

2 large egg whites

1 2-pound Branzino (sea bream or sea bass), cleaned

2 sprigs fresh rosemary

3 to 4 parsley stems

1 clove garlic

2 slices of a large lemon

Preheat the oven to 400°F. Line a heavy baking sheet with parchment paper.

In a small bowl, combine the sea salt and egg whites. Mix well (the mixture should feel like wet sand). Set aside.

Stuff the cavity of the fish with the rosemary, parsley, garlic, and lemon slices. Place the fish on the prepared baking sheet and cover with the salt mixture, packing down tightly. Bake the fish for 15 minutes, until the salt crust is golden brown around the edges. Transfer the fish with its salt crust to a large heated serving platter.

At the table, crack the crust, and peel off the skin if it doesn't come off with the crust. Using a flat fish spoon, remove the fish off the bone and serve.

MAKES 4 SERVINGS

Joslin Choices: 5 very-low-fat protein

Per Serving: 201 calories (19% calories from fat), 4 g total fat (1 g saturated fat), 38 g protein, 1 g carbohydrate, 0 dietary fiber, 81 mg cholesterol, 736 mg sodium, 539 mg potassium

Seafood Safety: A Statement from the Joslin Diabetes Center

While including seafood as part of a healthy meal plan can be beneficial to people with diabetes, eating raw seafood can be dangerous. Food-borne illness caused by improper handling, storage, and preparation of seafood presents the risk of serious illness or even death in people with diabetes and other chronic diseases.

It is recommended by the 1997 Food Code of the Food and Drug Administration (FDA) that most seafood be cooked to an internal temperature of 145°F (63°C) for 15 seconds so that bacteria or parasites which may be present in the seafood can be destroyed. Thawing and marinating seafood in the refrigerator, washing hands thoroughly before and after handling, and cooking immediately are additional food safety tips to keep in mind. Remember, keeping "Hot Foods Hot" (140°F [60°C] or higher) and "Cold Foods Cold" (41°F [5°C] or lower) are also important food safety tips to use when serving food.

We at Joslin Diabetes Center recommend, as does the FDA, that people with diabetes eat seafood that has been thoroughly cooked.

For further information, please reference "Critical Steps Toward Safer Seafood," reprinted with revisions, February 1998, from the FDA Consumer. FDA publication No. 98-2317.

Salad of Royal *Daurade* with Zucchini Flowers "Forville"

Stéphane Raimbault, L'OASIS

LA NAPOULE, FRANCE

On a recent trip to the south of France, Bonnie and her husband had the opportunity to dine at L'Oasis in the little village of La Napoule, located between Cannes and St. Raphaël. Stéphane Raimbault is the chef and owner of this most breathtaking and elegant restaurant, where one can dine in the garden under a canopy of leaves surrounded by flowers and lanterns, with the most gracious service that you can imagine. The meal rose to levels as grand as the setting. No wonder it is a member of *Les Grands Tables du Monde.*

This recipe calls for sea bream, a fish indigenous to the region, but difficult to purchase fresh in most of this country. As a substitute, try porgy, which has a similar flavor, but note that this fish has many small bones. You can also substitute a small red snapper, flounder, grouper fillets, rockfish, sea bass fillets, or any firm, flaky white fish.

1¼ pounds fresh fish fillets of royal *daurade* (sea bream)
1½ cups Fish Stock (page 93) or water
⅓ cup dry white wine
4 large zucchini flowers
1 large zucchini, 4 to 5 inches in diameter
additional small zucchini for a total of 1½ pounds, if needed
2 large plum (Roma) tomatoes, diced
¼ cup snipped fresh chives
2 teaspoons minced garlic
1 tablespoon grated lime zest
1 tablespoon fresh lime juice
¼ teaspoon kosher salt

freshly ground pepper to taste
1 head frisée or curly endive, about 1 pound, rinsed and drained on paper towels, separated into leaves
1 bunch rocket (arugula), rinsed and drained on paper towels, tough stems trimmed off and discarded
1 medium fennel bulb, trimmed and finely minced
¼ cup purple basil leaves
2 tablespoons chopped fresh chervil
2 tablespoons extra-virgin olive oil
1 tablespoon water
2 tablespoons aged balsamic vinegar
¼ teaspoon salt

Clean the fish and remove any small bones. Poach the fillets in the Fish Stock and wine to cover until just cooked, about 5 minutes. Cool and flake. Refrigerate until ready to use.

Working on a paper towel, carefully open the zucchini flowers very gently and remove the centers. Try to avoid tearing the flowers. Fill a large metal bowl with water and several ice cubes. Bring a pot of lightly salted water to a boil. Add the zucchini flowers and blanch for a few seconds. Remove and plunge into ice water to stop the cooking process. Drain on paper towels; chill.

Trim and wash the zucchini. Cut off an 8-inch-long piece of zucchini. Using a zester or a sharp knife, remove a lengthwise strip of the peeling about every ½ inch to form a decorative pattern. Cut into 4 rounds. Set aside. Peel and finely dice the remaining zucchini (if using), discarding any seeds.

In a large bowl, combine the flaked fish, finely diced zucchini, tomatoes, chives, garlic, lime zest, lime juice, salt, and pepper. In another bowl, combine the frisée, rocket, fennel, basil, and chervil.

Place the zucchini rounds on each of 4 large chilled plates. Top with the fish mixture and cover and surround with the frisée mixture, arranging it all in a decorative fashion to resemble a bouquet. In a cup, whisk together the olive oil, water, vinegar, and salt. Drizzle each plate with some of the mixture. Place a reserved zucchini blossom on top of each salad. Serve at once.

MAKES 6 SERVINGS

Joslin Choices: 3½ low-fat protein, ½ carbohydrate (bread/starch)

Per Serving: 235 calories (30% calories from fat), 8 g total fat (1 g saturated fat), 27 g protein, 12 g carbohydrate, 5 g dietary fiber, 51 mg cholesterol, 396 mg sodium, 1,206 mg potassium

Fish Stock

Use bones from non-oily fish (flounder, halibut, or any other white fish) for this wonderful stock. Your fish market will usually give you the bones at no charge. We developed this stock for our first cookbook, *The Joslin Diabetes Gourmet Cookbook* (Bantam Books).

1 pound fish bones, rinsed and cut into chunks
1 medium white onion, about 3 ounces, quartered
1 leek, white part only, rinsed and sliced
1 rib celery with leaves, sliced
8 shallots, diced
2 large cloves garlic, sliced
1 quart water
4 sprigs flat-leaf parsley
2 sprigs fresh thyme
2 small sprigs fresh tarragon
1 2-inch strip lemon zest
1 teaspoon fennel seeds
4 peppercorns
1 cup dry white wine

In a large stockpot or heavy saucepan, combine the fish bones, onion, leek, celery, shallots, garlic, and water. Bring to a boil over high heat. Skim off all the foam that rises to the surface. Add the parsley, thyme, tarragon, lemon zest, fennel seeds, and peppercorns. Cover, reduce the heat, and simmer for 15 minutes.

Add the wine and continue to simmer for another 15 minutes. Strain through a fine sieve or a colander lined with cheesecloth. Discard the solids. Cool to room temperature. Store in a sealed container in the refrigerator for up to 24 hours or freeze for up to 2 months.

MAKES 1 QUART

Joslin Choices: free food

Per 1-Cup Serving: 25 calories (6% calories from fat), trace total fat (0 saturated fat), 1 g protein, 3 g carbohydrate, 0 dietary fiber, 2 mg cholesterol, 14 mg sodium, 71 mg potassium

Steamed Halibut with Tomatoes, Lemongrass, and Fresh Coriander

Jonathan Eismann, PACIFIC TIME

MIAMI BEACH

Fusion cookery often turns out to be a jumble of confusing flavors, but in the hands of this talented Miami Beach chef, it works extremely well. Here chef-owner Eismann melds East with West and infuses his dishes with high flavor and lots of creativity. This halibut recipe is a prime example of his culinary talent. When we tested this recipe, we didn't count the cilantro leaves; we just grabbed a handful and threw them onto the fish. We probably ended up with more than 20 leaves per serving, but then we love cilantro.

2 tablespoons extra-virgin olive oil

6 teaspoons finely minced fresh ginger

4½ cups chopped, peeled, and seeded vine-ripened tomatoes with their juice

120 cilantro leaves with no stems

6 4-ounce center-cut fresh halibut fillets, cut 1- to 1½-inches thick

sea salt (optional)

freshly ground pepper

9 tablespoons fresh lemon juice

3 tablespoons fresh lime juice

3 large leeks, white part only, well washed and julienned

12 3-inch stalks fresh lemongrass, julienned

12 fresh lime leaves (optional)

1½ tablespoons finely minced flat-leaf parsley

1½ teaspoons finely grated lemon zest

Preheat the oven to 425°F.

Rub 1 teaspoon of the olive oil onto the bottom of each of 6 oven-to-table individual casseroles or gratin pans that are 8 to 9 inches in diameter and at least 1½ inches deep. Sprinkle each with 1 teaspoon of the ginger. Mound ¾ cup of the tomatoes in the center of each pan. Arrange 20 cilantro leaves on top of the tomatoes. Lightly season with salt (if using) and pepper.

Lightly season the halibut fillets with salt (if using) and pepper. Place on top of the tomatoes, skin side down. Combine the lemon and lime juice and drizzle 2 tablespoons over each fillet.

Arrange the leeks in 6 bundles and place 1 bundle on top of each fillet. Divide the lemongrass into 6 equal parts and arrange inside of each pan around the edge. Add 2 lime leaves (if using) around each edge.

Tightly seal each pan with aluminum foil. Place each sealed pan on top of the stove on high heat for 1 minute. Transfer each pan to the oven and bake for 20 minutes. Remove the pans from the oven and let rest, covered, for 4 minutes.

Mix the parsley and lemon zest. Divide into 6 equal parts. Quickly open each pan and toss the parsley/lemon mixture into the broth. Quickly re-cover each pan. Again place each pan on top of the stove over high heat for 1 minute.

Put a pan on each of 6 large serving plates that have been covered with a folded linen napkin. Serve immediately, letting your guests uncover their own pan, so they may enjoy the aroma.

MAKES 6 SERVINGS

Joslin Choices: 3 very-low-fat protein, 1 carbohydrate (bread/starch), 1 fat

Per Serving: 234 calories (29% calories from fat), 8 g total fat (1 g saturated fat), 26 g protein, 17 g carbohydrate, 2 g dietary fiber, 36 mg cholesterol, 82 mg sodium, 1,006 mg potassium

Fennel and Saffron Fish Soup

Robert Clark, " C "

VANCOUVER

"C" is the definitive fish restaurant in Vancouver, and Chef Robert Clark has a free hand to try new combinations of sauces with seafood and produce hand-picked from a variety of ethnic markets in Vancouver or flown in fresh daily from international waters.

Chef Clark is originally from Montreal and the Gaspé peninsula; he learned his craft at Ontario's George Brown College. He then worked at some of the most famous Toronto kitchens before he and his wife took a sabbatical in Southeast Asia and Australia. Designed by Dominic Smith, "C" has a somewhat industrial layout with open and airy seating areas in the glass-fronted two-story first floor, which overlooks the marina. This award-winning restaurant is the destination for many of us who travel to Vancouver, and to food lovers from around the world.

SOUP:

2 28-ounce cans no-salt-added plum
  (Roma) tomatoes

2 teaspoons saffron threads

1/4 teaspoon ground nutmeg

1 cup diced celery

3 cups diced fresh fennel

5 cloves garlic, sliced

3 cups loosely packed fresh basil leaves

8 cups water

1 teaspoon salt (optional)

1 teaspoon freshly ground pepper

GARNISH:

2 tablespoons olive oil

6 ounces sablefish, grouper, or monkfish fillet

6 ounces salmon fillet

6 ounces halibut fillet

6 ounces sea scallops

1/2 cup dry white wine

1 tablespoon tarragon vinegar

salt (optional)

freshly ground pepper

Mix all the ingredients for the soup in a heavy-bottomed stockpot. Bring to a boil. Lower the heat and simmer for 2 hours. Adjust the seasoning with salt (if using) and pepper.

Preheat the oven to 350°F. Brush a large baking dish with the olive oil.

Cut each kind of seafood into six 1-ounce pieces. Lay the seafood in one layer in the prepared baking dish, making sure the pieces do not touch. Sprinkle the white wine and vinegar over the top and season with salt (if using) and pepper. Place in the oven and bake until cooked (see page 90).

Pour the hot soup into 6 bowls. Lay the cooked seafood on top of the soup so each person can see the selection. Serve hot.

MAKES 6 SERVINGS

Joslin Choices: 2 medium-fat protein, 1 carbohydrate, 1 fat

Per Serving: 283 calories (45% calories from fat), 15 g total fat (3 g saturated fat), 19 g protein, 18 g carbohydrate, 5 g dietary fiber, 43 mg cholesterol, 154 mg sodium, 1,276 mg potassium

Steamed Lobster Dumplings with Saffron Cauliflower Sauce

Susanna Foo, SUSANNA FOO

PHILADELPHIA

We love to order dumplings at Susanna Foo's. They are always presented elegantly, and now we can make these gems at home. Only Chef Foo would combine lobster with cauliflower and make a dish that marries the best of East and West cuisines.

Most markets will steam whole lobsters for free; purchase the lobsters the day that you are going to use them.

meat from 2 steamed 1½-pound Maine lobsters

SAFFRON CAULIFLOWER SAUCE:

3 cups Chicken Stock (page 31) or Fish Stock
  (page 93)
½ teaspoon saffron threads
¼ cup warm water
1½ cups cauliflower florets, loosely packed
kosher salt (optional)
freshly ground pepper

LOBSTER STOCK:

1 tablespoon soybean or corn oil
2 cloves garlic, peeled and chopped
2 shallots, peeled and chopped
1 piece fresh ginger root, about 2 inches, scrubbed
  and smashed with the flat side of a mallet
reserved lobster shells and bodies
½ cup dry white wine
8 cups Chicken Stock or Fish Stock

DUMPLINGS:

1 tablespoon vodka
1 teaspoon dark sesame oil
½ teaspoon kosher salt
1¼ teaspoons white pepper
¼ pound medium shrimp (approximately 6 to
  8 shrimp), peeled and deveined
2 tablespoons minced scallions, white part only
2 tablespoons minced freshwater chestnuts or
  celery heart
reserved diced lobster meat
1 package very thin round Chinese dumpling or
  wonton wrappers

2 cups cleaned baby spinach
¼ cup snipped fresh chives
1 cup baby pea shoots or chervil

Reserve 8 nice chunks of the 2 steamed lobsters. Cut the remaining lobster meat into fine dice and set aside; reserve the shells and bodies to make the stock. Cover and refrigerate.

TO MAKE THE SAUCE: In a medium saucepan, heat the Chicken or Fish Stock. In a small bowl, mix the saffron threads with the water. Add the cauliflower and saffron to the saucepan; cover and simmer for 30 minutes, until the cauliflower is very soft. Puree the cauliflower and cooking liquid in a food processor. Season with salt (if using) and pepper to taste. (The sauce can be made 1 day ahead, covered, and refrigerated.)

TO MAKE THE STOCK: Heat the oil in a medium-size heavy pot. Add the garlic, shallots, and ginger, stirring for 1 minute. Add the reserved lobster shells and bodies. Add the white wine. Turn the heat low and cook for about 2 minutes, until the wine is almost evaporated. Add the Chicken or Fish Stock and simmer for about 45 minutes to 1 hour. Strain through a fine sieve. There should be about 3 to 4 cups of the lobster stock.

TO MAKE THE DUMPLINGS: In a small bowl, mix the vodka, sesame oil, salt, and pepper. Place the shrimp in a food processor, add the vodka mixture, and pulse to coarsely chop. Spoon the shrimp mixture into a large mixing bowl and add the scallions and water chestnuts. Mix well. Stir in the reserved diced lobster meat.

Line a large baking sheet with waxed paper. Fill a small bowl with cold water.

Trim each wrapper into a circle, about 2½ inches in diameter. Moisten around the edge with a little water. Place 1 tablespoon of the lobster mixture in the middle of 1 wrapper, lay another wrapper on top and seal the edges very tightly. Place each dumpling on the baking sheet and keep covered with wet paper towels. Repeat until the stuffing is used up. This should make 20 to 24 dumplings. (These can be made in advance and refrigerated for 1 day or frozen for 1 month.)

Fill the bottom of a large steamer with water and bring the water to a boil. While waiting for the water to boil, layer half the spinach on the bottom of the steamer rack, then place half the lobster dumplings on top of the spinach. Place the rack over the boiling water, cover, and steam about 5 minutes. Remove and keep the cooked dumplings in a large warmer; repeat with the remaining spinach and dumplings.

Spoon about ¼ cup of the hot cauliflower sauce into the center of 8 shallow soup plates. Top with some of the steamed spinach and three lobster dumplings. Top each with a reserved chunk of lobster. Sprinkle with the snipped chives and decorate with baby pea shoots or chervil.

MAKES 8 SERVINGS

Joslin Choices: 1 low-fat protein, 2 carbohydrate (bread/starch)

Per Serving: 247 calories (14% calories from fat), 4 g total fat (1 g saturated fat), 12 g protein, 37 g carbohydrate, 4 g dietary fiber, 25 mg cholesterol, 496 mg sodium, 485 mg potassium

East Comes West Dinner

Steamed Lobster Dumplings with Saffron Cauliflower Sauce (page 98)

Basil Shrimp in Coconut Ginger Broth with Asian Greens (page 123)

Clementines or Tangerines

Joslin Choices: 2 low-fat protein, 2½ carbohydrate (bread/starch),
389 calories (25% calories from fat)

Note: Items not referring to a specific recipe are not included in the nutritional analysis.
Consult the Joslin Food Choices (page 287) for that information.

Ganbas Sautés aux Epices

Guillaume Lubard, ALCAZAR

PARIS

Chef Lubard of Alcazar in Paris is a master of many cuisines. Here he shares a shrimp dish with spices that remind us of the Far East. You will love the sweetness of the shrimp with the sharp spices along with the luscious sauce that tastes indulgently rich.

24 frozen tiger prawns, about 1 pound total

1 large red bell pepper

2 medium leeks, white part only

2 medium zucchini

2 medium carrots

SAUCE:

1 green bell pepper

½ teaspoon ground ginger

1 teaspoon curry powder

½ teaspoon turmeric

¼ teaspoon ground cinnamon

¼ cup light cream

2 teaspoons olive oil

1 ounce preserved ginger (see Note below)

salt (optional)

freshly ground pepper

handful of chopped fresh coriander (cilantro)

Preheat the oven to 200°F.

Defrost the prawns just before you are going to use them. Shell and devein. Remove the seeds from the pepper and wash the leeks. Slice all the vegetables into thin julienne strips. Set aside.

TO MAKE THE SAUCE: Seed the bell pepper and cut into small pieces. Mix with the spices and bake for 1 hour. Place the mixture in a food processor or blender and add the light cream. Puree until smooth. Transfer the mixture to a saucepan and keep warm over a low heat until serving time.

Heat 1 teaspoon of the olive oil in a wok or heavy pan, and add the ginger and reserved vegetables. Cook for 2 to 3 minutes. Season to taste with salt (if using) and pepper. In another pan, heat the remaining oil, and sauté the prawns for 1 minute on each side.

Place the vegetables on a serving plate and top with the shrimp. Drizzle the plate with the sauce and sprinkle with the coriander.

MAKES 4 SERVINGS

Joslin Choices: 2 very-low-fat protein, 1 carbohydrate (bread/starch), 1 fat

Per Serving: 205 calories (28% calories from fat), 6 g total fat (2 g saturated fat), 18 g protein, 20 g carbohydrate, 5 g dietary fiber, 144 mg cholesterol, 195 mg sodium, 783 mg potassium

Note: Preserved ginger is available in Asian markets.

Herb-Crusted Prawns over Warm Potato Salad

David Reardon, BACARA RESORT & SPA
SANTA BARBARA, CALIFORNIA

Award-winning Chef Reardon has returned to the mainland from the Kohala Coast of the Big Island of Hawaii to take up the helm at this sprawling Spanish-style Santa Barbara resort and spa. Here he has three restaurants under his charge—Miro, serving organic French and California cuisine; the Bistro, an al fresco ocean-view dining area serving Continental and Mediterranean cuisine; and the Spa Café for nutritious and delicious poolside dining. This is a shining example of his flavorful "spa" cuisine.

SHRIMP STOCK:

1 teaspoon olive oil
¼ cup diced onion
1 medium carrot, diced
½ cup diced celery
shells from 12 prawns (see below)
¼ cup dry white wine
1 tablespoon tomato paste
2½ cups water
1 bay leaf
2 sprigs fresh thyme
5 whole peppercorns, crushed

PRAWNS:

12 prawns, shelled and deveined
1 egg white, lightly frothed
¼ cup chopped mixed fresh herbs (basil, tarragon, and parsley)
1 tablespoon olive oil

¼ cup sherry or white wine vinegar
1 cup Shrimp Stock (see above)
2 tablespoons unsalted butter
salt (optional)
freshly ground pepper to taste
juice of 1 large lemon

POTATO SALAD:

4 medium fingerling or white potatoes
2 tablespoons olive oil
freshly ground pepper
4 cups assorted mushrooms, sliced (oyster, porcini or cèpe, portobello, shiitake, chanterelle; see page 20)
¼ cup chopped shallots
reserved 2 tablespoons shrimp stock (see above)
salt (optional)
freshly ground pepper

TO MAKE THE STOCK: Heat the olive oil in a 2-quart saucepan. Add the onion, carrot, and celery, and sauté until lightly caramelized. Add the prawn shells, setting aside the prawns for later use. Stir the mixture until the shells turn pink, about 2 minutes. Deglaze the pan with the wine and reduce until almost dry. Stir in the tomato paste; add the water, herbs, and peppercorns. Bring to a boil; reduce the heat and simmer for 30 minutes. Strain the liquid, making sure to press down on the solids to extract all the flavor.

Return the liquid to the saucepan and, over medium-low heat, reduce until the liquid yields 1¼ cups. Reserve ¼ cup of the stock for preparing the mushrooms.

TO PREPARE THE PRAWNS: Dip the prawns in the egg white and dredge in the herb mix; cover and refrigerate. Measure out and set aside the remaining prawn ingredients until ready to cook.

TO PREPARE THE POTATO SALAD: Halve and slice the potatoes. Heat 1 tablespoon of the olive oil in a heavy sauté pan over medium heat. Add the potatoes and cook until golden brown and tender, about 10 minutes. Keep warm.

Heat the remaining 1 tablespoon olive oil in a large sauté pan over medium-high heat. Add the mushrooms in small batches and cook until golden brown. Add some of the shallots to each batch, transferring the mushrooms to a separate dish when each batch is done. When all the mushrooms have been cooked and removed from the pan, deglaze the pan with the reserved ¼ cup shrimp stock. Add the potatoes and mushrooms to the sauté pan. Gently mix together. Taste and season with salt (if using) and pepper. Keep warm.

Returning to the set-aside prawn ingredients, in a separate large sauté pan, heat the tablespoon of olive oil over medium heat. Add the herbed prawns and sauté for 2 minutes, turning once. Remove the prawns from the pan and deglaze it with the sherry vinegar. Let reduce until dry: add the 1 cup shrimp stock. Bring to a boil and reduce the heat. Swirl in the butter. Season with salt (if using), pepper, and lemon juice.

TO ASSEMBLE THE DISH: In the middle of each of 6 shallow soup plates, place a generous spoonful of the warm potato salad. Pour some of the reduced shrimp-lemon mixture over each serving and place 2 prawns on top. Serve immediately.

MAKES 6 SERVINGS

Joslin Choices: ½ very-low-fat protein, 1½ carbohydrate (bread/starch), 2 fat

Per Serving: 222 calories (44% calories from fat), 12 g total fat (3 g saturated fat), 8 g protein, 25 g carbohydrate, 4 g dietary fiber, 34 mg cholesterol, 62 mg sodium, 848 mg potassium

Potato-Crusted Sea Bass with Grilled Eggplant, Tomato, and Mint Salad

Phillip R. Bouza, BARTON CREEK RESORT

AUSTIN, TEXAS

Barton Creek Resort has a collection of awards from around the world attesting to its maintenance of the highest standards in amenities and service. It boasts four of the best golf courses in Texas, designed by Ben Crenshaw, Arnold Palmer, and Tom Fazio. The resort also offers a spa with fitness facilities, as well as an array of European personal services to help you relax, unwind, and recharge after all that golf. A recent renovation added more luxurious guestrooms, as well as new dining space to showcase the talents of Chef Bouza.

½ pound russet potatoes
½ medium onion, minced
salt (optional)
freshly ground pepper
1 pound fresh sea bass fillets, cut into 4 portions
½ cup unbleached all-purpose flour

½ cup egg wash, made from 1 large egg beaten
   with ¼ cup water
2 tablespoons olive oil
Grilled Eggplant, Tomato, and Mint Salad
   (recipe follows)

Preheat the oven to 350°F.

Peel and grate the potatoes. Stir in the minced onion and season to taste with salt (if using) and pepper. Dredge the sea bass fillets in the flour, and dip into the egg wash. Press the potato mixture as a coating onto the top of each sea bass piece.

Place the olive oil in an ovenproof skillet and heat until hot. Place the fish, potato side down, in the hot oil and allow to cook until the potato coating is golden brown, 3 to 5 minutes. Flip the fish and continue to cook for another 1 to 2 minutes. Finish cooking in the oven for approximately 5 to 7 minutes.

Serve on a bed of Grilled Eggplant, Tomato, and Mint Salad.

MAKES 4 SERVINGS

Joslin Choices (fish only): 2½ low-fat protein, 1½ carbohydrate (bread/starch)

Per Serving: 273 calories (34% calories from fat), 10 g total fat (2 g saturated fat), 22 g protein, 22 g carbohydrate, 1 g dietary fiber, 102 mg cholesterol, 88 mg sodium, 460 mg potassium

Grilled Eggplant, Tomato, and Mint Salad

1 medium eggplant
2 tablespoons olive oil
½ large onion
1 tablespoon honey

4 Roma (plum) tomatoes, seeded and julienned
1 tablespoon lime juice
½ cup fresh mint leaves, shredded

Peel the eggplant and slice lengthwise into 8 slices. Soak the eggplant in lightly salted water for 30 minutes. Drain, rinse with water, and drain again. Light a grill or preheat the broiler. Brush the eggplant with ½ tablespoon of the olive oil and grill or broil for 10 to 12 minutes, turning once. Set aside.

In a large sauté pan, caramelize the onion in ½ tablespoon of the olive oil for 6 to 8 minutes over medium-high heat. Stir in the honey. Add the grilled eggplant, tomatoes, and lime juice. Gently toss for 30 seconds. Remove from the heat and add the mint leaves. Drizzle with the remaining tablespoon of oil. Use as directed in the main recipe.

MAKES 4 SERVINGS

Joslin Choices (salad only): 1 carbohydrate (bread/starch), 1 fat

Per Serving: 120 calories (50% calories from fat), 7 g total fat (1 g saturated fat), 2 g protein, 15 g carbohydrate, 3 g dietary fiber, 0 cholesterol, 9 mg sodium, 362 mg potassium

Salmon with Verjus and Caper Sauce

David Hay, THORN PARK COUNTRY HOUSE

SEVENHILL, SOUTH AUSTRALIA

Gourmet food editors once noted that Chef Hay has a "special talent" when cooking salmon. The recipe here proves this to be true. Serve this dish with some steamed baby potatoes and his recipe for Green Pear, Fennel, and Witloof (Endive) Salad (page 63).

4 shallots, finely chopped

1 teaspoon olive oil

1 cup verjus (see page 108)

½ cup dry white wine

2 tablespoons fresh lime juice

6 4-ounce salmon fillets, skin removed

1 teaspoon chopped fresh lemon thyme

2 tablespoons chopped chives

2 tablespoons small capers, washed and drained

1 to 2 tablespoons light olive oil

sea salt (optional)

freshly ground pepper

lemon or lime wedges for garnish

Gently cook the shallots in the olive oil and a little of the verjus until soft but not colored, about 5 minutes. Add the rest of the verjus, wine, and lime juice, and boil rapidly to reduce until about ½ cup of liquid remains. (This can be done well in advance.)

Just before serving, steam the salmon for several minutes or roast in a very hot oven (450°F) on a parchment paper–lined baking sheet for 5 minutes

Warm the reduced liquid and add the herbs and capers; whisk in the light olive oil to thicken. The sauce should not be boiled. Add salt (if using) and pepper to taste.

Place each of the fillets onto a plate and spoon over some of the sauce. Garnish with the lemon or lime wedges. Serve at once.

MAKES 6 SERVINGS

Joslin Choices: 3 very-low-fat protein, 1 carbohydrate (bread/starch), ½ fat

Per Serving: 211 calories (31% calories from fat), 7 g total fat (1 g saturated fat), 23 g protein, 10 g carbohydrate, 1 g dietary fiber, 53 mg cholesterol, 150 mg sodium, 517 mg potassium

Verjus

A wonderful alternative to vinegar or lemon juice in sauces, marinades, and salad dressings, verjus (pronounced vair-ZHOO) is the unfermented juice of unripe wine grapes. The French have known about this "green juice" since medieval and Renaissance times and have been cooking with it for nearly 800 years. Although it's still a little expensive, we're sure that you will be thrilled with the results and agree it's well worth the effort of ordering it. It's now become a staple in our own pantries.

Verjus contributes a subtle note of acidity to food, heightening flavors and refreshing the palate at the same time. Acidity controls the balance of the main taste sensations of saltiness, bitterness, and fat on our palate; this is why vinegar or lemon juice is used in many recipes. Verjus does not contain any acetic acid—a main component of vinegar. Its acidity is gentler and better balanced than the citric acid in lemon juice. Could this be the secret ingredient that has made so many great restaurant dishes hard to duplicate in the home kitchen? You'll find that verjus is an ingredient called for several times in this wonderful collection of recipes from some of the great chefs of the world. For recipes using verjus, see pages 107, 109, and 252.

Citrus-Crusted Scallops with Mango, Avocado, and Fusion Vinaigrette

Susan Spicer, BAYONA
NEW ORLEANS

Co-owner and chef of Bayona, Susan Spicer is a New Orleans native who honed her skills from Bangkok to London, and from France to California. In her ever-evolving style of "contemporary global" cooking nuances of Alsace, India, and the American Southwest have been augmented with Mediterranean flavors. In the course of her career, she has received many awards from national magazines such as *Gourmet,* and, significantly, the James Beard Award for Best Chef, Southeast Region. As if Bayona could not keep Chef Spicer busy enough, she has opened a new casual restaurant, Herbsaint, and also actively supports local charities. Food is one reason visitors come to New Orleans. Some of the best food, from our experience, is the result of Chef Spicer's talents.

Here she transforms various ingredients into a melding of textures and tastes to produce a meal that is light, beautiful, and not a daunting task for you to prepare at home. You can do the time-consuming parts ahead of time and put the dish together at the last minute.

zest of 2 oranges and 2 limes
$\frac{1}{2}$ teaspoon Szechuan peppercorns
$\frac{1}{4}$ teaspoon black peppercorns
$\frac{1}{2}$ teaspoon fennel seeds
kosher salt (optional)
1 pound sea scallops

DRESSING:
juice of 2 large oranges and 2 large limes
$\frac{1}{4}$ cup Fusion verjus (see Note below)
2 tablespoons shallots, finely minced
1 teaspoon minced fresh ginger
$\frac{1}{2}$ teaspoon dark sesame oil

$\frac{1}{2}$ cup olive or peanut oil
salt (optional)
ground Szechuan pepper
Sambal Oelek (see page 144) to taste

1 teaspoon olive or peanut oil
2 cups mixed greens, preferably with some Asian greens, such as mizuna, tat soi, Japanese mustards, or pea sprouts (see Note below)
1 ripe mango, peeled and cut into slices or diced
1 ripe avocado, peeled and cut into slices or diced
$\frac{1}{2}$ cup finely chopped scallions or red onion
cilantro for garnish

Place a wire rack on a baking sheet and lay the strips of zest on the rack. Dry in a 170°F oven until crisp, about $1\frac{1}{2}$ to $1\frac{3}{4}$ hours. Grind the dried zest in a spice grinder with the Szechuan peppercorns, black peppercorns, and fennel seeds. Sprinkle a little salt (if using) on the scallops, and dust one side with the spice mixture. Set aside.

TO MAKE THE DRESSING: In a saucepan, combine the orange juice, lime juice, and verjus. Bring to a boil and reduce to ¼ cup. Remove from the heat and whisk in the shallots, ginger, sesame oil, and olive oil. Add salt (if using), Szechuan pepper, and Sambal Oelek to taste (makes 14 tablespoons).

In a sauté pan, bring the 1 teaspoon oil almost to the smoking point, then add the scallops, spice side down, and sear for about 1 minute. Turn and sear on the other side for 1 minute. The scallops should be tender, not chewy.

Divide the greens among 4 large plates and place the scallops around them. Arrange the mango, avocado, and scallions around the scallops. Dress each plate with 1 tablespoon of the vinaigrette. Serve immediately. Refrigerate the remaining vinaigrette for another use.

MAKES 4 SERVINGS

Joslin Choices: 1 low-fat protein, 1 carbohydrate (fruit), 3 fat

Per Serving: 268 calories (60% calories from fat), 19 g total fat (3 g saturated fat), 11 g protein, 17 g carbohydrate, 5 g dietary fiber, 18 mg cholesterol, 127 mg sodium, 665 mg potassium

Note: Fusion, also known as Fusion Foods, is the newest venture of Duckhorn Vineyards and is the largest maker of verjus in California's Napa Valley wine region. See Sources (page 296). You'll find mizuna, tat soi, Japanese mustards, and pea sprouts at Asian markets and specialty produce stores.

Prosciutto-Wrapped Scallops with Mesclun in Tomato Vinaigrette

Rémi Cousyn, CALORIES

SASKATOON, SASKATCHEWAN, CANADA

Chef Rémi Cousyn grew up in Provence and honed his craft in his native France. He was honored as "best apprentice" and invited to represent his region in the contest *Le Meilleur Apprenti de France.* After receiving his national cooking diploma, Chef Cousyn trained under Roger Vergé (Michelin 3-star chef) and then worked in France, Switzerland, Montreal, and Whistler (British Columbia). In 1995, he and his wife, Janis, bought Calories in Saskatoon. It was not long before it was named one of Canada's top 100 restaurants by readers of Air Canada's *enRoute* magazine. In 1999, it was named one of western Canada's top 10 restaurants, and for 14 years it has been included in *Where to Eat in Canada.* Chef Cousyn's recipes have been published in Anita Stewart's recent book *The Flavours of Canada, Homemaker's Magazine, Châteleine, Gourmet,* and by the Canadian Broadcasting Company.

When asked to be a part of this book, Chef Cousyn was pleased to show that French food can be enjoyed in a healthy eating plan. Janis and Rémi pride themselves in educating people on the joys of wholesome and creative food served in their friendly bistro-style setting.

12 thin slices prosciutto, about 2 ounces total
24 large sea scallops, about 1 pound total

TOMATO VINAIGRETTE:
4 small vine-ripened plum (Roma) tomatoes
1 tablespoon red wine vinegar
2 cloves garlic, peeled

salt (optional)
freshly ground pepper
5 sprigs fresh thyme
3 tablespoons olive oil

½ pound mesclun or mixed baby greens
½ teaspoon olive oil

Trim the prosciutto of all fat. Cut in half lengthwise and wrap the prosciutto around the perimeter of each scallop without covering the 2 flat sides. Secure with a toothpick.

TO MAKE THE VINAIGRETTE: Cut the tomatoes into quarters and put in a blender. Add the vinegar, peeled garlic, salt (if using), pepper, and the leaves from 1 sprig of thyme. While blending, add the olive oil through the lid hole.

Wash and dry the mesclun.

Place the ½ teaspoon olive oil in a sauté pan. Over high heat, sauté the wrapped scallops on 1 side until caramelized, about 2 minutes. Turn the scallops over and let them sit in the pan while plating.

Toss the mesclun with some of the Tomato Vinaigrette. Pile the mesclun in the middle of each of 4 large serving plates. Decorate the rim of the plates with a drizzle of the remaining dressing. Place the scallops artistically around the salads. Garnish each with a sprig of thyme. Serve at once.

MAKES 4 SERVINGS

Joslin Choices: 3 very-low-fat protein, 1 vegetable, 2 fat

Per Serving: 225 calories (51% calories from fat), 13 g total fat (2 g saturated fat), 21 g protein, 7 g carbohydrate, 2 g dietary fiber, 40 mg cholesterol, 540 mg sodium, 584 mg potassium

Sopa de la Mar

Bill Wavrin, RANCHO LA PUERTA
TECATE, MEXICO

Rancho La Puerta is a 3,000-acre spa in Tecate, Mexico, started by Edmond Szekely and his wife, Deborah, in 1940. Since then the spa, a bus ride from the airport in San Diego, has grown from a bunch of tents to an elegant spa where exercise, nutrition, and the beauty of the mountains and lush plantings make city stresses disappear. The 150 guests spend a week in some of the 40 exercise classes or relax with the latest in massage and other pampering by the spa's knowledgeable staff. Chef Bill Wavrin is the hero of the ranch. His cookies and dark bread are legendary, and his meals, which use fresh vegetables and herbs from the spa's organic garden, make eating healthy a joy.

This great soup from Chef Wavrin is good anytime, particularly when you do not know what to do when you have 6 guests coming over for lunch or dinner and all you have is a few shrimp and 1 fish fillet. Any firm-fleshed fish will do. You can make and serve this outstanding soup in 30 minutes flat and it is a guaranteed crowd pleaser! Enjoy!

1 teaspoon olive oil
½ teaspoon minced fresh ginger
½ medium onion, chopped
½ large rib celery, chopped
½ medium carrot, sliced
½ medium red bell pepper, julienned
2 cups button mushrooms, quartered
¼ medium thin-skinned potato, scrubbed and chopped
½ medium tomato, chopped
2 large cloves garlic, sliced
1 jalapeño chile pepper, seeded and minced

½ medium zucchini, chopped
2 quarts Vegetable Stock (page 115)
½ cup fresh or frozen corn kernels
½ pound red snapper, boned and chopped
½ pound medium shrimp, peeled and deveined, chopped
2 tablespoons chopped cilantro
juice of 2 large limes
salt (optional)
freshly ground pepper
2 cups shredded green cabbage
6 lime wedges

In a soup pot, heat the olive oil over medium-high heat. Add the ginger, onion, celery, carrot, red bell pepper, and mushrooms and sauté, stirring, until the onion wilts, about 5 minutes. Stir in the potato, tomato, garlic, jalapeño, zucchini, and Vegetable Stock. Bring to a boil. Reduce the heat and simmer for 15 minutes.

Add the corn and red snapper. Simmer for 5 minutes. Add the shrimp and simmer for another 2 minutes. Add the cilantro and lime juice. Season to taste with salt (if using) and pepper.

TO SERVE: Ladle into wide, shallow soup bowls. Sprinkle some of the shredded cabbage on top and pass the lime wedges for squeezing onto each serving.

MAKES 6 SERVINGS

Joslin Choices: 2 very-low-fat protein, 1 carbohydrate (bread/starch)

Per Serving: 164 calories (18% calories from fat), 3 g total fat (1 g saturated fat), 19 g protein, 17 g carbohydrate, 3 g dietary fiber, 71 mg cholesterol, 465 mg sodium, 751 mg potassium

Vegetable Stock

Making and freezing this stock is a wonderful way to clean out your vegetable bin. The recipe was first published in our *Joslin Diabetes Gourmet Cookbook* (Bantam Books). Roasting the vegetables first intensifies their wonderful flavor.

1 large carrot, scrubbed and cut into large chunks

1 large leek, white part only, well rinsed and cut into large pieces

1 large onion, about 8 ounces, cut into 8 pieces

2 large ribs celery with leaves, coarsely chopped

1 cup coarsely chopped fresh fennel bulb

1 cup coarsely chopped tomato

¾ pound fresh spinach, rinsed and trimmed

2 sprigs fresh thyme

4 sprigs flat-leaf parsley

2 bay leaves

½ teaspoon salt (optional)

4 whole peppercorns

10 cups water

Preheat the oven to 400°F.

Arrange the carrot, leek, onion, celery, and fennel in a shallow roasting pan. Roast for 30 to 45 minutes, until the vegetables begin to brown.

Transfer the vegetables to a stockpot or a large heavy saucepan. Add the remaining ingredients and bring to a boil. Reduce the heat and simmer, uncovered, for 30 minutes. Remove the pot from the stove and let sit for another 30 minutes.

Strain through a fine sieve or colander lined with cheesecloth. Discard the solids. Return the stock to the stove and reduce at a slow simmer to 1 quart.

MAKES 1 QUART

Joslin Choices: free food

Per 1-Cup Serving: 16 calories (trace calories from fat), trace total fat (0 saturated fat), 1 g protein, 4 g carbohydrate, 1 g dietary fiber, 0 cholesterol, 41 mg sodium, 185 mg potassium

Thai-Style Seafood Salad

Peter Gorton, THE HORN OF PLENTY
TAVISTOCK, ENGLAND

Bonnie first met Chef Gorton while visiting relatives in Plymouth. This recipe shows the influences of Thai cuisine in England, where it is sweeping the nation there much as it is here in the States. While some people like their food mildly hot, others prefer it scorching. You be the judge of the type of chile pepper to use. They vary greatly in their heat (see page 78). If in doubt, use the mild Anaheim chile pepper; you can always add more heat, but you can never take it out once it is in.

½ large cucumber, seeded and cut into matchstick-size julienne strips

2 pounds cooked mixed seafood (salmon, shrimp, scallops, etc.)

1 fresh chile pepper (Anaheim, jalapeño, or serrano, depending on the heat desired—see Headnote above), seeded and cut into fine julienne strips

4 shallots, minced

1 tablespoon grated fresh ginger

2 large cloves garlic, minced

¼ cup fresh lime juice

2 tablespoons Thai fish sauce

2 teaspoons to 1 tablespoon sugar

2 tablespoons olive oil

1 bunch fresh coriander, chopped

freshly ground pepper to taste

leaves of 1 head lettuce—Boston, Bibb, romaine, or red or green loose-leaf lettuce, washed and crisped

½ cup seeded and finely chopped tomato for garnish

In a large bowl, combine the cucumber strips and the seafood mixture. In another bowl, mix together the chile pepper, shallots, ginger, and garlic. Toss with the lime juice, fish sauce, sugar, and olive oil. Add to the seafood mixture and combine thoroughly. Stir in the coriander and season with pepper.

Arrange the lettuce leaves on a large serving platter. Top with the seafood salad and garnish with the chopped tomatoes. Serve cold.

MAKES 8 SERVINGS

Joslin Choices: 3½ low-fat protein, 1 vegetable

Per Serving: 218 calories (40% calories from fat), 10 g total fat (1g saturated fat), 26 g protein, 6 g carbohydrate, 1 g dietary fiber, 105 mg cholesterol, 537 mg sodium, 642 mg potassium

Insalata di Frutti di Mare (Mediterranean Seafood Salad)

Carole Peck, GOOD NEWS CAFÉ
WOODBURY, CONNECTICUT

We have known and admired this chef for years and always try to dine at her restaurant whenever we are in this picturesque region of Connecticut. Nightly, you are likely to dine next to a celebrity from television, film, or the literary world. Recognized by the food media to be one of the most talented chefs cooking today, Chef Peck was one of only 4 chefs chosen from a group of 900 to cook for the Julia Child Cookbook Awards. This marvelous seafood salad is a shining example of her uncanny talent for combining flavors in new ways and her artist's eye for making the food look as beautiful as a painting.

3 tablespoons extra-virgin olive oil
4 pounds mussels, scrubbed and debearded
  (see page 118)
2 pounds little clams or cockles, scrubbed
2 pounds fresh octopus, cleaned and tenderized
2 pounds medium shrimp, shells on
1 head romaine lettuce, leaves washed and dried

juice of 3 large lemons
$2/3$ cup extra-virgin olive oil
kosher salt (optional)
6 sprigs fresh oregano, coarsely chopped
6 sprigs flat-leaf parsley, coarsely chopped
freshly ground pepper

FRESH HERB DRESSING:
2 teaspoons Dijon mustard
2 large cloves garlic, finely chopped

Pour the olive oil into a large pan. Add the mussels and clams. Cook, covered, over high heat, shaking the pan occasionally, until the mussels and clams have opened, 3 to 5 minutes. Remove the mussels and clams, reserving all of the cooking liquid.

Place the octopus in a large pan and pour on the reserved cooking liquid. Cover and simmer gently until tender, about 2 hours. Add the shrimp and continue cooking until they turn pink, 2 to 3 minutes.

Remove the octopus and shrimp from the pan. Cut the octopus into small pieces and shell the shrimp, mussels, and clams. Mix all the seafood together in a large bowl. Set aside.

Wrap the romaine leaves in paper towels and chill to crisp.

TO PREPARE THE FRESH HERB DRESSING: In a medium bowl, whisk together the mustard, garlic, lemon juice, and olive oil. Sprinkle with the salt (if using), oregano, parsley, and pepper. Pour over the seafood and toss to mix. Cover and chill for about 2 hours.

TO SERVE: Shred the romaine lettuce and spread on a large, shallow serving platter. Spoon the seafood mixture over the lettuce and serve.

SERVES 30 AS PART OF A BUFFET

Joslin Choices: 3 low-fat protein, 1 vegetable

Per Serving: 205 calories (40% calories from fat), 9 g total fat (1 g saturated fat), 25 g protein, 5 g carbohydrate, 0 dietary fiber, 95 mg cholesterol, 325 mg sodium, 552 mg potassium

Cleaning Mussels

In the United States we can purchase not only blue mussels, both farm-raised and wild, but the green-lipped variety, which comes from New Zealand. They can be used interchangeably in recipes. Frozen, cleaned mussels are available in some fish markets. These come with half the shell removed. When you bring fresh mussels home, store them uncovered, so they will not suffocate in the refrigerator. They can remain refrigerated for up to 1 day before using.

Scrub the shells well with a stiff brush, and rinse in several changes of cold water until the water runs clear. Sort through the mussels and discard any with damaged shells. Just before cooking them, cut or pull off the beards, the hairy growth attached to the shell, using a sharp knife. If you remove the beards ahead of time, the mussels will die and become unsuitable for eating. When you cook the mussels discard any that do not open.

Cilantro and Kaffir Lime–Marinated Scallops with Port Wine Reduction and Mixed Herb Salad

Eric Faivre, THE ORCHID AT MAUNA LANI
KOHALA COAST, BIG ISLAND, HAWAII

Chef Faivre oversees three restaurants at this luxurious hotel on the pristine Kohala Coast on the Big Island of Hawaii. The Grill is an innovative, upscale, and distinctly Hawaiian restaurant. Fine china and crystal table settings are used, which cast dancing lights against the warmth of rich, dark koa-wood tables. Brown's Beach House offers beachside dining with Hawaiian regional cuisine. The Orchid is the perfect place for family-style dining amid a garden of tropical foliage and ever-blooming orchids, koi-filled ponds, and waterfalls.

36 medium-size sea scallops
2 tablespoons chopped cilantro
4 kaffir lime leaves (see page 120)
2 teaspoons extra-virgin olive oil
1 cup port wine
1 tablespoon fresh or unsweetened pineapple juice
1 tablespoon fresh lemon juice
½ teaspoon mustard

¼ cup chopped fresh chervil
¼ cup loosely packed small fresh basil leaves
¼ cup loosely packed fresh tarragon leaves
¼ cup chopped fresh chives
¼ cup small whole watercress leaves
vegetable cooking spray
salt (optional)
freshly ground pepper to taste

Marinate the scallops overnight in the refrigerator with the cilantro, kaffir lime leaves, and 1 teaspoon of the olive oil.

In a small saucepan, reduce the port wine to a syrup consistency. Cool down before using.

Mix together the pineapple juice, lemon juice, remaining 1 teaspoon olive oil, and mustard to make a vinaigrette. Place the fresh herbs in a bowl and drizzle with the pineapple vinaigrette. Toss and set aside.

Lightly coat the grid of a hot grill with cooking spray. Drain off and discard the excess olive oil mixture from the scallops. Before grilling, season the scallops to taste with salt (if using) and pepper. Grill the scallops 4 to 6 inches from the heat source, until the scallops are opaque throughout (cut to test), about 5 to 7 minutes, turning once.

TO SERVE: Drizzle the port wine reduction in a decorative pattern on each of 6 large plates. Top each with equal portions of the mixed herb salad and 6 scallops. Serve warm.

MAKES 6 SERVINGS

Joslin Choices: 3 low-fat protein, ½ carbohydrate (bread/starch)

Per Serving: 203 calories (16% calories from fat), 3 g total fat (0 saturated fat), 23 g protein, 8 g carbohydrate, 0 dietary fiber, 55 mg cholesterol, 297 mg sodium, 367 mg potassium

Kaffir Lime Leaves

Kaffir lime leaves are glossy dark leaves that have a unique double shape and look like two leaves that are joined end to end, much like a figure eight. Closely identified with Thai cooking for their distinct citrus aroma, fresh kaffir lime leaves are hard to come by in some areas. Look for them at Asian markets, where you are more likely to find them frozen in plastic bags. Frozen leaves can be used instead of fresh with no difference in taste. Dried leaves are much less flavorful, so double the amount when adding to a recipe. If you are unable to find kaffir lime leaves, substitute grated lime zest. One tablespoon zest is equivalent to 6 kaffir lime leaves.

Pan-Fried Scallops with Beetroot and Walnut Oil

Martin Lam, RANSOME'S DOCK
LONDON

We first read about this chef in the British *Waitrose Food Illustrated,* a beautiful magazine that keeps us abreast of the culinary happenings in the U.K. There, the restaurant received an excellent review accompanied by a full-page photo of this dish. It looked so enticing, we were ready to head for the kitchen to cook, but alas, no recipe was run with the article and photo. Surfing the Internet the next day, Fran found Chef Lam's Web site and invited him to participate in this cookbook. Within a few hours, the recipe arrived. Since that time, we have sent friends to dine at Ransome's Dock restaurant in Battersea, London, and they have assured us the rest of the menu offers innovative, delicious, and healthy dishes.

6 medium beetroots (beets), scrubbed and
  trimmed
olive oil
rock salt (optional)
2 tablespoons walnut oil
1 teaspoon aged sherry vinegar

salt (optional)
freshly ground pepper
½ tablespoon sunflower oil
12 large sea scallops with roe, sliced in half
  horizontally
1 tablespoon snipped fresh chives

Preheat the oven to 350°F.

Roll the beetroots first in the olive oil, then in the rock salt (if using). Place in a heavy baking dish and roast for 2 hours. Remove from the oven and cool until they can be easily handled. Peel and cut into ¼-inch slices. (If prepared the day before and refrigerated, return to room temperature before continuing.)

Dress the beetroot slices with the walnut oil, vinegar, salt (if using), and pepper to taste. Allow to sit for 20 minutes to allow the flavors to develop before arranging the slices in a soup plate or on large dinner plates. Spoon some of the dressing on each serving.

Heat the sunflower oil in a heavy nonstick skillet. When the pan is very hot, cook the pink scallop roe first for 1 minute, then add the white meat for 45 seconds on each side. Turn off the heat. Season the scallops with salt (if using) and pepper.

Immediately arrange the scallop slices on the beetroot slices, and scatter the chives on the beetroot. Serve at once.

MAKES 4 SERVINGS

Joslin Choices: 1 low-fat protein, 1 carbohydrate (bread/starch), 1 fat

Per Serving: 183 calories (43% calories from fat), 9 g total fat (1 g saturated fat), 10 g protein, 17 g carbohydrate, 1 g dietary fiber, 15 mg cholesterol, 287 mg sodium, 586 mg potassium

Basil Shrimp in Coconut Lime Ginger Broth with Asian Greens

Ris Lacoste, 1 7 8 9

WASHINGTON, D.C.

Chef Lacoste can bring any recipe to haute cuisine, and here she marries Thai with classic touches to present a dish that is elegant to both the eye and palate. With this dish, she has fulfilled her fondest wish to have all plates come back to the kitchen empty. When you serve this recipe, you can be sure that the dish will disappear before your eyes.

BROTH:

3 12-ounce cans light coconut milk

4 ounces fresh ginger, scrubbed and coarsely chopped with skin on

4 ounces lemongrass, coarsely chopped

1 kaffir lime leaf (see page 120)

1½ ounces Thai fish sauce

3 tablespoons sugar

18 large shrimp, peeled and deveined

2 tablespoons chopped fresh basil

1 tablespoon chopped fresh garlic

2 tablespoons peanut or olive oil

1 pound shiitake mushrooms, sliced

3 cups fresh Asian greens or mesclun

1 medium red bell pepper, finely julienned

1 bunch scallions, trimmed and diced, white part only

salt (optional)

freshly ground pepper

Thai chili paste or Chinese chili paste with garlic

2 tablespoons chopped fresh cilantro

2 tablespoons basil, cut into a chiffonade

1 large lime, cut into 6 wedges

PREFERABLY, THE DAY BEFORE SERVING, PREPARE THE BROTH: In a heavy-bottomed 2-quart saucepan, combine the coconut milk, ginger, lemongrass, and lime leaf. Bring just to a boil and let simmer for 10 minutes. Stir in the fish sauce and sugar. Strain, cover, and refrigerate overnight or up to 3 days. If time does not allow, let the broth simmer for approximately 30 minutes to infuse the flavors. You can then strain and use immediately.

Marinate the shrimp in the basil, garlic, and oil. This can also be done a day ahead; store the shrimp covered, in the refrigerator.

TO SERVE: Sauté the shrimp for a minute or two until the centers are barely opaque. Add the mushrooms, cook for a minute longer, and then add the greens, red pepper, and scallions. Toss once or twice in the pan. Season with salt (if using) and pepper. Place a dab of the chili paste in the bottom of each of 6 shallow soup bowls. Top with equal parts of the shrimp-vegetable mixture.

Strain about ¾ cup of the hot broth over the shrimp-vegetable mixture and top with the chopped cilantro, basil chiffonade, and a squeeze of fresh lime juice.

MAKES 6 SERVINGS

Joslin Choices: 1 very-low-fat protein, ½ carbohydrate (½ bread/starch), 1 fat

Per Serving: 143 calories (43% calories from fat), 7 g total fat (2 g saturated fat), 9 g protein, 12 g carbohydrate, 3 g dietary fiber, 32 mg cholesterol, 333 mg sodium, 276 mg potassium

Indochine Shrimp Salad

Jonathan Eismann, PACIFIC TIME
MIAMI BEACH

This is another great recipe from Chef Eismann that fuses the flavors of the East and West. We have made this wonderful salad with the shrimp as called for, and substituting an equal amount of boneless chicken breast. Both were superb!

1½ pounds large shrimp, peeled and deveined
2 quarts water
1 cup dry white wine
½ cup fresh lemon juice
1 teaspoon salt (optional)

CITRUS VINAIGRETTE:
6 tablespoons fresh lemon juice
6 tablespoons fresh lime juice
¼ cup sugar
2 large cloves garlic, minced
¼ cup loosely packed flat-leaf parsley leaves
¼ cup loosely packed cilantro leaves

CUCUMBER MARINADE:
1 large cucumber, seeded and diced
¾ cup rice wine vinegar
¼ cup honey
pinch salt

2 ounces rice noodles
30 small basil leaves
30 small mint leaves
2½ cups cubed, peeled mango

Steam or blanch the shrimp in the water combined with wine, lemon juice, and salt (if using) until the shrimp turn bright pink and are opaque throughout. Drain and shock in ice water. After 1 minute, drain again and refrigerate.

TO MAKE THE CITRUS VINAIGRETTE: Combine the lemon and lime juices. Add the sugar and stir until dissolved. Blend in the garlic, parsley, and cilantro leaves. Refrigerate.

FOR THE CUCUMBER MARINADE: Combine the cucumber, vinegar, honey, and salt. Let stand to marinate for 20 minutes, then drain. Refrigerate the cucumber, discarding the marinade.

Break the rice noodles into 3-inch pieces and soak in warm water for 10 minutes. Drain the noodles and blanch in boiling water until al dente, about 5 minutes. Drain and shock in ice water. Drain again and reserve.

Cut the cooked shrimp in half lengthwise. In a large nonreactive bowl, mix together the shrimp, Citrus Vinaigrette, cucumber, cooked rice noodles, basil and mint leaves, and mango. Place in the refrigerator for 5 minutes, then transfer to a serving dish. Serve cold.

MAKES 6 SERVINGS

Joslin Choices: 2½ very-low-fat protein, 2½ carbohydrate (bread/starch)

Per Serving: 283 calories (7% calories from fat), 2 g total fat (0 saturated fat), 24 g protein, 36 g carbohydrate, 2 g dietary fiber, 172 mg cholesterol, 185 mg sodium, 461 mg potassium

Grilled Tuna with Leeks and Roasted Tomato and Red Pepper *Nage*

Tamara Murphy, BRASA
SEATTLE, WASHINGTON

When we visit the San Juan Islands in Puget Sound, we fly into Seattle and head to Brasa before taking the ferry to the islands. Chef Tamara Murphy marries Mediterranean ingredients with the wood grill and a wood-burning oven using local ingredients. She delivers meals so varied and robust that Brasa was named the best restaurant in Seattle by *Food & Wine* in 2000, and the same editors named Chef Murphy Best New Chef in 1994. *Gourmet* named Brasa one of the Top 5 in Seattle in 2000.

olive oil cooking spray

NAGE:
1 tablespoon grapeseed or canola oil
4 plum (Roma) tomatoes
2 large red bell peppers
½ cup fresh orange juice

2 tablespoons fresh lime juice
salt (optional)
freshly ground pepper

4 medium leeks
4 4-ounce fresh tuna fillets, such as ahi, cut about
  1 inch thick

Lightly spray a grill grid or a broiler pan with the cooking spray. Light the grill or preheat the broiler.

TO MAKE THE *NAGE:* Rub about ¼ teaspoon oil on each tomato. Cut the tomatoes in half lengthwise. Grill the tomatoes and peppers, turning occasionally, until the skins blister, about 4 to 5 minutes. Place in a bowl and cover with plastic wrap. Wait until cool to peel off the skins. Place the tomatoes and peppers in a food processor blender, along with the orange juice and lime juice. Process until smooth. Season to taste with salt (if using) and pepper. Set aside.

Trim the green tops and root ends off the leeks. Starting at the green tip, slice each leek down the center to within 1 inch of the end. Wash under cold running water. Re-form into the shape of a leek and place in a large nonstick skillet. Add water to cover, bring to a boil, reduce the heat, and simmer until the leeks are tender, about 10 minutes. Drain and return the leeks to the skillet. Drizzle the remaining 2 teaspoons oil over the leeks. Place the leeks on the hot grill until grill marks form, turning once. Set aside.

Season the tuna fillets with salt (if using) and pepper. Grill the tuna to the desired doneness, about 3 to 4 minutes per side for medium-rare, turning once.

TO SERVE: Ladle equal amounts of the tomato-pepper *nage* on each of 4 large heated serving plates. Place the leeks on the sauce with the root end of the leek at the bottom of the plate, forming a circle with the leek halves. Slice each tuna fillet into thirds and attractively arrange the fillets in the center of the leek circle. Serve at once.

MAKES 4 SERVINGS

Joslin Choices: 3 very-low-fat protein, 1½ carbohydrate (1½ bread/starch)

Per Serving: 254 calories (18% calories from fat), 5 g total fat (1 g saturated fat), 28 g protein, 25 g carbohydrate, 4 g dietary fiber, 53 mg cholesterol, 67 mg sodium, 975 mg potassium

Note: Nage is a French word that means "swimming." It is an aromatic poaching liquid much like a court-bouillon, but *nage* is also a style of presentation in which the fish or shellfish is served surrounded by the poaching liquid. The vegetables used in the poaching liquid are part of the final presentation.

Dinner on the Patio

Grilled Tuna with Leeks and Roasted Tomato and Red Pepper Nage (page 127)

Grilled Corn

Fresh Fruit Sorbet (page 277)

Joslin Choices: 3 very-low-fat protein, 2½ carbohydrate (1½ bread/starch, 1 fruit), 325 calories (15% calories from fat)

Note: Items not referring to a specific recipe are not included in the nutritional analysis. Consult the Joslin Food Choices (page 287) for that information.

Seared Tuna with Cucumber and Rice Noodles, Tamarind Coulis, and Pepper Brunoise

Scott Barton, PULSE SPORTS CLUB/LA
NEW YORK CITY

When selecting the tuna for this dish, look for yellowfin tuna that is at least 1 inch thick so you will get a firm exterior and a pale pink interior when it is cooked. We used a cast-iron skillet when testing this dish, as it gives an exceptional sear to the fish. The play of herbs and spices in this recipe makes it exceptional.

The freshest-quality tuna is sometimes call sushi-quality tuna. Brunoise is a chef's term for a mixture of vegetables that have been shredded or finely diced, then cooked very slowly, usually in butter. The brunoise is then used to flavor sauces or soups, or, as in this recipe, as a flavorful and decorative garnish.

BASIL-ORANGE OIL:
1 bunch fresh basil
½ tablespoon grated orange zest
1½ cups extra-virgin olive oil

GINGER JUICE:
1 2-inch piece ginger

SPICE POWDER:
1 tablespoon coriander seeds, toasted
1 tablespoon white peppercorns, toasted
1 tablespoon paprika
1 teaspoon Aleppo pepper (see Note below)
1 teaspoon chipotle chili powder
1 tablespoon kosher salt (optional)

2 pounds sushi-quality tuna loin
   (see Headnote above)
olive oil

NOODLE SALAD:
1 7-ounce package rice stick noodles
2 medium cucumbers, shredded into very thin
   julienne strips
1 cup very thinly sliced red cabbage

1 tablespoon chopped chives
1 tablespoon fresh lime juice or to taste
½ cup tomato, peeled, seeded, and finely diced

3 Japanese eggplant, sliced ½ inch thick on the
   diagonal
olive oil cooking spray
salt (optional)
freshly ground pepper

TAMARIND COULIS:
¼ cup red chili paste
1 cup tamarind juice
1 tablespoon extra-virgin olive oil
salt (optional)
freshly ground pepper

PEPPER BRUNOISE:
1 habanero chile, seeded and finely minced
1 tablespoon finely chopped cilantro
1½ teaspoons unsalted butter
2 tablespoons finely minced red bell pepper
2 tablespoons finely minced yellow bell pepper
2 tablespoons finely minced purple bell pepper

TO MAKE THE BASIL-ORANGE OIL: In advance, blanch the fresh basil in boiling water for 10 seconds. Shock in ice water and dry. Place in a blender with the orange zest and olive oil. Blend to puree. Strain the mixture through a coffee filter, cheesecloth, or fine strainer. Keep the liquid product refrigerated until each use.

TO MAKE THE GINGER JUICE: In advance, peel and grate the ginger. Using a fine strainer or cheesecloth, squeeze the pulp to extract the juice. Discard the pulp. Keep refrigerated until each use.

TO MAKE THE SPICE POWDER: Using a spice grinder or a mortar and pestle, grind the spices to form a fine powder. If using, stir in the salt. Roll the tuna in the spice powder. Sear in a lightly oiled sauté pan over medium-high heat, turning once, for about 3 minutes per side for medium-rare, longer if you like medium to medium-well tuna. Chill 30 minutes and then slice.

TO MAKE THE NOODLE SALAD: Boil the rice stick noodles in a large pot of unsalted boiling water for 3 minutes. Drain and toss with the cucumbers, red cabbage, and chives. Whisk together the lime juice, 1 tablespoon of the Basil-Orange Oil, and ½ tablespoon of the Ginger Juice. Pour over the noodles and toss all with the tomato. Set aside.

Light a grill. Lightly coat the eggplant slices with the cooking spray. Season with salt (if using) and pepper. Grill over medium-hot coals for 10 to 12 minutes, turning once. Set aside.

TO MAKE THE TAMARIND COULIS: Whisk together the chili paste, tamarind juice, and olive oil. Season to taste with salt (if using) and pepper. Set aside.

TO MAKE THE PEPPER BRUNOISE: In a small sauté pan, sauté the habanero and cilantro in ½ teaspoon of the unsalted butter for 5 to 6 minutes, until thoroughly cooked. Set aside. In a separate small sauté pan, sauté the bell peppers in the remaining 1 teaspoon unsalted butter for 5 to 6 minutes, until thoroughly cooked. Set aside.

Place a portion of the noodle salad at the top of each of 12 large plates. Fan the slices of eggplant off the noodles. Lay the slices of tuna over the eggplant. Finish with a few dots of Tamarind Coulis and the Pepper Brunoise.

MAKES 12 SERVINGS

Joslin Choices: 2 very-low-fat protein, 2 carbohydrate (bread/starch)

Per Serving: 248 calories (19% calories from fat), 5 g total fat (2 g saturated fat), 21 g protein, 30 g carbohydrate, 5 g dietary fiber, 39 mg cholesterol, 243 mg sodium, 708 mg potassium

Note: Aleppo pepper is available at specialty food stores, or see Sources, page 296.

Asparagus Verona-Style

Stefano Manfredi, BEL MONDO
SYDNEY

Chef Manfredi and his restaurant in The Rocks district, with spectacular views of Sydney Harbour, first caught our attention when *The New York Times* described his cuisine as the "best Italian food in Australia." Combining the timeless tradition of Northern Italian cuisine with the best of Australia's seasonal products, he has created an innovative blend of the old and the new to the delight of the locals, tourists, the editors of *Australian Vogue,* and the NBC team from the *Today* show. While covering the 2000 Summer Olympics in Sydney, they invited Chef Manfredi to appear on the show.

You'll appreciate how easy this dish is to prepare, and you will marvel as we did at its exquisite flavor. How can anything so simple be so good?

1 pound fresh asparagus, trimmed	salt (optional)
4 large eggs	freshly ground pepper
2 tablespoons white wine vinegar	1 2½-ounce piece Parmesan cheese,
4 teaspoons extra-virgin olive oil	shaved thin

Steam the asparagus in a small amount of water until al dente, 3 to 7 minutes depending on the size of the spears. Distribute them evenly onto 4 large serving plates.

Gently poach the eggs in simmering water with the vinegar until the eggs are set, 3 minutes for soft yolks.* Using a slotted spoon, remove the eggs from the water, drain briefly, and place on the servings of asparagus. Drizzle each serving with 1 teaspoon of the olive oil. Season with salt (if using) and pepper and scatter the Parmesan shavings over all. Serve at once.

MAKES 4 SERVINGS

Joslin Choices: 2 medium-fat protein, 1 vegetable, 1 fat

Per Serving: 229 calories (60% calories from fat), 16 g total fat (6 g saturated fat), 17 g protein, 6 g carbohydrate, 1 g dietary fiber, 226 mg cholesterol, 394 mg sodium, 434 mg potassium

*For recipes that call for eggs that are raw or undercooked when the dish is served, use either shell eggs that have been treated to destroy *Salmonella,* by pasteurization or another approved method, or pasteurized egg products. Treated shell eggs are available from a growing number of retailers and are clearly labeled, while pasteurized egg products are widely available. (source: FDA)

Baked Eggplant Pie with Smoked Tomato Coulis

Ernie Briggs, ERNIE'S MEDITERRANEAN GRILL
FREDERICKSBURG, TEXAS

Amid the hustle and bustle of Fredericksburg, a mecca for tourists in the Texas Hill Country, is a culinary oasis created by Ernie and his wife and pastry chef, Anne Briggs. The restaurant is surrounded by brick-paved patios with blooming begonias, fire-engine-red salvia, and bubbling ornamental fountains. Ernie presents a fusion of Italian flavor with generous helpings of southern French and Greek influences and a sprinkling of Middle Eastern aromas to an eclectic clientele that ranges from ranchers and cowboys to Who's Who in Texas industry.

BAKED EGGPLANT PIE:
2 medium eggplant, about 1½ pounds total
olive oil for lightly coating pie plate and
   rubbing eggplant
2 tablespoons chopped fresh garlic
1 teaspoon kosher salt (optional)
1 teaspoon freshly ground pepper
3 tablespoons chopped fresh basil
1 teaspoon chopped fresh thyme
½ teaspoon chopped fresh rosemary
3 large eggs, lightly beaten
¼ cup grated Romano cheese

1 tablespoon olive oil
1 cup fresh bread crumbs

SMOKED TOMATO COULIS:
6 large ripe plum (Roma) tomatoes, cut in
   half lengthwise
6 large cloves garlic, peeled and left whole
1 tablespoon chopped fresh basil
¼ teaspoon chopped fresh rosemary
salt (optional)
freshly ground pepper to taste

Preheat the oven to 350°F. Lightly coat a 9-inch pie plate with olive oil. Set aside.

Using a skewer, poke each eggplant 10 to 12 times. Lightly rub the eggplant with olive oil. Place the eggplant in a dish, cover with aluminum foil, and bake for 20 to 25 minutes, until soft. Remove from the oven and uncover, saving the foil for use later.

When the eggplant are cool, cut in half, taking care not to damage the skin as it will be used later. With a kitchen spoon, remove the pulp and place it in the work bowl of a food processor fitted with a metal blade. Reserve the skin and puree the pulp.

Transfer the pulp to a mixing bowl and beat in the garlic, salt (if using), pepper, basil, thyme, rosemary, beaten eggs, Romano cheese, 1 tablespoon olive oil, and bread crumbs. Mix well.

Line the inside of the prepared pie plate with half the eggplant skin, outer skin facing down. Fill the pie plate with the eggplant mixture, packing it down. Place the remaining eggplant skin on top, outer skin facing up. Bake in the oven for 30 to 40 minutes, until the filling is set.

Meanwhile, preheat the grill. Place the tomatoes and garlic on the reserved aluminum foil. Smoke on the grill at low to moderate heat for 30 to 40 minutes (Ernie uses mesquite or pecan wood for this step). The tomatoes should remain firm with the skin peeling off. Peel the tomatoes, puree them in a food processor, then strain. Place in a bowl and stir in the basil, rosemary, salt (if using), and pepper.

TO SERVE: Slice the partially cooled pie into 6 wedges. Serve each slice on a plate with some of the Smoked Tomato Coulis. Serve warm or at room temperature.

MAKES 6 SERVINGS

Joslin Choices: ½ medium-fat protein, 1½ carbohydrate (bread/starch), 1 fat

Per Serving: 204 calories (35% calories from fat), 8 g total fat (2 g saturated fat), 9 g protein, 26 g carbohydrate, 4 g dietary fiber, 111 mg cholesterol, 247 mg sodium, 490 mg potassium

Warm Napoleon of Grilled Eggplant, Riviera-Style

Gilles Ajuelos, LA BASTIDE ODÉON
PARIS

Chef Ajuelos of La Bastide Odéon in Paris shares a recipe that one might enjoy in the south of France. The presentation of these beautiful napoleons is rivaled only by the combination of ingredients the chef has used. If you do not have molds, see page 135 to learn how to make them out of PVC pipe. Unmolding is a cinch: Just lightly push the napoleon onto the plate.

12 large plum (Roma) tomatoes, about
  3 pounds total
6 small Japanese eggplant, about 1½ pounds total
¼ teaspoon kosher salt
freshly ground pepper
2 tablespoons olive oil
1 bunch fresh basil

7 ounces low-fat ricotta cheese
7 ounces fresh spinach
¼ cup egg substitute
1 small head garlic, peeled, about 12 small cloves
3½ ounces grated Parmesan cheese
¼ cup pureed black olives (tapenade)
¾ teaspoon extra-virgin olive oil

Preheat the oven to 200°F. Line 2 baking sheets with racks.

Blanch the tomatoes and remove their skins. Cut the tomatoes into quarters and scoop out the seeds. Lay the tomatoes on racks and bake for 3 hours to dry.

Preheat the oven to 400°F.

Slice the eggplant lengthwise into thin strips (less than ½ inch) and place them on a baking sheet. Salt and pepper them and brush with ½ tablespoon of the olive oil. Bake for 15 minutes. Set aside.

Chop half the basil and mix with the ricotta. Season with pepper. Set aside.

Blanch the spinach in boiling water for 1 minute; then drain and cool. In a food processor, place the spinach, egg substitute, cloves of garlic, and Parmesan. Puree with the remaining 1½ tablespoons olive oil. Strain though a sieve. You should have a thick green sauce.

Reduce the oven temperature to 375°F. Line a baking sheet with parchment paper.

TO ASSEMBLE THE NAPOLEONS: Using 6 lightly oiled 4-inch ring molds (see page 135) placed on the prepared baking sheet, layer the grilled eggplant, the ricotta mixture, and the olive puree. Arrange the oven-dried tomatoes on top. Unmold the napoleons by pressing down slightly on the tomato layer while removing the ring mold. Heat in the oven for 5 minutes.

Carefully cut each napoleon into 6 wedges and arrange with the wedges slightly apart, but still forming a circle on individual plates. Top each serving with 2 tablespoons of the green sauce and drizzle with ⅛ teaspoon extra-virgin olive oil. Decorate with some of the whole basil leaves. Serve at once.

MAKES 6 SERVINGS

Joslin Choices: 2 medium-fat protein, 1 carbohydrate (bread/starch), 1 fat

Per Serving: 269 calories (51% calories from fat), 16 g total fat (6 g saturated fat), 16 g protein, 19 g carbohydrate, 5 g dietary fiber, 23 mg cholesterol, 580 mg sodium, 840 mg potassium

Ring Molds

Several of the chefs' recipes call for the use of a 4-inch ring mold. You can buy these molds at restaurant supply stores, some specialty kitchenware shops, or you can purchase a piece of PVC pipe at the hardware store that is 4 inches in diameter. Secure the pipe in a vise and, using a hack-saw, cut the pipe into 4-inch lengths. Or, you can have the PVC pipe cut at the hardware store. Wash in hot, sudsy water and dry and the molds are ready to use time and time again.

Lunch for the Girls

Warm Napoleon of Grilled Eggplant, Riviera-Style (page 134)

Raspberry Soufflés with Fresh Raspberry Sorbet (page 280)

Joslin Choices: 3 medium-fat protein, 3 carbohydrate (1 bread/starch, 2 fruit), 415 calories (34% calories from fat)

Chayote Stuffed with Crabmeat

Paul Ramsey, PINEHURST

PINEHURST VILLAGE, NORTH CAROLINA

Chef Ramsey uses local recipes as well as fresh local ingredients to create menus that reflect the flavors of the area. North Carolina is famous for its crab. Here he serves this East Coast delicacy with Southwest flair.

2 chayote squash, about ¾ pound total

1 tablespoon canola oil

1 clove garlic, minced

1 jalapeño chile pepper, seeded and minced

¾ cup medium diced green bell pepper

¾ cup medium diced yellow bell pepper

1 medium tomato, peeled, seeded, cut into medium dice

½ cup fresh corn, cut off the cob

1 tablespoon chopped cilantro

½ pound crabmeat (Alaskan king, Dungeness, lump, stone)

1 tablespoon low-fat, low-salt canned chicken broth

Preheat the oven to 350°F.

Peel the chayote squash and cut in half through the natural indentation in the sides. Cut a small piece off the curved bottom of each half so that it will lie flat on a plate. Cut out and discard the seeds. With a melon scoop, remove enough flesh from each half to make a shell about ½ inch thick on the sides and bottom. Dice the removed flesh and reserve.

Heat the canola oil in an 8-inch skillet. Add the garlic and jalapeño. Cook for 1 minute, and then add the bell peppers and tomato, along with the reserved diced squash. Cook for about 2 minutes. Put the mixture in a bowl. Add the corn, cilantro, and crabmeat. Mix well.

Place the chayote shells in a shallow baking dish. Divide the crabmeat mixture among the shells, mounding up the filling. Pour the broth into the baking dish. Cover with aluminum foil and seal. Bake for 20 minutes. Open the foil and spoon any liquid in the plate over the stuffing. Re-cover and bake another 25 minutes, or until the squash is tender and cooked through.

Carefully transfer filled shells to 4 plates. Serve hot.

MAKES 4 SERVINGS

Joslin Choices: 1½ low-fat protein, 1 carbohydrate (bread/starch)

Per Serving: 154 calories (28% calories from fat), 5 g total fat (0 saturated fat), 14 g protein, 16 g carbohydrate, 4 g dietary fiber, 40 mg cholesterol, 218 mg sodium, 537 mg potassium

Lunch for Four

Chayote Stuffed with Crabmeat (page 137)

Fresh Fruit Sorbet (page 277)

Joslin Choices: 1½ low-fat protein, 2 carbohydrate (1 bread/starch, 1 fruit),
226 calories (20% calories from fat)

Haricots Verts, Couscous, and Mint Salad

Jimmy Schmidt, RATTLESNAKE
DETROIT, MICHIGAN

The first Rattlesnake was opened in 1985 in Denver, and the opening of the Detroit restaurant followed in 1988. The big dining rooms are filled with stunning art. Awards are as familiar to Jimmy Schmidt as are the raves for his American food with an international twist.

1 pound haricots verts or very young green beans, stems trimmed leaving the pointed growth tip
sea salt (optional)
1¼ cups water
1 tablespoon ground turmeric
freshly ground black pepper
½ cup instant couscous

DRESSING:
¾ cup extra-virgin olive oil
4 cloves garlic, finely minced
2 tablespoons minced fresh ginger

½ cup aged sherry vinegar
½ cup fresh lemon juice
¼ cup snipped fresh chives

1 small sweet onion, peeled and cut into very fine julienne
1 red bell pepper, stem, seeds and white inner ribs removed, cut into fine julienne
2 cups loosely packed mizuna, Red Mustard, Red Oak, or Spoon Leaf spinach, cleaned and stems trimmed as necessary
¼ cup chiffonade of fresh mint leaves

TO COOK THE HARICOTS VERTS: Bring a large pot of water to a boil. Add salt (if using). Add the beans, cooking until al dente, firm to the bite, yet tender and tasting very sweet, not raw green. Transfer to a colander and drain. Cool immediately under running water. Transfer to a dish, cover loosely with plastic wrap, and refrigerate.

TO COOK THE COUSCOUS: In a small saucepan, bring the 1¼ cups water to a boil; add the turmeric, and season with sea salt (if using) and black pepper. Place the couscous in a medium bowl and add the hot liquid. Cover and allow to sit until all the liquid has been absorbed, about 10 minutes. Transfer to a cookie sheet to cool. Stir to fluff with a fork. Adjust the seasonings to your taste.

TO MAKE THE DRESSING: In a medium nonstick skillet, heat 2 tablespoons of the olive oil. Add the garlic and ginger, cooking slowly until the garlic is tender but not brown, about 5 minutes. Add the sherry vinegar and lemon juice, turning the heat to high and bringing to a boil. Cook until reduced to ½ cup. Remove from the heat and allow to cool to room temperature. Transfer to a blender and puree until smooth. Leaving the blender running, slowly add the remaining olive oil. Add the chives. Transfer to a sealed container and refrigerate for up to 3 days, if not using immediately.

In a large bowl, combine the haricots verts, sweet onion, red pepper, and spinach with ¼ cup of the dressing to coat. Add the couscous and drizzle on an additional 1 to 2 tablespoons of the dressing as needed to lightly coat the ingredients; toss thoroughly. Refrigerate the remaining dressing to drizzle over grilled chicken breasts or grilled salmon. Add half the mint and toss to combine. Transfer the salad to a large serving bowl; mound in the center. Top with the remaining mint and a generous sprinkling of black pepper. Serve slightly chilled.

MAKES 6 SERVINGS

hoices: 1 carbohydrate (bread/starch), 1 fat

Per Serving: 150 calories (42% calories from fat), 7 g total fat (1 g saturated fat), 3 g protein, 18 g carbohydrate, 3 g dietary fiber, 0 cholesterol, 6 mg sodium, 208 mg potassium

Lasagne of French Mushroom and Lovage with Fava Bean Coulis

James Boyce, MARY ELAINE'S AT THE PHOENICIAN
SCOTTSDALE, ARIZONA

Travel + Leisure recently named The Phoenician one of the Top 100 Hotels in the United States, and Mary Elaine's has helped the hotel earn that honor. Here the food is delicious, yet well within the guidelines of a health-conscious meal plan. Chef Boyce really has a talent with vegetables.

FAVA BEAN COULIS:
1 tablespoon olive oil
1 tablespoon minced shallots
½ cup shelled fresh fava beans (see page 222)
½ cup Vegetable Stock (page 115)
½ cup fresh spinach leaves
salt (optional)
freshly ground pepper

LASAGNE:
1 tablespoon olive oil
½ cup thinly sliced cipollini onion

3 large cloves garlic, minced
4 cups assorted mixed mushrooms—morels, chanterelles, and porcini—sliced (see page 20)
¼ cup heavy cream
2 tablespoons Devonshire cream
¼ cup lovage leaves, chopped (see page 142)
1 tablespoon snipped chives

12 2 x 2-inch sheets fresh pasta

TO MAKE THE FAVA BEAN COULIS: Place the olive oil in a medium saucepan over medium heat. Add the shallots and cook for 1 minute, not allowing the shallots to color. Add the fava beans and continue to cook for an additional 2 minutes, stirring occasionally. Add the Vegetable Stock and simmer for 5 minutes.

Remove from the heat and stir in the spinach. When the spinach is wilted, place the mixture in a blender or food processor. Blend until smooth. Adjust the seasonings with salt (if using) and pepper. Keep warm.

TO PREPARE THE LASAGNE: In a large sauté pan, heat the olive oil over medium heat. Add the onion and garlic; cook for 1 minute. Add the mushrooms and continue to cook for 5 minutes or until the mushrooms are cooked through.

Add the heavy cream and cook for 2 minutes. Remove from the heat and mix in the Devonshire cream. Add the chopped lovage and chives; mix thoroughly.

Cook the pasta in boiling lightly salted water to al dente. Strain and drain the pasta sheets on paper towels.

Place 1 piece of pasta in the middle of a warm dinner plate. Spread a small amount of the mushroom mixture on top and cover with another pasta sheet. Spread with more of the mushroom mixture and another pasta sheet. Set aside and keep warm. Fill the remaining plates.

TO SERVE: Surround the pasta with the coulis and garnish with any leftover mushroom mixture. Serve at once.

MAKES 4 SERVINGS

Joslin Choices: 1 very-low-fat protein, 1 carbohydrate (bread/starch), 3 fat

Per Serving: 272 calories (47% calories from fat), 15 g total fat (5 g saturated fat), 10 g protein, 27 g carbohydrate, 7 g dietary fiber, 26 mg cholesterol, 36 mg sodium, 582 mg potassium

Lovage

Lovage is a perennial herb with a strong celery flavor that is enjoying renewed popularity as a result of the growing interest in vegetarian cooking. Because of its great size (lovage is the largest of the kitchen herbs; it can grow to heights of more than six feet), it's not a plant suitable for container gardening. The Pilgrims brought lovage to America to use as a digestive. Back in the Middle Ages, lovage was known as "love parsley" for its reputed aphrodisiac qualities.

In cooking, use lovage sparingly, as a little goes a long way. Fresh, it has a very pungent celery flavor with a hint of lemon and anise. Cooking tames this Mediterranean herb and you can use all of it—the leaves, stalks, and the roots. The latter, when grated, make a refreshing and interesting herb tea that many claim aids digestion.

Grilled Ricotta Salata with Flame-Roasted Peppers, Walla Walla Sweet Onions, and Fennel Slaw

Greg Higgins, HIGGINS
PORTLAND, OREGON

Higgins is housed in a historic building with a pressed-tin ceiling and polished wood floors. From his open kitchen, Chef Higgins can see every seat in the restaurant, while behind him are two windows that expose all of the kitchen action to passersby on the busy downtown Portland street. With strong connections to the local farming community, he shares the bounty of the Northwest with his discriminating patrons. An avid organic gardener, he grows many of his own herbs, vegetables, and fruits. He has been cooking since he was a young boy, when he experimented with recipes from *Fannie Farmer* in his mother's kitchen.

2 large green bell peppers
2 large red bell peppers
2 large yellow bell peppers
2 large Walla Walla or other sweet onions, about 1 pound total, cut into 6 wedges each with root end still attached
2 tablespoons minced garlic
4 tablespoons extra-virgin olive oil

2 tablespoons red wine vinegar
salt (optional)
freshly ground pepper
3 medium fennel bulbs, about 1 ½ pounds total
1 teaspoon Sambal Oelek (see page 144)
6 ounces hard Ricotta Salata, cut ½ inch thick (see page 62)
sprig of fennel-top for garnish

Light a grill. Char the peppers on the grill. Place in a plastic bag to sweat for 10 minutes. Peel, seed, and julienne the peppers. Grill the wedges of onion until evenly browned, 3 to 4 minutes per side. Place the peppers and onion wedges in a container. Whisk together with 1 tablespoon of the garlic, 2 tablespoons of the olive oil, and 1 tablespoon of the vinegar. Pour over the peppers and onion. Season to taste with the salt (if using) and pepper. Set aside to marinate.

Trim the fennel bulbs. Cut 6 pieces off the feathery top for a final garnish. Finely chop 2 tablespoons of the fennel tops. Using a very sharp knife or mandolin, thinly shave the bulbs. Toss with the chopped tops, the remaining garlic, olive oil, vinegar, and the Sambal Oelek. Adjust the seasoning with salt (if using) and pepper.

Grill the Ricotta Salata for 1 to 2 minutes per side, turning once. Cut into 6 equal pieces. Drain the peppers and onion. Fan an onion wedge on each of 6 large plates. Arrange a small pile of marinated peppers and the fennel salad on the plate and top with a piece of the grilled ricotta. Garnish with a sprig of fennel top.

MAKES 6 SERVINGS

Joslin Choices: 1 high-fat protein, 1 carbohydrate (bread/starch), 1 fat

Per Serving: 266 calories (51% calories from fat), 15 g total fat (7 g saturated fat), 8 g protein, 23 g carbohydrate, 7 g dietary fiber, 7 mg cholesterol, 132 mg sodium, 843 mg potassium

Sambal Oelek

A multipurpose condiment, sambals are very popular in Indonesia, Malaysia, and southern India. Sambal Oelek is the most basic of these, and you'll find it called for several times in this cookbook. Made of chiles, brown sugar, and salt, it's available in Asian markets, specialty shops, and on the Internet (see Sources, page 296). Sambal Oelek is not a condiment to dip one's finger into and then taste. It's very hot, so add it sparingly. You can always put in more, but you can never remove the heat once it's added.

You can make your own Sambal Oelek by pulsing hot fresh chile peppers in your food processor or blender until they form a paste. Add a smidgen of brown sugar, a few drops of water, and a dash of salt. Include the seeds of the chile peppers if you *really* like it hot. In a pinch, substitute another bought chill paste, hot pepper sauce, or red pepper flakes.

Spaghetti *à la Crudaiola*

Ricardo Ullio, SOTTO SOTTO

ATLANTA

The name of this restaurant means "hush-hush," but according to every review of this Atlanta restaurant it is no longer a secret— ". . . it's a sensation." Chef Ullio, a native of Milan, is known for the simplicity and freshness of his presentations. His elegant restaurant features hand-rolled pasta and perfect risotto, as well as dishes cooked in a modern wood oven. He wins kudos as a chef, but he used his engineering skills when he transformed empty stores into the elegant open-space Sotto Sotto.

1 pound dried spaghetti
4 cups diced ripe tomatoes, preferably organically
  grown heirloom tomatoes
2 tablespoons julienned fresh basil

3 tablespoons olive oil
splash 12-year-old balsamic vinegar
sea salt (optional)
freshly ground pepper to taste

In a large pot of boiling lightly salted water, cook the spaghetti to al dente, about 9 minutes.

Meanwhile, put the tomatoes in a large pasta bowl with the basil, olive oil, balsamic vinegar, salt (if using), and pepper. When the pasta is done, drain, and then toss with the tomato mixture. Serve immediately.

MAKES 8 SERVINGS

Joslin Choices: 3 carbohydrate (bread/starch), 1 fat

Per Serving: 269 calories (22% calories from fat), 7 g total fat (1 g saturated fat), 8 g protein, 46 g carbohydrate, 3 g dietary fiber, 0 cholesterol, 12 mg sodium, 311 mg potassium

Cold Vegetable Cannelloni with Gazpacho Andalou

Gilles Ajuelos, LA BASTIDE ODÉON
PARIS

When we began calling Paris to enlist chefs for this cookbook, the very first to respond was Chef Ajuelos, who stated that although he was very busy, he would like to participate. His restaurant, which is across from the Odéon Theater, opened in 1995 and has been serving Mediterranean cuisine to raves ever since. The food is that of Provence, which is where Chef Ajuelos trained. It is the pairing of Provençal recipes with the unexpected that keeps this restaurant busy day and night. Renowned cookbook author Patricia Wells praises the chef by saying that he presents food that people want: ". . . modern, light, of the moment, and well thought out." *Bon Appétit* says that the food ". . . could transport you from the Left Bank to Provence."

The gazpacho is quick to prepare, and in the summer it makes a perfect light lunch.

GAZPACHO:
14¼ ounces plum (Roma) tomatoes
2 slices white good-quality sandwich bread
1 small rib celery
2 large cloves garlic
½ medium white onion
1 tablespoon tomato paste
1 tablespoon white wine vinegar
1 tablespoon olive oil
freshly ground pepper

3½ ounces celeriac (celery root), trimmed
1 medium bulb fennel
3½ ounces broad beans (fresh fava beans), shelled
   (see page 222)
4 ounces green beans, trimmed
1 tablespoon olive oil
¼ teaspoon kosher salt
freshly ground pepper
½ cup chopped fresh basil
6 lasagne noodles

CANNELLONI:
3½ ounces zucchini, trimmed
3½ ounces carrots, peeled

TO PREPARE THE GAZPACHO: Put the tomatoes, bread, celery, garlic, onion, and tomato paste in a food processor and puree to the consistency of soup. Add a bit of water if too thick. Put through a sieve and add the vinegar, olive oil, and pepper to taste. Chill.

Cut the zucchini, carrots, and celeriac into fine julienne strips. Cut the fennel in two, remove the heart, and then chop very fine. Cook the broad beans and green beans in boiling water for 4 to 5 minutes, until crisp-tender. Drain.

TO MAKE THE CANNELLONI: Sauté the zucchini, carrots, and celeriac in a heavy nonstick sauté pan with the 1 tablespoon olive oil until crisp-cooked. Season with the salt and pepper. Mix with the broad beans and green beans and 1 tablespoon of the chopped basil. Reserve the remaining basil for garnish. Cover the vegetable and beans mixture and refrigerate. Cook the lasagne noodles in lightly salted boiling water to al dente, following the package directions. Drain and chill. Roll the vegetable and bean mixture in the noodles, making sure to roll the noodles tightly to form a wheel.

TO SERVE: Place a cannelloni upright in a shallow pasta bowl. Ladle on some of the chilled gazpacho and garnish with some of the reserved chopped basil. Serve cold.

MAKES 6 SERVINGS

Joslin Choices: ½ very-low-fat protein, 2 carbohydrate (bread/starch), 1 fat

Per Serving: 258 calories (21% calories from fat), 6 g total fat (1 g saturated fat), 10 g protein, 42 g carbohydrate, 9 g dietary fiber, 0 cholesterol, 185 mg sodium, 806 mg potassium

Large Plates—
Over 300 Calories

Lemon-Oregano Chicken with Vegetable Stacks

Maha Jeha Arnondin, MEZZA
ARLINGTON, TEXAS

The first time we dined at this popular Mediterranean restaurant, this entrée was not on the menu. On a subsequent visit, however, Chef Maha described the dish and prepared it for us, saying that it was going to be added soon. It was so delicious, with just a hint of lemon and wonderfully heady with oregano, that we asked her for the recipe. It's a superb way to serve chicken.

4 5-ounce skinless chicken breast halves, trimmed of all visible fat and cut into ½-inch cubes
½ cup fresh lemon juice
½ cup dry white wine
¼ cup extra-virgin olive oil
4 teaspoons crushed dried oregano

1 teaspoon salt (optional)
1 teaspoon white pepper
4 small Idaho potatoes, peeled and cut into ¾-inch cubes
Vegetable Stacks (recipe follows)

Place the chicken cubes in a shallow dish. Whisk together the lemon juice, wine, olive oil, oregano, salt (if using), and white pepper. Pour over the chicken. Cover and refrigerate for at least 1 hour or overnight.

Preheat the oven to 450°F. Spread the potatoes in a shallow roasting pan. Roast for 15 minutes. Add the chicken with its marinade. Cover with foil and bake for 30 minutes. Uncover, stir the potato-chicken mixture, and continue to bake for another 15 minutes. Remove from the oven and let stand for 5 minutes before dividing among 4 heated dinner plates. Serve with a Vegetable Stack alongside.

MAKES 4 SERVINGS

Joslin Choices (chicken-potato mixture only): 4 low-fat protein, 1½ carbohydrate (1½ bread/starch), 3 fat

Per Serving: 477 calories (52% calories from fat), 27 g total fat (6g saturated fat), 32 g protein, 21 g carbohydrate, 2 g dietary fiber, 91 mg cholesterol, 97 mg sodium, 899 mg potassium

Vegetable Stacks

1 large carrot, peeled and sliced thinly on the diagonal

2 small yellow summer squash, trimmed and sliced in thin julienne strips the same length as the snow peas

½ pound fresh snow peas, trimmed

Place the carrot slices and squash strips in a vegetable steamer over simmering water. Cover and steam for 2 minutes. Add the snow peas to the steamer and continue to steam for another 1 to 2 minutes, until all the vegetables are crisp-tender.

Divide the snow peas among the 4 dinner plates, arranging closely together lengthwise to form a flat base. Arrange the carrot slices on top of the snow peas and top with the strips of squash in the same direction as the snow peas. Serve hot.

MAKES 4 SERVINGS

Joslin Choices (vegetables only): 1 vegetable

Per Serving: 48 calories (2% calories from fat), 0 total fat (0 saturated fat), 3 g protein, 9 g carbohydrate, 3 g dietary fiber, 0 cholesterol, 12 mg sodium, 378 mg potassium

Friday Night Supper

Lemon-Oregano Chicken with Vegetable Stacks *(page 148)*

Chopped Red Onion, Horseradish, and Watercress Salad *(page 74)*

Apple Strudel with Fresh Berry Sauce *(page 264)*

Joslin Choices: 4 low-fat protein, 3½ carbohydrate (1½ bread/starch, 2 fruit), 1 vegetable, 3 fat, 689 calories (39% calories from fat)

Vietnamese Charred Chicken Breast with Lemon–Black Pepper Dipping Sauce over Purple Sticky Rice with Sautéed Asian Greens

Denise Appel, ZINC
NEW HAVEN, CONNECTICUT

When we asked our colleagues on the East Coast to let us know of chefs and restaurants that have come into the limelight since our last trip there, this talented chef and her restaurant ended up on each shortlist of several people "in the know." When one friend e-mailed us Elise Maclay's review of Zinc for *Connecticut* magazine, we knew we had a winner, as we have always agreed with Elise's judgment of restaurants. Chef Appel is someone we will be hearing about for years to come because of her ability to produce brilliantly original dishes, each with an interplay of colors, textures, and tastes.

CHICKEN:
4 8-ounce bone-in chicken breasts,
    wings attached
1 teaspoon toasted sesame oil
¼ teaspoon cayenne pepper
½ teaspoon chopped garlic
¼ teaspoon freshly ground black pepper
1 teaspoon Thai fish sauce

DIPPING SAUCE:
zest and juice of 4 large lemons
1 teaspoon kosher salt (optional)
1 teaspoon freshly ground pepper
1 teaspoon sugar

RICE:
1 cup purple sticky rice (see Note below)
2 cups cold water

SAUTÉED GREENS:
1 medium bok choy, about 1½ pounds
1 medium Napa (Chinese) cabbage,
    about 1½ pounds
1 tablespoon toasted sesame oil
½ cup mirin (Asian rice wine)
salt (optional)
freshly ground pepper

½ cup teriyaki sauce
1 bunch scallions, white part and 2 inches green,
    thinly sliced
2 tablespoons toasted sesame seeds

TO PREPARE THE CHICKEN: Combine the sesame oil, cayenne pepper, garlic, black pepper, and Thai fish sauce. Rub over the skin side of the chicken and place on a plate. Cover with plastic wrap and refrigerate for at least 1 hour or overnight.

TO MAKE THE DIPPING SAUCE: In a bowl, combine the lemon zest and juice, salt (if using), pepper, and sugar. Stir until dissolved. (Sauce may be made ahead, but must be used the same day as made). Keep at room temperature.

FOR THE RICE: Do not pre-rinse the rice. Put the rice in a heavy pot with the water. Bring to a boil, lower the heat to simmer, and cook, covered, until all the water is absorbed. Remove from the heat and keep warm.

TO PREPARE THE GREENS: Slice the cabbages on the bias. Heat the sesame oil in a large, non-stick skillet or wok over high heat until the oil ripples. Add the cabbage and quickly stir-fry for about 2 minutes. Add the mirin, salt (if using), and pepper. Remove from the heat and keep warm.

Light a grill. Place the chicken on the grill over hot coals, skin side down. Grill for 2 to 3 minutes until nicely charred. Flip the chicken over and continue to grill until the chicken is cooked through—until the juices run clear, about 3 to 5 minutes. Cut to test with the point of a knife. Transfer the chicken to a cutting board and let rest for 3 minutes. Then cut off the wings, saving them for another purpose, and carve the breast on the bias into even slices, discarding all the skin.

TO ASSEMBLE: Mound ½ cup of the hot rice in the center of 4 large heated plates. Divide the dipping sauce into 4 condiment bowls and place on each plate. Arrange the greens on the plates. Spoon the teriyaki sauce into a small circle in front of the rice. Top the rice with the chicken slices and sprinkle the plate with the scallions and sesame seeds. Serve immediately.

MAKES 4 SERVINGS

Joslin Choices: 4 low-fat protein, 2 carbohydrate (bread/starch)

Per Serving: 446 calories (24% calories from fat), 12 g total fat (2 g saturated fat), 36 g protein, 43 g carbohydrate, 9 g dietary fiber, 79 mg cholesterol, 635 mg sodium, 1,215 mg potassium

Note: Purple sticky rice is available at Asian stores; in a pinch, substitute white short-grain jasmine rice.

Sautéed Chicken Paillards over Cucumber, Tomato, Parsley, and Coriander Salad with Rice Vinegar Dressing

Jean-Marie Lacroix, THE FOUNTAIN AT
THE FOUR SEASONS HOTEL

PHILADELPHIA

Growing up in Philadelphia, Bonnie knew that to dine well she had to travel to New York City—that is, until the Four Seasons opened and her family was treated to this elegant hotel and the talents of Chef Lacroix. He has been instrumental in the development of regional sources for meat, produce, and breads since 1983, when the hotel opened. Both the Fountain Restaurant and Swann Lounge and Café have received numerous awards, including being named one of the Top 25 restaurants in the United States by *Food & Wine*. A *Condé Nast Traveler* readers' poll named it as number 2 in the country. Since giving us this recipe, Chef Lacroix has retired. We wish him good fortune in his new endeavors in the culinary world.

A paillard is a pounded piece of meat or chicken that is very thin and quickly grilled. Do try to buy free-range chicken for this dish. The superb flavor makes it worth the extra price.

4 5-ounce boneless, skinless free-range chicken
  breast halves

MARINADE:
3 tablespoons olive oil
1 handful parsley sprigs
1 teaspoon chopped shallot
1 teaspoon fresh lemon juice

2 English cucumbers, cut lengthwise and sliced on
  bias ¼ inch thick

3 medium tomatoes, cored, seeded, and cut into
  ¼-inch dice
1 cup good-quality rice vinegar
salt (optional)
freshly ground pepper
2 tablespoons chopped flat-leaf parsley
1 tablespoon chopped cilantro

Remove all the visible fat and sinew from the chicken breast halves. Place each half between 2 sheets of plastic wrap or waxed paper and pound very thin. Place the chicken breast halves on a large plate. In a small bowl, combine the olive oil, parsley sprigs, shallot, and lemon juice. Spoon over the chicken. Cover with the plastic wrap and refrigerate for 1 to 2 hours.

In a medium bowl, toss the cucumbers, tomatoes, and rice vinegar. Season with salt (if using) and pepper to taste.

Remove the chicken from the plate and scrape off the marinade. Place a large, nonstick skillet over high heat. Add the chicken paillards to the pan, 2 at a time, and quickly sauté for about 1½ minutes per side, turning once. Do not crowd the pan. Transfer to a platter and keep warm. Repeat, cooking the remaining 2 paillards.

Using a slotted spoon, place one-quarter of the cucumber mixture in the center of each of 4 dinner plates. Drizzle with some of the remaining vinegar. Place 1 chicken paillard over each salad and sprinkle with parsley and coriander. Serve at once.

MAKES 4 SERVINGS

Joslin Choices: 4 low-fat protein, 1 carbohydrate (bread/starch), 2 fat

Per Serving: 401 calories (54% calories from fat), 24 g total fat (5 g saturated fat), 31 g protein, 15 g carbohydrate, 2 g dietary fiber, 91 mg cholesterol, 105 mg sodium, 695 mg potassium

Fried Bean Curd with Shredded Chicken and Bean Sprouts

Foo Loon Kiang, KOPI TIAM AT THE SWISSHÔTEL SINGAPORE, THE STAMFORD

SINGAPORE

If you want the native food in Singapore, go to Kopi Tiam at this luxury hotel in Singapore. When we invited Chef Kiang to participate, he became very excited and submitted several recipes. We settled on this one; it is superb and you won't have any problem finding all of the ingredients at your local market. You will make it often.

½ pound firm bean curd (tofu), drained and pressed (see page 247), cut into 2 rectangular portions

2 tablespoons plus 1 teaspoon cornstarch

1 tablespoon peanut oil

3½ ounces mung bean sprouts, rinsed and drained

¾ cup plus 1 tablespoon Chicken Stock (page 31) or canned low-fat, low-salt broth

6 ounces cooked chicken breast, shredded

1 large egg white

½ teaspoon salt (optional)

½ teaspoon freshly ground white pepper

¾ teaspoon sugar

¼ teaspoon reduced-sodium soy sauce

Pat the bean curd dry with paper towels and sprinkle with the 2 tablespoons cornstarch. Place the wok over high heat and, when very hot, add the peanut oil. Add the bean curd and fry until golden brown and crispy on all sides, about 6 to 8 minutes. Transfer the bean curd to 2 large plates.

Add the bean sprouts to the skillet and stir-fry for 1 minute. Toss in the Chicken Stock and shredded chicken. Whisk the egg white, remaining 1 teaspoon cornstarch, salt (if using), pepper, sugar, and soy sauce. Add to the skillet and continue to stir-fry for another 1 to 2 minutes, until the chicken is heated through and the sauce has slightly thickened. Spoon the sprouts and chicken mixture over the bean curd and serve at once.

MAKES 2 SERVINGS

Joslin Choices: 5½ low-fat protein, 1 carbohydrate (bread/starch), 1 fat

Per Serving: 417 calories (45% calories from fat), 21 g total fat (4 g saturated fat), 41 g protein, 17 g carbohydrate, 3 g dietary fiber, 51 mg cholesterol, 182 mg sodium, 540 mg potassium

Grilled Turkey and Vegetable Tacos with Mango and Avocado

Bruce Auden, BIGA ON THE BANKS
SAN ANTONIO, TEXAS

Turkey is an important ingredient for Texas-style cooking, as it can be used in regional dishes like these tacos. Turkey's flavor characteristics hold up well to the robust flavors of the Southwest and Mexico. Chef Auden said that you might add salsa if you like, but if the poblano has enough heat (see page 78), you should not need to add it. No matter, this takes the taco to a gourmet level that even Tex-Mex taco lovers will enjoy.

MARINADE:

1 tablespoon fresh lime juice

2 tablespoons vegetable oil, not canola

1 teaspoon ground cumin

6 turkey cutlets, about 4 ounces each

3 whole poblano chile peppers (see page 78)

6 plum tomatoes

12 whole scallions, trimmed, leaving
  2 inches green

2 ripe mangoes, peeled and seeded

2 small ripe Haas avocados, pitted and peeled

12 7-inch tortillas, flour or corn, grilled or warmed

1 bunch cilantro sprigs, washed and dried,
  for garnish

coarse salt (optional)

lime wedges (optional)

Combine the ingredients for the marinade and pour over the turkey cutlets. Marinate in the refrigerator for up to 3 hours. When your grill is ready with glowing coals (no flames), start grilling the turkey until cooked through, the poblano peppers until their skins are charred and blistered, the tomatoes until charred and blistered, and the scallions until charred. If you want the mangoes warm, place them on a sheet of foil on the grill for 2 to 3 minutes.

As each item is grilled enough, remove, and keep warm until everything is done. Cut the turkey, peppers, tomatoes, mangoes, and avocadoes into slices. Leave the scallions whole. Divide everything into 12 piles near the edge of each of the tortillas, and roll them up. Garnish with the cilantro sprigs, and sprinkle with coarse salt (if using) and a squeeze of lime, if desired.

MAKES 6 SERVINGS

Joslin Choices: 4 medium-fat protein, 3 carbohydrate (2 bread/starch, 1 fruit)

Per Serving: 542 calories (35% calories from fat), 22 g total fat (3 g saturated fat), 35 g protein, 56 g carbohydrate, 9 g dietary fiber, 60 mg cholesterol, 157 mg sodium, 1,055 mg potassium

Tex-Mex Dinner

Jicama with Fire-Roasted Salsa *(page 263)*

Grilled Turkey and Vegetable Tacos with Mango and Avocado *(page 155)*

Joslin Choices: 4 medium-fat protein, 3 carbohydrate (2 bread/starch, 1 fruit), 563 calories (35% calories from fat)

Note: Items not referring to a specific recipe are not included in the nutritional analysis. Consult the Joslin Food Choices (page 287) for the information on jicama.

Garlic- and Cilantro-Rubbed Game Hens with Roasted Potatoes, Haricots Verts, and Cilantro Vinaigrette

Marlin Kaplan, ONE WALNUT

CLEVELAND, OHIO

Chef Kaplan positively loves cilantro. To him, it has more impact than most other herbs, sending a dish in a new direction and adding an almost indescribable dimension with its clean fresh flavor. This is evident when dining at One Walnut, a downtown restaurant studded with sleek Art Deco lighting where several items on the menu feature cilantro.

His cuisine is best described as upscale "comfort food," often encrusted with a combination of herbs and spices. Eating a Cornish game hen is a bit of work, but, as with crab legs, the effort is rewarded with immense flavor. You can eliminate the haricots verts and this dish will still be complex and delicious.

1 tablespoon ground cumin

2 tablespoons good-quality chili powder

2 tablespoons paprika, plus extra for garnish

2 1-pound Cornish game hens or *poussins,*
  cut in half lengthwise

2 tablespoons unbleached all-purpose flour

4 tablespoons roasted garlic puree

2 shallots, minced

1 bunch cilantro, cleaned, leaves picked and
  finely chopped

1 tablespoon olive oil

1 pound small red bliss potatoes, quartered

1 tablespoon olive oil

2 tablespoons crushed dried rosemary

coarse salt (optional)

freshly ground black pepper

½ pound haricots verts or young green beans,
  stem ends removed

2 teaspoons unsalted butter

CILANTRO VINAIGRETTE:

1 clove garlic

½ shallot

1 tablespoon rice wine vinegar

1 tablespoon lemon juice

¼ teaspoon crushed red pepper flakes

salt (optional)

freshly ground pepper

1 bunch cilantro, cleaned and leaves picked

1 ice cube

1 cup canola oil or vegetable oil

Preheat the oven to 400°F.

Combine the cumin, chili powder, and paprika and sprinkle evenly over the hens. Dust the hens with the flour and brush with the garlic puree. Roll them in the shallots. Set aside 2 tablespoons of the cilantro. Roll the hens in the remaining cilantro. In a heavy-bottomed sauté pan, heat the olive oil. Add the hens and sear on each side until the skin is golden brown, about 5 minutes per side.

Transfer the hens to a baking pan and bake until the juices run clear when pricked in the thigh, about 30 to 35 minutes.

Meanwhile, combine the potatoes, olive oil, rosemary, salt (if using), and pepper. Toss until the potatoes are coated evenly, then spread in a single layer on a baking sheet and roast in the middle of the oven for 30 to 35 minutes, until the potatoes are golden brown and tender.

While the potatoes and hens are roasting, bring a medium pot of lightly salted water to a boil and blanch the haricots verts for 2 minutes. Drain and plunge into a bath of ice water to stop the cooking process. Drain again. Melt the butter in a medium saucepan. When it foams, add the haricots verts and season with salt (if using) and pepper to taste. Keep warm, but do not cover or they will lose their color.

TO PREPARE THE VINAIGRETTE: In a food processor or blender, place the garlic, shallot, rice wine vinegar, lemon juice, red pepper flakes, salt (if using), and pepper. Puree the mixture. Add the cilantro leaves and the ice cube. Puree again, slowly adding the oil through the feed tube. Turn off the machine as soon as the oil is added, being careful not to overmix as the heat of the processor will turn the vinaigrette dark brown. The emulsion should be a vibrant green.

TO ASSEMBLE THE DISH: Using a paper towel, rub the rims of 4 large heated plates with a little oil. Sprinkle the rims with the cilantro reserved from the hens and lightly dust with paprika. Drizzle 1 tablespoon of the vinaigrette onto the center of each plate. Place a small mound of the roasted potatoes on the vinaigrette and lean equal portions of the beans against the potatoes. Lay a half hen over the potatoes. Drizzle with another ½ tablespoon of the vinaigrette. Refrigerate the remaining vinaigrette to use another time over vegetables or fish. Serve immediately.

MAKES 4 SERVINGS

Joslin Choices: 4½ medium-fat protein, 2 carbohydrate (bread/starch), ½ fat

Per Serving: 545 calories (46% calories from fat), 28 g total fat (5 g saturated fat), 38 g protein, 36 g carbohydrate, 9 g dietary fiber, 155 mg cholesterol, 145 mg sodium, 1,331 mg potassium

Joslin Choices (vinaigrette only): 2 fat

Per 1½-Tablespoon Serving: 110 calories (99% calories from fat), 12 g total fat (1 g saturated fat), 0 protein, 0 carbohydrate, 0 dietary fiber, 0 cholesterol, 1 mg sodium, 7 mg potassium

Sunday Dinner with the Family

Garlic- and Cilantro-Rubbed Game Hens
   with Roasted Potatoes, Haricots Verts,
   and Cilantro Vinaigrette (page 157)

Chocolate Grand Marnier Soufflé with Raspberry Coulis (page 269)

Joslin Choices: 5 medium-fat protein, 3½ carbohydrate (2 bread/starch, 1½ fruit), 666 calories (41% calories from fat)

Braised Rabbit with Port Wine Pipérade and Garlic Cannellini Bean Puree

Greg Higgins, HIGGINS
PORTLAND, OREGON

Chef Higgins first caught our attention when he was in Atlanta to teach cooking classes for *Cooking Light* magazine a few years back. Since then, we have heard about him from our colleagues at the James Beard Foundation, who nominated him for "Best Chef in the Northwest and Hawaii" in 2001. His cooking focuses on Pacific Northwest ingredients and traditional French techniques.

When we called him about this cookbook, he responded, "That's how I cook. So, no problem." This recipe shows he really understands how to infuse complex flavors into low-fat dishes. The whole meal has only 12 grams of fat. Follow this with a piece of fresh fruit and you're truly eating well while watching your fat grams.

A pipérade is a side dish from the Basque region of France, and it always contains tomatoes and bell peppers cooked in olive oil, in addition to whatever else the cook decides to add.

BEAN PUREE:

1 pound dried cannellini beans, rinsed and picked over

1 cup oven-roasted garlic cloves, about 3 large bulbs

2 tablespoons finely chopped fresh rosemary

1 teaspoon crushed red pepper flakes

2 quarts Vegetable Stock (page 115)

2 tablespoons extra-virgin olive oil

salt (optional)

freshly ground pepper

RABBIT:

4 hindquarters fresh rabbit, about 6 ounces each (see Note below)

salt (optional)

freshly ground pepper

½ tablespoon olive oil

PIPÉRADE:

1 cup julienned onion

3 tablespoons minced garlic

1 cup julienned green bell pepper

1 cup julienned red bell pepper

2 tablespoons chopped fresh marjoram or oregano

½ teaspoon crushed red pepper flakes

3 cups canned no-salt-added diced tomatoes in puree

1 cup port wine

red wine vinegar to taste

¼ cup chopped parsley

TO PREPARE THE BEAN PUREE: Soak the beans overnight in cold water to cover or use the quick-soak method. Drain and place the beans in a medium saucepan with the roasted garlic, rosemary, red pepper flakes, and Vegetable Stock. Simmer over medium heat, stirring occasionally, until the beans are splitting open and tender, 20 to 30 minutes. Remove from the heat and drain, reserving the broth. Puree the bean mixture in a food processor or food mill with the olive oil, salt (if using), and pepper to taste, adding the reserved bean cooking liquid as needed to attain the desired smooth texture. Keep the puree warm until needed.

Season the rabbit legs with salt (if using) and pepper. In an ovenproof saucepan or casserole, heat the olive oil until it begins to smoke over high heat. Sear the rabbit pieces in the hot oil, 3 to 5 minutes per side. Remove the rabbit and keep warm.

TO PREPARE THE PIPÉRADE: Reduce the heat to medium and add the onion, garlic, green and red peppers, marjoram, and chili flakes to the hot pan, and sauté until the vegetables are just tender, about 3 to 5 minutes. Add the tomatoes and wine. Bring to a simmer and reduce to thicken, stirring often, about 15 minutes. Season the sauce to taste with the vinegar, salt (if using), and pepper.

Preheat the oven to 400°F.

Place the seared rabbit legs in the pipérade (it need not cover them entirely). Cover the pan and place in the oven for 15 to 20 minutes, until the rabbit is firm to the touch and cooked through (cut to test).

Remove from the oven and stir in the chopped parsley. Serve on a portion of the garlic cannellini bean puree with the pipérade sauce spooned around.

MAKES 4 SERVINGS

Joslin Choices: 4½ low-fat protein, 2 carbohydrate (bread/starch)

Per Serving: 491 calories (22% calories from fat), 12 g total fat (3 g saturated fat), 39 g protein, 43 g carbohydrate, 8 g dietary fiber, 80 mg cholesterol, 180 mg sodium, 980 mg potassium

Joslin Choices (bean puree only): 1 very-low-fat protein, 1 carbohydrate (bread/starch)

Per ½-Cup Serving: 220 calories (18% calories from fat), 4 g total fat (2 g saturated fat), 14 g protein, 34 g carbohydrate, 8 g dietary fiber, 0 cholesterol, 96 mg sodium, 666 mg potassium

Note: You may substitute bone-in skinless chicken thighs or breasts for the fresh rabbit.

Grilled Duck Breast with Sautéed Peaches and Tuscan Bread Salad

Don Pintabona, TRIBECA GRILL
NEW YORK CITY

We have eaten this delicious salad at this restaurant, which occupies the first two floors of the Tribeca Film Center building. Owned by Oscar-winning actor Robert De Niro in partnership with restaurateur Drew Nieporent, Tribeca Grill under the guiding hand of Chef Pintabona offers the cross-cultural creative influences of many different cuisines. No wonder it's become one of New York City's most popular restaurants.

BREAD SALAD:
½ 1-pound baguette, diced
2 medium ripe peaches, peeled and diced
2 teaspoons sugar
20 black olives
2 large beef steak tomatoes, diced
1 medium red onion, finely minced
2 tablespoons capers, rinsed and drained
½ cup chiffonade-cut fresh basil

1 tablespoon minced garlic
¼ cup red wine vinegar
¼ cup extra-virgin olive oil
¼ cup sugar
salt (optional)
freshly ground pepper to taste

6 5-ounce duck breasts

Preheat the oven to 300°F.

Arrange the bread cubes in a shallow roasting pan and place in the oven until the bread is nicely toasted, about 10 to 15 minutes. Stir the bread cubes occasionally for even toasting. Set aside.

While the bread is toasting, sauté the peaches, sprinkled with the 2 teaspoons sugar, in a nonstick pan until lightly glazed. Set aside.

Mix all the remaining salad ingredients together and set aside.

Light a grill.

Remove the skin and any fat from the duck breasts. Lightly score the breasts with a sharp knife. When the coals are hot, grill the duck breasts to medium-rare, about 2 to 3 minutes per side.

While the duck is grilling, mix the bread, peaches, and salad ingredients, tossing to evenly coat the bread with the wet ingredients. Let sit at least 1 minute (do not mix too far in advance or the salad will become soggy).

Divide the salad among 6 large plates. Slice the duck breasts and serve over the salad. Serve at once.

MAKES 6 SERVINGS

Joslin Choices: 3 medium-fat protein, 3 carbohydrate, 2 fat

Per Serving: 581 calories (44% calories from fat), 28 g total fat (5 g saturated fat), 32 g protein, 49 g carbohydrate, 4 g dietary fiber, 154 mg cholesterol, 584 mg sodium, 348 mg potassium

Grilled Ostrich over Rösti with Duxelles and Red Wine Sauce

Tony Howorth, CAFÉ DU JARDIN AT COVENT GARDEN

LONDON

We enjoy ostrich as an excellent substitute for filet mignon, so when this recipe came in, we were excited to try it. We pass by countless ostrich ranches driving between our homes in Oklahoma and Texas. Rösti are shredded potatoes formed into a pancake and crisply fried. A cast-iron skillet makes it easy to get the right crispness without a lot of added fat.

Chef Howorth's recipe for the wine sauce called for a calf's foot, something we can't easily get here in the United States, so we left the calf's foot out and thickened the sauce by reduction. The sauce was delicious.

DUXELLES:

3 cloves garlic, minced

2 tablespoons finely minced yellow onion

¼ cup minced fresh tarragon

4 medium white button mushrooms, cleaned and finely chopped

2 teaspoons olive oil

1 teaspoon Dijon mustard

4 teaspoons dry white wine

salt (optional)

freshly ground pepper

RÖSTI:

1 8-ounce russet potato, peeled

½ teaspoon salt (optional)

1 teaspoon olive oil

RED WINE SAUCE:

4 shallots, minced

½ teaspoon olive oil

½ cup dry red wine

1 cup Chicken Stock (page 31)

1 large plum tomato, peeled, seeded, and finely chopped

OSTRICH:

1 large red bell pepper

⅓ cup port wine

2 tablespoons minced fresh thyme

4 4-ounce ostrich fillets

salt (optional)

freshly ground pepper

TO MAKE THE DUXELLES: In a nonstick sauté pan, cook the garlic, onion, tarragon, and mushrooms in the olive oil over medium heat until the onion is wilted, about 5 minutes. Add the mustard and wine. Season with salt (if using) and pepper to taste. Sauté, stirring occasionally, until all the liquid has evaporated. Remove from stove and reserve. Keep warm.

TO PREPARE THE RÖSTI: Shred the potato and season with salt (if using). Wrap the potato in a piece of cheesecloth and wring out all the liquid, leaving the potatoes very dry. Place a 3-inch skillet over medium-high heat and add ¼ teaspoon of the olive oil. When the pan is very hot, put one-quarter of the potatoes in a thin layer on the bottom of the pan. Sauté without disturbing the potatoes until crispy and nicely browned on the bottom, forming a thin pancake. Carefully turn the potato pancake over and continue to cook until it is nicely browned and crisp on the bottom. Turn out onto a paper towel to drain. Repeat, making 4 potato pancakes. Keep warm.

FOR THE SAUCE: Sauté the shallots in a nonstick sauté pan with the olive oil over low heat until the shallots are wilted, about 4 minutes. Add the wine, stock, and tomato. Simmer, stirring occasionally, until reduced and thickened, about 15 minutes. Keep warm.

Light a grill. Place the bell pepper on the grill about 4 inches from the source of heat, turning until the skin is blistered and blackened on all sides. Transfer the pepper to a plastic bag, close, and let stand for 10 minutes.

Meanwhile, bring the red wine sauce back to a boil. Add the port. Peel and seed the pepper. Slice the pepper into julienne strips and add to the sauce along with the thyme. Reduce the heat and simmer until the sauce reaches the desired consistency. Keep warm.

FOR THE OSTRICH: Salt (if using) and pepper the ostrich fillets, then grill for 2 to 3 minutes per side, turning once for rare, 3 to 4 minutes for medium.

TO ASSEMBLE: Place a warm potato rösti in the center of each of 4 large serving plates. Place a grilled ostrich filet on top of each rösti and spoon some of the duxelles on top of the ostrich. Spoon the wine sauce around the rösti and serve at once.

MAKES 4 SERVINGS.

Joslin Choices: 4 very-low-fat protein, 1 carbohydrate (bread/starch), 1 fat

Per Serving: 324 calories (24% calories from fat), 9 g total fat (2 g saturated fat), 29 g protein, 22 g carbohydrate, 3 g dietary fiber, 92 mg cholesterol, 170 mg sodium, 685 mg potassium

Medallion of Braised *Ñandú* (Ostrich) on Rose-Hip Sauce with Wild Patagonian Mushrooms, Served in a Nest of Whole-Wheat Pasta

Guido Stütz, CRYSTAL GARDEN AT THE SHERATON PARK TOWER
BUENOS AIRES

We cannot get Patagonian mushrooms here (the World Wide Web lists some 50 varieties grown in Patagonia), but you can substitute shiitakes, cèpes, or morels in this recipe by a talented Argentinean chef. Fresh rose hips are also hard to find. If you use rose hips from your own garden, they must be pesticide-free. Better to use (as Chef Stütz suggested) another type of wild fruit. We did not have any "wild" fruit, so we used pomegranate seeds and the result was delicious.

4 4-ounce fillets *ñandú* (ostrich)
sea salt (optional)
freshly ground pepper
1 tablespoon walnut oil
6 ounces Patagonian or other wild mushrooms
¼ cup minced shallots
4 ounces rose hips or other wild fruit
   (see Headnote above)

⅔ cup dry red wine
1⅓ cups Beef Stock (page 167) or low-fat,
   low-sodium canned beef broth
5 small sprigs fresh rosemary
8 ounces whole-wheat pasta such as fettuccine

Season the ostrich with sea salt (if using) and pepper. Sear on both sides in a hot skillet in the walnut oil. Remove the ostrich and keep warm.

In the same skillet, sauté the mushroom slices for 4 to 5 minutes. Add the shallots and the rose hips. Return the ostrich to the skillet and add the red wine. Let the liquid reduce slightly and add the Beef Stock and 1 sprig fresh rosemary.

Cook, turning the ostrich occasionally so that it cooks evenly. Reduce the sauce until it forms a thick gravy.

Meanwhile, prepare the whole-wheat pasta according to package directions. Drain and arrange a "nest" of the pasta in the center of each of 4 large plates. Place a fillet of ostrich in each nest and coat liberally with the sauce. Garnish with the remaining rosemary sprigs and serve at once.

MAKES 4 SERVINGS

Joslin Choices: 4 very-low-fat protein, 3 carbohydrate (bread/starch)

Per Serving: 452 calories (15% calories from fat), 8 g total fat (2 g saturated fat), 37 g protein, 53 g carbohydrate, 6 g dietary fiber, 91 mg cholesterol, 181 mg sodium, 651 mg potassium

Beef Stock

Ask your butcher to collect the bones you will need for making this stock. For an even richer flavor, return the strained stock to the stove and reduce it further.

5 pounds mixed beef and veal bones (marrow, knuckle, and shin)
2 large onions, peeled and cut in half
1 leek, white part only, well rinsed and cut into large pieces
2 carrots, scrubbed and cut into chunks
2 ribs celery with leaves, cut into large pieces

4 cloves garlic, peeled
about 6 quarts water
5 fresh thyme sprigs
6 sprigs fresh flat-leaf parsley
1 bay leaf
8 peppercorns or to taste

Preheat the oven to 400°F.

Place the bones in a single layer in a large roasting pan. Scatter the onions, leek, carrots, celery, and garlic among the bones. Roast for 1 hour, until the bones and the vegetables begin to brown.

Transfer the bones and vegetables to a large stockpot. Add the water and bring to a vigorous boil. Skim and discard the foam that rises to the top. Reduce the heat to a simmer, add the remaining seasonings, and cook, uncovered, for 6 hours.

Strain through a fine sieve or a colander lined with cheesecloth. Discard the solids. Return the stock to the stove and boil slowly until reduced to 2 quarts. Set aside to cool to room temperature. Skim off and discard any fat that rises to the surface. Refrigerate, covered, or freeze for up to 6 months.

MAKES 2 QUARTS

Joslin Choices: free food

Per 1-Cup Serving: 22 calories (26% calories from fat), 1 g total fat (0 saturated fat), 2 g protein, 2 g carbohydrate, 0 dietary fiber, 7 mg cholesterol, 34 mg sodium, 71 mg potassium

Thai Beef Salad with Noodles, Scallions, and Red Curry Vinaigrette

Michael Herschman, MOJO CAFÉ
CLEVELAND, OHIO

This is one of the most popular dishes at Mojo Café. Sambal Oelek is almost a staple with our chefs, and is likely to become one in your own kitchen. The recipe also calls for Vietnamese or Thai potato noodles. You will find both at Asian markets. The Red Curry Vinaigrette makes a lot (about 3 cups), so you will have plenty left over for another use. We spooned some over grilled shrimp and served them with steamed rice. Delicious!

1 pound top beef sirloin
kosher salt (optional)
freshly ground pepper
1 8-ounce package Vietnamese or
    Thai potato noodles
3 scallions, white part only

RED CURRY VINAIGRETTE:
2 tablespoons roasted shallots
2 tablespoons Thai red curry paste

½ cup brown sugar
1 tablespoon Sambal Oelek (see page 144)
½ cup red wine vinegar
½ cup reduced-sodium soy sauce
¾ cup dark sesame oil
½ cup blended safflower and olive oil

2 tablespoons sesame seeds, toasted

Light a grill or preheat a broiler. Season both sides of the steak with salt (if using) and pepper. Grill for about 3 minutes per side, turning once, just until the meat is richly browned on both sides. Remove from the grill and let rest for 5 minutes. Thinly slice across the grain, then julienne. Set aside.

Reconstitute the potato noodles by briefly boiling in lightly salted water, then shock in ice water to cool and stop the cooking process. Drain and set aside. Cut the scallions lengthwise into thin julienne strips. Set aside.

TO PREPARE THE RED CURRY VINAIGRETTE: In a blender, combine the roasted shallots, red curry paste, brown sugar, Sambal Oelek, red wine vinegar, and soy sauce. Blend until smooth. With the blender still running, drizzle in the sesame oil and blended oil to form the vinaigrette. Transfer to a container and chill. Makes about 3 cups. (Any unused vinaigrette can be covered and refrigerated for use within 3 days.)

In a large stainless-steel mixing bowl, combine 1 cup of the vinaigrette, the strips of grilled beef, the potato noodles, and the scallions. Mix well. Divide among 8 bowls and sprinkle each serving with some of the toasted sesame seeds. Serve at once.

MAKES 8 SERVINGS

Joslin Choices: 2 medium-fat protein, 2 carbohydrate (bread/starch), 1 fat

Per Serving: 352 calories (46% calories from fat), 18 g total fat (4 g saturated fat), 18 g protein, 29 g carbohydrate, 1 g dietary fiber, 50 mg cholesterol, 300 mg sodium, 257 mg potassium

Joslin Choices (Red Curry Vinaigrette per 1-tablespoon serving): 1 fat

Per Serving: 63 calories (82% calories from fat), 6 g total fat (1 g saturated fat), 0 protein, 3 g carbohydrate, 0 dietary fiber, 0 cholesterol, 126 mg sodium, 10 mg potassium

Herb-Crusted Pork Tenderloin with Grilled Pears and Wilted Spinach

Todd Gray, EQUINOX
WASHINGTON, D.C.

Pork with grilled pears and spinach? In the hands of Chef Gray, this combination becomes as American as apple pie. The combination is so delightful that you may want to try it with chicken or veal. How nice to have a chef of Todd Gray's talents cooking for you.

3 10-ounce pork tenderloins
freshly ground pepper
¼ teaspoon salt (optional)
vegetable cooking spray
2 cups dried unseasoned bread crumbs
¼ cup chopped parsley
1 tablespoon whole-grain mustard

1 tablespoon Dijon mustard
6 tablespoons canned low-sodium vegetable broth
½ cup peeled shallots, thinly sliced
1 pound baby spinach, washed
3 Bartlett pears, peeled, cored, and each cut into
   6 lengthwise wedges

Heat a grill or a broiler to a high temperature; season the pork with pepper and ⅛ teaspoon of the salt (if using). Coat the grill grid or broiler pan with the cooking spray. Grill the pork tenderloins to medium, about 10 minutes per side, until an instant-read meat thermometer registers 140°F. While the tenderloins are grilling, on a plate, combine the bread crumbs and parsley. In a small bowl, combine the mustards. Set both aside. Preheat the oven to 350°F.

Remove the tenderloins from the grill and brush with the mustard mixture. Roll each tenderloin in the breadcrumb mixture and place in a large baking pan that has been lightly coated with the cooking spray. Bake until the pork is cooked medium-well and the meat thermometer registers 160°F, about 10 minutes.

Meanwhile, place a large sauté pan over medium heat. Add the stock, shallots, and spinach. Allow to wilt. Add the pepper and the remaining ⅛ teaspoon salt (if using). Remove from the heat and keep warm.

Season the sliced pears with pepper and grill or broil on high heat until grill marks are set, about 2 minutes per side. Remove and keep warm.

Remove the pork tenderloins from the oven. Cut each tenderloin on the diagonal into 6 medallions. Mound a small amount of spinach mixture in the middle of 6 large heated serving plates. Arrange the pears around the edges and top with sliced medallions of crusted pork. Serve immediately.

MAKES 8 SERVINGS

Joslin Choices: 4½ very-low-fat protein, 3 carbohydrate (2 bread/starch, 1 fruit), 1 fat

Per Serving: 402 calories (18% calories from fat), 8 g total fat (2 g saturated fat), 38 g protein, 45 g carbohydrate, 4 g dietary fiber, 84 mg cholesterol, 542 mg sodium, 1,136 mg potassium

Christmas Dinner

Asparagus and Red Grape Tomato Salad with Citrus Vinaigrette (page 59)

Herb-Crusted Pork Tenderloin with Grilled Pears and Wilted Spinach (page 170)

Zabaglione and Fresh Fruit (page 283)

Joslin Choices: 4½ very-low-fat protein, 4½ carbohydrate (2 bread/starch, 1 low-fat milk, 1½ fruit), 2 vegetable, 2 fat, 642 calories (24% calories from fat)

Wild Boar Ragout with Herbed Gnocchi

Kevin Thomas Ascolese, SALVE!

DALLAS, TEXAS

Once when Bonnie called for our fourth chat of the day, she had just returned from lunch with a group of friends who included a couple from Dallas. All excited, she told me that we needed to contact the chef at Salve! I was happy to reply that I had just received Chef Ascolese's recipe contributions in that morning's crop of e-mails, sent only hours before he left for Rome. From there, he and the owners of Salve! and its sister restaurant, Mi Piaci, another Dallas establishment, would spend the next few weeks driving through Tuscany, garnering new ideas and recipes for the restaurants.

You can find wild boar at specialty shops and on the World Wide Web (see Sources, page 296), or you can substitute boneless pork shoulder or boneless beef. Either way, this is a savory dish to be enjoyed whenever you want something warm and comforting. Italians call the cooking sauce used in this recipe *soffrito*.

1 tablespoon olive oil
2 pounds boneless wild boar shoulder or lean
   boneless pork shoulder, cut into 1-inch cubes
   (see Headnote above)

2 tablespoons balsamic vinegar
½ cup red wine vinegar
1 cup Chicken Stock (page 31)
1 cup Beef Stock (page 167)

SOFFRITO:
2 ounces Canadian bacon or
   pancetta, diced
1 medium yellow onion, diced
1 large clove garlic, minced
1 teaspoon olive oil
1 sprig fresh rosemary
2 sprigs fresh thyme
3 sprigs fresh sage
⅛ teaspoon ground cinnamon
⅛ teaspoon ground cloves
2 tablespoons tomato paste

HERBED GNOCCHI:
3 pounds russet potatoes, scrubbed and pierced
   2 or 3 times with the point of a sharp knife
3 large eggs
1 cup unbleached all-purpose flour, plus extra
   for the work surface
3 tablespoons grated Parmesan cheese
1 teaspoon crushed dried oregano
½ teaspoon crushed dried thyme
1 teaspoon minced parsley
1½ teaspoons salt (optional)
1 teaspoon freshly ground pepper

In a Dutch oven, heat the olive oil over medium-high heat. Add the wild boar and brown the boar on all sides, about 5 minutes total. Remove from the heat and set aside.

TO MAKE THE *SOFFRITO:* In a 10-inch cast-iron skillet, brown the Canadian bacon, onion, and garlic in the olive oil for 3 minutes, stirring often. Add the herbs and continue to cook, stirring, for another 2 minutes. Add the cinnamon, cloves, and tomato paste. Remove from the heat and reserve.

Return the Dutch oven to the stove and reduce any pan juices by one-third. Add the balsamic vinegar, red wine vinegar, Chicken Stock and Beef Stock, and the reserved *soffrito.* Bring to a boil, reduce the heat to a simmer, and let the ragout cook, uncovered, for 45 minutes. Cover and simmer for another 45 minutes, until the meat is very tender.

WHILE THE RAGOUT IS SIMMERING, PREPARE THE GNOCCHI: Microwave or bake the potatoes, following your oven manufacturer's instructions, until tender. While they are still hot or warm, cut the potatoes in half and scoop out the potato flesh. Put it through a ricer or mash with a potato masher. Let stand until it reaches room temperature.

Add the eggs, flour, Parmesan cheese, herbs, salt (if using), and pepper to the potato. With a wooden spoon, mix gently until everything is incorporated. Be careful to not overwork the mixture.

Cut the mixture into 3 equal parts. Dust a work surface with flour, and with the palms of your hands, roll the dough into 3 long thin logs. Cut the logs into ¾-inch gnocchi. To make the traditional marks on the gnocchi quickly, roll a wire whisk over the top of the gnocchi.

Cook the gnocchi in boiling water until they float to the surface, about 2 to 3 minutes. Remove and keep warm.

TO SERVE: Combine the hot ragout with the gnocchi. Ladle into shallow pasta bowls and serve at once.

MAKES 8 SERVINGS

Joslin Choices: 4 very-low-fat protein, 2½ carbohydrate (bread/starch), 1 fat

Per Serving: 395 calories (21% calories from fat), 9 g total fat (3 g saturated fat), 35 g protein, 42 g carbohydrate, 3 g dietary fiber, 151 mg cholesterol, 235 mg sodium, 988 mg potassium

Sun-Dried Tomato–Crusted Lamb with Feta Cheese, Eggplant, and Niçoise Olive Pasta Salad

Marlin Kaplan, ONE WALNUT
CLEVELAND, OHIO

Chef Kaplan wrote, "This recipe is an all-out Mediterranean affair with sun-dried tomatoes, eggplant, Niçoise olives, and pasta. It began with the rather innocent notion of making a red pesto of sun-dried tomatoes and using it to coat delicate lamb noisettes. This worked out better than I could have hoped—because the pesto is so moist, it behaves very much like a marinade, infusing the lamb itself with a lightly acidic tomato flavor rather than simply coating it. From there, I kept building up the flavors until the dish became the one presented here."

Thank you, Chef Kaplan. You made our job with this recipe so simple and delightful (it was a joy to make and delicious to eat). By the way, a noisette is a small, tender, round slice of meat (in this case ') cut from the rib or loin. When searing the lamb, take great care not to scorch or burn the toma-.; they can go from perfect to ruined in a matter of seconds.

LAMB:
6 sun-dried tomatoes (dry-pack)
⅓ cup warm water, mixed with the juice of
    1 large lemon
4 4-ounce lamb noisettes
kosher salt (optional)
freshly ground pepper
3 tablespoons dry unseasoned bread crumbs
2 tablespoons ground cumin
2 tablespoons crushed dried thyme
1 teaspoon olive oil

2 whole Japanese eggplant
2 teaspoons olive oil

PASTA SALAD:
1 tablespoon red wine vinegar
1 teaspoon minced shallot

1 teaspoon minced garlic
1 teaspoon crushed dried oregano
3 tablespoons extra-virgin olive oil
¼ cup Niçoise olives, pitted and chopped
2 cups bow-tie pasta, cooked al dente following
    package directions, drained, and cooled to
    room temperature
1 red bell pepper, stems, seeds, and ribs removed,
    cut into small dice

2 ¾-ounce containers arugula, rinsed and drained
¼ cup crumbled feta cheese
chopped parsley

Cover the sun-dried tomatoes with the warm water–lemon juice mixture. Set aside.

Season the lamb noisettes with salt (if using) and pepper. Mix together the dry bread crumbs, cumin, and thyme. Use to lightly dredge the noisettes on both sides and all edges. When the sun-dried tomatoes are rehydrated, finely chop and gently press them onto the lamb. Refrigerate the lamb for 10 minutes.

Meanwhile, warm the olive oil in a large nonstick sauté pan over high heat. When the pan is hot, remove the lamb from the refrigerator and sauté for 3½ to 4 minutes per side for medium-rare or to desired doneness, turning once and being careful not to burn the tomatoes. When the lamb is done, remove from the pan and keep warm.

Slice the eggplant on the bias into ½-inch-thick rounds. Brush with the olive oil and season with salt (if using) and pepper. Working in batches, place the eggplant in the same sauté pan and sauté over medium-high heat until lightly browned and tender, turning once, about 4 to 5 minutes per side. Transfer the eggplant to a platter and keep warm. Repeat until all eggplant is cooked.

TO MAKE THE PASTA SALAD: In a mixing bowl, combine the vinegar, shallot, garlic, and oregano. Whisk the olive oil in slowly. Toss with the olives, pasta, and diced pepper.

TO ASSEMBLE: Place small piles of arugula on the center of each of 4 plates. Next, place a small portion of the pasta salad on top of the arugula. Arrange the eggplant slices on the pasta. Carve the sautéed lamb into thin diagonal slices, and place in piles on the pasta. Garnish with the feta cheese and parsley. Serve immediately.

MAKES 4 SERVINGS

Joslin Choices: 4 medium-fat protein, 2 carbohydrate (bread/starch), 1 fat

Per Serving: 552 calories (45% calories from fat), 28 g total fat (7 g saturated fat), 35 g protein, 42 g carbohydrate, 11 g dietary fiber, 93 mg cholesterol, 380 mg sodium, 1,232 mg potassium

Easter Dinner

Sun-Dried Tomato–Crusted Lamb with Feta Cheese, Eggplant, and
  Niçoise Olive Pasta Salad (page 174)

Le Soufflé Leger à la Pomme et Citron Vert (page 271)

Joslin Choices: 5½ medium-fat protein, 3 carbohydrate (2 bread/starch, 1 fruit), ½ fat,
  552 calories (45% calories from fat)

Olives for All

*T*aste should be your guideline in purchasing olives, not size. Kalamata olives, from Greece, are deep purple to black with a soft texture and very rich taste. Italian Gaeta olives are brown to black, soft and earthy in taste. The French Niçoise olive, the taste of Provence, is a small, medium-purple olive, with a large pit for its size. They are cured for several months and become chewy. You can also find them cured in lemon and garlic. Two other ripe olives to try are the Chilean Alfonso, which are vinegary, and the Lebanese Phonecia, packed in a garlicky olive oil. The United States also packs Greek-style olives and dry-pack olives, some of which are certainly worth buying. The common olives you will find canned in grocery stores are black, or Mission, olives that come from California, but they lack the flavor and texture of the ones the chefs use.

There are, of course, green cocktail olives that frequently are pitted and stuffed with pimiento. One recipe that calls for green olives specifically uses Picholine olives, grown in Provence and bottled in Nice. The French love these relatively small green olives with pointed bottoms for their intense green olive flavor and meaty texture. They are packed in lightly salted brine. We've even found them at an "olive bar" at a local supermarket. Specialty food stores also sell these little gems, and they can be purchased from the Internet (see Sources, page 296).

If you're making a recipe or hors d'oeuvres that calls for olives, taste a selection and choose your favorites. When buying loose olives, select those that are uniform in color with no blemishes. You can keep them for 2 weeks refrigerated. Store bottled olives in the pantry until ready to use them and refrigerate after you open. Remember, olives can be used to flavor foods, but use them sparingly as they are high in fat and salt.

Braised Lamb Shanks with Spelt

Jean-Marie Lacroix, THE FOUNTAIN AT THE
FOUR SEASONS HOTEL

PHILADELPHIA

Chef Lacroix is a native of France and received his formal training at Thonon-les-Bains on Lake Geneva. He has cooked in restaurants in France, Switzerland, Scotland, and Canada. A Maître Cuisinier de France, he became the first Philadelphia chef to receive the Robert Mondavi Award for Culinary Excellence. In 1999, he was a nominee for a James Beard Award as Best Chef, Mid-Atlantic United States. His trainees call themselves "Papa's graduates" and have gone on to excel as chefs.

2 cups spelt grain

4 cups water

4 lean lamb shanks, about 12 ounces each

2 tablespoons olive oil

1 tablespoon unbleached all-purpose flour

1 medium carrot, peeled and sliced

1 medium onion, peeled and sliced

1 large clove garlic, peeled and crushed

2 medium tomatoes, peeled, seeded, and chopped

1 tablespoon tomato paste

1 rib celery, chopped

1 cup dry white wine

½ 12-gram vegetable bouillon cube, crushed

TO COOK THE SPELT: Place the spelt in a large pot and cover with the 4 cups of water. Bring to a boil, lower the heat, and simmer gently for 2 hours, adding additional water if needed.

Meanwhile, trim as much fat as possible from the lamb shanks. Heat the olive oil in a large cast-iron pot and sauté the lamb shanks until golden brown all over. Transfer the lamb shanks to a plate and pour out the oil. Sprinkle the flour over the bottom of the pot and stir, scraping up the browned bits. Cook, stirring, for 1 minute. Add the carrot, onion, garlic, tomatoes, tomato paste, and celery. Return the shanks to the pot and pour the wine over the lamb and the vegetables. Cook over medium heat until the liquid is reduced by half. Add enough boiling water so that the lamb is covered by 1 inch of cooking liquid. Stir in the ½ vegetable bouillon cube. Cover and cook slowly over low heat for about 1½ hours. The gravy should barely simmer.

When the lamb shanks are cooked through and very tender, transfer them to a platter using a slotted spoon. Keep warm. Boil the pan juices until reduced by half to form a gravy.

Drain any remaining water from the spelt and add three quarters of the gravy; keep the remainder hot. Place the lamb shanks on top of the spelt and simmer another 5 to 8 minutes so that the grain absorbs the lamb flavor. Add the rest of the gravy.

TO SERVE: Spoon the spelt and vegetables into 4 shallow soup plates. Top with the lamb shanks and nap with any remaining gravy. Serve hot.

MAKES 4 SERVINGS

Joslin Choices: 3 low-fat protein, 3½ carbohydrate (bread/starch)

Per Serving: 478 calories (24% calories from fat), 13 g total fat (3 g saturated fat), 32 g protein, 53 g carbohydrate, 2 g dietary fiber, 81 mg cholesterol, 200 mg sodium, 857 mg potassium

Comfort Food Supper

Braised Lamb Shanks with Spelt (page 178)

Chai Rice Pudding (page 274)

Joslin Choices: 3 low-fat protein, 5½ carbohydrate (bread/starch), 638 calories (22% calories from fat)

Brodetto di Pesce Da Fiore (Fish Soup Da Fiore)

Mara Zanetti, DA FIORE

VENICE

When Bonnie asked a dear friend if she knew a chef from Italy, she never thought she would be given Marcella Hazan's phone number. Not only do we own her cookbooks and use them as references, we have often aspired to attend her cooking school in Italy. Her son, who works and writes with her, responded to Bonnie's phone call and gave her one name when asked for an excellent restaurant in Italy—Da Fiore. When we began to read about this excellent restaurant, we both realized that we had dined there and agreed with every rave review that has been written about the *cucina* there. Chef Zanetti starts with only the finest-quality fresh fish and vegetables, which are then given the simplest treatment.

Some of these fish names may be unfamiliar to you. Go to your fishmonger and ask for a variety of fish, some firm and others not. Also, ask for fish trimmings to make the fish broth if you do not wish to clean your own fish. Add the fish and seafood depending on the amount of time needed to cook through. The result will be a bit of Italy on your table.

4½ pounds various seafood (such as scorpion fish, catfish, monkfish, dogfish, baby calamari, mullet, and shrimp), cleaned for cooking, heads removed and reserved, fish cut into slices or fillets

1 medium onion, peeled

1 medium carrot, peeled

1 rib celery

1 bouquet garni (1 sprig flat-leaf parsley, 1 sprig fresh thyme, and 2 bay leaves, tied in a square of cheesecloth)

5 cups water

salt to taste (optional)

⅓ cup extra-virgin olive oil

¼ cup minced onion

2 bay leaves

1 clove garlic, peeled

1 tablespoon minced flat-leaf parsley

1 tablespoon minced fresh basil

freshly ground pepper to taste

1 cup dry white wine

1 pound ripe tomatoes, peeled, seeded, and diced

12 slices Italian country bread, toasted

TO MAKE THE FISH BROTH: In a large pot, combine the reserved fish heads, whole onion, carrot, celery, and bouquet garni. Add the water and season with salt (if using). Bring to a boil, then lower the heat and simmer for 20 minutes. Strain the resulting broth. You should have 4¼ cups broth. Discard the solids. If necessary, supplement the broth with additional water. Return the broth to the pot and bring it back to a simmer.

In a large pot, heat the olive oil. Add the minced onion, bay leaves, and garlic. Brown. Discard the garlic. Add the minced parsley and basil. Stir and immediately add the baby calamari. Season to taste with pepper. Add the wine and allow to evaporate almost completely. Add the tomato pieces and salt to taste (if using). Discard the bay leaves. Add the prepared fish broth and simmer 5 minutes, stirring occasionally. Return to a boil. Add the dogfish and cook 5 minutes. Add any remaining seafood, except for the mullet and shrimp. Simmer for 10 minutes, stirring occasionally. Add the mullet and shrimp. Return to a boil, then turn down the heat and simmer for 5 minutes. Remove from the heat.

Divide the seafood among 8 soup bowls. Pour the cooking liquid over the fish. Place 2 pieces of toasted bread in each bowl. Serve immediately.

MAKES 8 SERVINGS

Joslin Choices: 5 low-fat protein, 2 carbohydrate (bread/starch)

Per Serving: 481 calories (36% calories from fat), 19 g total fat (4 g saturated fat), 40 g protein, 31 g carbohydrate, 3 g dietary fiber, 221 mg cholesterol, 434 mg sodium, 868 mg potassium

Crisp Striped Bass with Artichokes Fricassee, Wilted Turnip Greens, and Meyer Lemon Jus

Josiah Citrin, MÉLISSE

SANTA MONICA, CALIFORNIA

Mélisse is named for a lemon-scented herb from the Mediterranean region. Owner and chef Josiah Citrin has been recognized as a "rising star" among chefs by the press. Mélisse was voted "Best New Restaurant" in July 2000 by *Food & Wine,* "Best Newcomer" in the collector's edition of the *Gourmet Guide to America's Best Restaurants* in 2000, and one of "The World's Most Exciting New Restaurants" by *Condé Nast Traveler* in 2000. This is an exciting and unusual way to prepare striped bass, and it mirrors the flavors of the Mediterranean.

12 baby artichokes, about 1½ pounds total

1 quart water mixed with the juice of
   1 large lemon

½ medium onion, sliced

1 medium carrot, sliced

sea salt (optional)

freshly ground pepper

2 cups dry white wine

2 cups water

1 bay leaf

2 sprigs fresh thyme

1 tablespoon finely diced carrot

1 tablespoon finely diced celery

1 tablespoon finely diced leek white

1 tablespoon chopped parsley

6 6-ounce center-cut striped bass fillets, skin on

2 tablespoons plus 1 teaspoon extra-virgin
   olive oil

1 tablespoon unsalted butter

1 large Meyer lemon, seeds removed and lemon
   cut into small dice, including rind (see Note
   below)

2 cups chopped turnip greens

TO PREPARE THE ARTICHOKES: Using a small knife, trim away the stem and outer leaves from each artichoke. Cut off the tips and place in the lemon water. Set aside.

Place a pot over medium heat. Add the sliced onion, cover, and allow the onion to sweat until it is translucent. Add the carrot and cook for a few more minutes. Add the drained artichokes. Season to taste with sea salt (if using) and pepper. Add the white wine, water, bay leaf, and thyme. Bring to a boil, then reduce to a simmer. Cover and let cook until the artichokes are tender, about 20 minutes.

Transfer the cooking liquid to a small saucepan. Set the artichokes aside. Place the cooking liquid over medium-high heat and reduce by one-half. Remove from the heat and set aside. Discard the carrot, onion, and bay leaf.

TO PREPARE THE VEGETABLE GARNISH: Bring a saucepan of water to a boil. Add the diced carrot and cook for 1 minute. Using a small strainer or slotted spoon, remove the carrot pieces and refresh in a bowl of ice water. Repeat, cooking the celery and then the leek, refreshing each in ice water. Drain the vegetables on paper towels, then place in a bowl and mix with the parsley. Set aside.

Preheat the oven to 400°F.

Heat a large cast-iron pan over high heat. Season the fish fillets on the flesh side with sea salt (if using) and pepper. Add 1 teaspoon of the extra-virgin olive oil to the pan and place the fish fillets skin side down. After 30 seconds, press the fish down with a spatula. Reduce the heat and let cook for 4 minutes. Transfer the fish to the oven. Bake for another 3 minutes. Remove from the oven and keep warm.

While the fish is cooking, heat the artichokes in the reduced broth. When the mixture boils, swirl in the unsalted butter and 1 tablespoon of the olive oil. Add the diced Meyer lemon and the reserved diced vegetable mixture.

In a sauté pan, wilt the turnip greens in the remaining 1 tablespoon olive oil. Season lightly with sea salt (if using) and pepper.

TO SERVE: Spoon the artichokes and broth into 6 wide, shallow soup bowls. Place the turnip greens around the edges and a fish fillet on top. Serve immediately.

SERVES 6

Joslin Choices: 5 very-low-fat protein, 1 carbohydrate (bread/starch), 1 fat

Per Serving: 426 calories (23% calories from fat), 12 g total fat (3 g saturated fat), 40 g protein, 34 g carbohydrate, 16 g dietary fiber, 141 mg cholesterol, 387 mg sodium, 1,617 mg potassium

Note: If Meyer lemon is not available, use a regular lemon.

Fillet of Sea Bream and Clams in an Olive Oil and White Wine Sauce, Served with Creamed Potatoes and Basil

Guido Stütz, CRYSTAL GARDEN AT THE SHERATON PARK TOWER

BUENOS AIRES

Provided for you by the very talented Chef Stütz, this is a wonderful dish to serve to your most discriminating guests. We have it on good authority from several different sources that the Crystal Garden is the place to dine in Buenos Aires if you want impeccable food and service. The hotel is situated in the heart of the city, close to businesses, shops, and theaters.

CREAMED POTATOES:
¾ pound peeled potatoes, cut into small chunks
sea salt
2 tablespoons extra-virgin olive oil, warmed
¼ cup chopped fresh basil

4 4-ounce sea bream or porgy fillets, skin on and
    scales removed
juice of 1 lemon

freshly ground pepper
1 tablespoon extra-virgin olive oil
¼ cup minced onion
4 cloves garlic, minced
12 fresh littleneck or other hard-shell clams,
    shucked
⅔ cup dry white wine
sea salt (optional)
2 tablespoons chopped fresh coriander (cilantro)

TO MAKE THE CREAMED POTATOES: Boil the potatoes in lightly salted water until tender, 10 to 14 minutes. Drain and mash thoroughly. Add the 2 tablespoons warmed olive oil and basil. Mix until smooth and creamy. Set aside and keep warm.

Meanwhile, season the fish with the lemon juice and pepper. Heat 2 teaspoons of the olive oil in a large nonstick skillet. Add the onion and garlic. Cook over medium heat, stirring, until the onion is limp but not browned, about 4 minutes. Add the clams and sauté until golden, turning once, about 2 minutes total. Add the sea bream fillets and brown for 2 minutes per side, turning once.

Remove the sea bream from the skillet and arrange on 4 large plates with the creamed potatoes. Add the white wine to the skillet with the clams and heat through until boiling. Remove the clams and place them around the fish fillets.

Puree the white wine mixture in a food processor or blender, adding the remaining teaspoon of olive oil to form a sauce. Taste the sauce and season with sea salt (if using). Stir in the coriander and spoon the sauce over and around the fish and the clams. Serve at once.

MAKES 4 SERVINGS

Joslin Choices: 3 medium-fat protein, 1½ carbohydrate (bread/starch)

Per Serving: 352 calories (39% calories from fat), 15 g total fat (2 g saturated fat), 26 g protein, 22 g carbohydrate, 2 g dietary fiber, 55 mg cholesterol, 299 mg sodium, 802 mg potassium

Pan-Seared Cod Fillets in a Clear Broth with Lime Leaves and Rice Noodles

Stan Frankenthaler, SALAMANDER

BOSTON

Chef Frankenthaler wrote, "Cod is king. Sweet, large, tender creamy white flakes make cod one of the most enjoyable and popular of seafoods, and also one of the toughest to cook. As the fillet cooks it can literally fall apart if mishandled. I think one of the best things you can use your nonstick pan for is to sauté delicate fish fillets. Not only can you cook with less oil, but the fillet will also never stick and so you will be able to cook fish with ease." Just follow his recipe and you have a dish worthy of your most discriminating company, from one of Boston's most popular chefs.

1 pound center-cut cod fillet, divided into 4 equal portions

2 teaspoons light sesame oil

1 tablespoon plus 2 teaspoons reduced-sodium soy sauce

2 teaspoons minced fresh ginger

1 teaspoon cracked coriander seeds

1 teaspoon salt (optional)

1 teaspoon cracked pepper

2 cups clear Fish Stock (page 93), chicken broth, or vegetable broth

1 1-inch piece fresh ginger, peeled and finely julienned

4 kaffir lime leaves (see page 120), center spine discarded, leaves finely julienned

1 medium carrot, peeled and finely julienned

½ pound pencil-thin asparagus, trimmed and cut into 2-inch lengths

juice of 1 large lime

1 7-ounce package rice stick noodles, rehydrated in cold water until al dente, and drained

fresh cilantro leaves for garnish

2 scallions, white part and 1 inch green, thinly sliced for garnish

4 large lime wedges for garnish

Rinse the cod pieces and pat dry with paper towels. Place in a shallow nonreactive dish. Mix together the sesame oil, 2 teaspoons soy sauce, minced ginger, coriander seeds, salt (if using), and pepper. Spread over the cod, cover, and refrigerate 2 to 6 hours.

Heat a nonstick sauté pan over medium-high heat. Add the cod and sear 2 to 4 minutes before turning. Reduce the heat to medium and cook 3 to 4 minutes longer. Cod should flake under gentle pressure when done. Transfer the cod to 4 shallow soup plates.

Add the broth to the sauté pan and bring to a boil. Add the julienned ginger, lime leaves, carrot, asparagus, remaining 1 tablespoon soy sauce, and lime juice. Bring back to a boil. Remove ⅔ cup of the broth mixture; strain and set aside. Return all the solids to the sauté pan. Ladle the remaining broth and vegetables into 4 heated soup plates.

Return the reserved broth to the pan. Add the softened noodles to the strained broth. When the noodles are heated through, divide them among the soup plates. Garnish with the cilantro leaves, scallions, and lime wedges. Serve hot.

MAKES 4 SERVINGS

Joslin Choices: 1½ very-low-fat protein, 3 carbohydrate (bread/starch)

Per Serving: 307 calories (12% calories from fat), 4 g total fat (1 g saturated fat), 19 g protein, 47 g carbohydrate, 2 g dietary fiber, 31 mg cholesterol, 598 mg sodium, 423 mg potassium

Steamed Cod on Broccoli Mousse with Red Bell Pepper Salsa, Watercress Pesto, Oven-Dried Celery Root, and Balsamic Reduction

Giancarlo di Francesco, PREGO AT THE WESTIN PLAZA
SINGAPORE

A beautiful restaurant in one of the city's finest hotels, Prego offers imaginative modern Italian dishes created by Chef di Francesco. There are several recipes grouped together here; add them to your repertoire as separate items. The Red Bell Pepper Salsa is wonderful with chicken, the Watercress Pesto is superb with pasta, and the Oven-Dried Celery Root makes a great crunchy topping for salads. How creative these chefs are! We can all learn much from them.

OVEN-DRIED CELERY ROOT:

1 small celery root
½ cup water mixed with 2 tablespoons fresh
   lemon juice

BROCCOLI MOUSSE:

1 10-ounce baking potato, scrubbed
½ pound fresh broccoli florets
1 tablespoon finely chopped fresh mint
2 teaspoons extra-virgin olive oil

RED BELL PEPPER SALSA:

1 small red bell pepper, roasted, skin removed and
   thinly sliced
2 tablespoons capers, rinsed and drained
⅛ large lemon, seeds removed and finely chopped
   (including rind)
2 cloves garlic, minced
2 tablespoons minced flat-leaf parsley
4 teaspoons extra-virgin olive oil

WATERCRESS PESTO:

1 quart loosely packed watercress, tough stems
   discarded, rinsed and dried
½ cup packed flat-leaf parsley leaves
6 tablespoons pine nuts
4 cloves garlic, minced
3 tablespoons plus 1 teaspoon extra-virgin
   olive oil
2 teaspoons hot water
salt (optional)
freshly ground pepper

BALSAMIC REDUCTION:

⅓ cup plus 4 teaspoons balsamic vinegar

1 cod fillet, cut about 1 inch thick, 1¼ pounds total
1 quart Fish Stock (page 93)

FOR THE OVEN-DRIED CELERY ROOT: Cut off a 1½-ounce piece of the celery root. Tightly wrap the rest of the root and refrigerate for another use. Peel the piece of celery root and slice very thinly with a mandolin or sharp knife. Place the slices in the water-lemon mixture for a few minutes, then drain. Spread the slices on a parchment paper–lined baking sheet and oven-dry at 250°F until thoroughly dried, about 25 to 30 minutes, stirring occasionally for even drying. Remove from the oven and set aside.

MEANWHILE, PREPARE THE BROCCOLI MOUSSE: Prick the potato several times and microwave until tender, following your microwave oven manufacturer's instructions (exact time will depend on the wattage power of your microwave), or bake the potato at 400°F in your oven for about 1 hour, until tender. Cool slightly, peel, and work the potato through a vegetable mill or mash thoroughly with a potato masher.

While the potato is baking, cook the broccoli in boiling water until tender, about 10 minutes. Drain and work the broccoli through the vegetable mill or mash thoroughly with the potato masher. Mix the mashed potato, broccoli, mint, and olive oil. Shape the mixture into 4 flat round patties. Set aside.

TO MAKE THE SALSA: In a bowl, mix together the red bell pepper, capers, lemon, garlic, parsley, and olive oil. Set aside. (Makes 1 cup.)

FOR THE WATERCRESS PESTO: In a food processor or blender, pulse the watercress, parsley, pine nuts, and garlic until finely minced. With the motor running, add the olive oil and hot water through the feed tube to form a smooth pesto. Season with salt (if using) and pepper to taste. Set aside.

TO MAKE THE BALSAMIC REDUCTION: Place the balsamic vinegar in a small saucepan and simmer over low heat until reduced to about 3 tablespoons. Remove from the heat and place in a squirt bottle. Set aside.

TO COOK THE COD: Cut the fillet into 4 equal portions and steam the cod in the Fish Stock for about 10 minutes, until the cod flakes when prodded with a fork. Remove the cod from the stock and keep warm.

While cod is cooking, sauté the Broccoli Mousse patties in a nonstick skillet until warmed through, about 3 minutes per side, turning once. Place the heated patties in the center of each of 4 large heated plates. Top each patty with a cod fillet.

TO SERVE: Place 6 tiny mounds of the salsa in a circular pattern around the cod and Broccoli Mousse, each mound containing 1 heaping teaspoon and placed an equal distance apart. Place 1 heaping teaspoon of the Watercress Pesto in the middle of each salsa mound. Squirt some of the Balsamic Reduction in a decorative pattern around the edge of the plate and scatter the Oven-Dried Celery Root over all. Serve at once.

MAKES 4 SERVINGS

Joslin Choices: 3 very-low-fat protein, 1 carbohydrate (bread/starch), 2 fat

Per Serving: 315 calories (41% calories from fat), 15 g total fat (2 g saturated fat), 23 g protein, 23 g carbohydrate, 4 g dietary fiber, 38 mg cholesterol, 374 mg sodium, 759 mg potassium

Fish in Its Own Glass

Paul Minchelli, PAUL MINCHELLI
PARIS

For years, the best fish restaurant in Paris was in Montparnasse, where the Minchelli brothers held court. In 1994, Paul Minchelli, the cooking partner, went out on his own and remodeled a restaurant on boulevard de la Tour-Maubourg. The result is Paul Minchelli, a restaurant where fish and shellfish are served fresh and pure. Patricia Wells's *The Food Lovers' Guide to Paris* (Workman, 1999, fourth edition) says Chef Minchelli "does very little to his fish and shellfish, but what he does is inevitably the right thing." This recipe came handwritten by the chef over the fax line. It was a joy to receive because we knew the results would be perfect, and they are.

1 22-ounce royal *daurade* (sea bream), red
  snapper, grouper, or sea bass
1 12 x 12-inch piece dried seaweed
  (see Note below)
1 Pyrex-style baking dish with transparent lid, just
  large enough to hold fish

1 bamboo mat for making sushi (see Note below)
½ cup hot water
about 1 tablespoon olive oil
salt (optional)
freshly ground pepper to taste

Preheat the oven to 325°F.

Skin, bone, and fillet the fish. Rinse and pat dry.

Crumble the seaweed in the bottom of the Pyrex dish. Place the bamboo mat on top of the seaweed. Add the water to the dish and place the fillets on top of the bamboo mat, making sure the fish does not touch the sides of the dish.

Cover the dish and place in the oven. Bake until the fish flakes easily when prodded in the thickest part, about 4 to 5 minutes. Cut into 4 portions and remove from the dish. Serve with a splash of olive oil, salt (if using), and pepper.

MAKES 4 SERVINGS

Joslin Choices: 3½ very-low-fat protein, 1 fat

Per Serving: 161 calories (35% calories from fat), 6 g total fat (1 g saturated fat), 25 g protein, 0 carbohydrate, 0 dietary fiber, 56 mg cholesterol, 92 mg sodium, 344 mg potassium

Note: Dried seaweed and bamboo mats are available in health food stores and Asian markets.

Sea Bass in Banana Leaf with Aromatics

Mark McEwan, NORTH 44°
TORONTO

When we inquired about the best restaurant in Toronto, the answer came back time and time again, North 44°. Owner and chef Mark McEwan is American-born and French-trained. The restaurant is elegant, airy, and intimate, with impeccable service and exceptional cuisine that includes the essence of Italian cuisine with nuances of Asian flavors and California cooking style.

Chef McEwan uses only the freshest locally grown fruits and vegetables, fish, poultry, and meat. Sauces and seasonings are simple, allowing the main ingredients to take center stage. Oils and butter are used sparingly, with many items poached in broth.

We found frozen banana leaves at a local Latino grocery store. They are also in some Asian markets, but, in a pinch, aluminum foil will work. In addition, you may substitute high-quality hearts of palm sold in a glass jar for the fresh.

DRY RUB FOR FISH:
1 tablespoon toasted crushed coriander seeds
1 teaspoon freshly ground black pepper
1 teaspoon grated lemon zest
1 teaspoon grated orange zest
1 teaspoon fresh thyme leaves
pinch cumin
pinch curry powder
pinch salt

2 5-ounce Chilean sea bass fillets
12 pearl onions
4 small beets, preferably 2 yellow and 2 red, trimmed and scrubbed

4 pieces banana leaf, about 12 inches in length and as wide as possible
4 pieces hearts of palm, fresh if possible and steamed until tender (see Headnote above)
4 sprigs parsley or chervil
2 pieces lemongrass, lightly pulverized with hammer
2 generous tablespoons slivered fresh ginger
2 fresh jalapeño or serrano chile peppers, cut in half and seeded
⅛ teaspoon salt (optional)
freshly ground pepper
2 tablespoons coriander oil

Preheat the oven to 375°F.

TO MAKE THE RUB: Blend together the crushed coriander seeds, black pepper, lemon and orange zests, thyme leaves, cumin, curry powder, and salt. Rub on one side of the sea bass, forming a crust. Place a nonstick skillet over high heat and sear the sea bass, crust side down, until lightly charred. Turn and sear the opposite side. Remove from the pan and cool. Fish should still be medium-rare or opaque on the outside, raw and warm on the inside. It will finish cooking in the oven.

Meanwhile, cook the pearl onions in boiling water until almost tender, about 10 minutes. Drain and run under cold water. When cool enough to handle, slip off their skins. Set aside.

In a separate pot, cook the beets in boiling water until almost tender, about 10 minutes. Drain and run under cold water. When cool enough to handle, slip off their skins and cut each beet in half. Set aside.

Place 2 banana leaves on a work surface, laying 1 leaf on top of the other at opposing angles with the center of one directly over the center of the other. Repeat, using the other 2 banana leaves. Place the hearts of palm on the banana leaves and top with the pearl onions and beets. Lay the sea bass on top.

Place the parsley or chervil, lemongrass, ginger, and the chile peppers on top of the fish. Add the salt (if using) and pepper to taste. Drizzle 1 tablespoon of the coriander oil over each piece of fish.

Fold the closest layer of banana leaf first, then fold over the second layer, creating as neat and airtight a package as possible. Tie each package with kitchen string in both directions as you would a gift. Place the fish in the oven for approximately 15 to 18 minutes or until the fish registers 140°F on an instant meat thermometer.

Place on a plate, cut the string and discard it. Unfold the leaves and serve.

MAKES 2 SERVINGS

Joslin Choices: 3 low-fat-protein, 2 carbohydrate (bread/starch), 2 fat

Per Serving: 400 calories (43% calories from fat), 20 g total fat (3 g saturated fat), 27 g protein, 32 g carbohydrate, 6 g dietary fiber, 51 mg cholesterol, 129 mg sodium, 1,507 mg potassium

Chilean *Congrio con Pebre* (Sea Bass with Pepper Sauce)

Mary Sue Milliken and Susan Feniger, BORDER GRILL

SANTA MONICA, CALIFORNIA, AND LAS VEGAS

Every time Fran has dined at Border Grill, either in Santa Monica or in Las Vegas, these busy and talented "Two Hot Tamales" have always been elsewhere. In addition to their running three restaurants (they also own Ciudad in Los Angeles), writing cookbooks, and their Food Network series, they keep a tight reign on the kitchen staff so that their splendid recipes come across as if they cooked the dishes themselves.
We happen to love Chilean sea bass and this is a terrific way to prepare it.

PEBRE:

1 bunch parsley, washed and dried
1 bunch cilantro, washed and dried
½ cup diced onion
3 large cloves garlic, peeled
¼ cup extra-virgin olive oil
2 tablespoons fresh lemon juice
1 serrano chile, seeded (see page 78)
salt (optional)
freshly ground pepper to taste

FISH:

½ tablespoon olive oil
10 white button mushrooms, sliced
½ cup sliced onion

2 large cloves garlic, peeled, pounded, and sliced
pinch saffron threads
1 cup dry white wine
4 cups Fish Stock (page 93) or bottled clam juice
reserved parsley stems (see *pebre,* below)
8 small white creamer potatoes, about ½ pound total, scrubbed, thinly sliced, and covered with cold water
4 4-ounce Chilean sea bass fillets, ling cod, monkfish, or other oily whitefish
20 cockles or baby clams
2 bunches leeks, white and light green parts only, washed thoroughly and cut into ½-inch dice
1 large tomato, seeded and diced

TO MAKE THE *PEBRE:* Pick off the parsley leaves and reserve the stems. Pick off the cilantro leaves and discard the stems. Puree the parsley and cilantro leaves, onion, garlic, olive oil, lemon juice, serrano chile, salt (if using), and pepper together in a food processor or mini chopper. (Makes about ¾ cup.)

TO MAKE THE FISH: In a large pot, heat the olive oil over medium heat. Add the mushrooms, onion, garlic, and saffron and cook for 5 to 10 minutes, until the vegetables are limp but not browned. Add the wine and reduce by half. Add the Fish Stock and parsley stems and simmer for 20 minutes. Strain into a large wide skillet or pot and bring to a slow boil. Discard the solids.

Drain the potatoes and add to the broth, along with the fish, cockles, and diced leeks. Simmer, covered, for 8 to 10 minutes.

Divide evenly among 4 large soup plates or individual pasta bowls: 1 fish fillet, 5 cockles, equal parts of the vegetables, and 1 cup of the broth. Top each fish fillet with 1 teaspoon of the *pebre*, and sprinkle with the diced tomato. Serve immediately. Refrigerate the remaining *pebre* to use with grilled chicken or pork.

MAKES 4 SERVINGS

Joslin Choices: 4 very-low-fat protein, 1½ carbohydrate (bread/starch), 1 fat

Per Serving: 346 calories (22% calories from fat), 8 g total fat (2 g saturated fat), 35 g protein, 23 g carbohydrate, 3 g dietary fiber, 64 mg cholesterol, 486 mg sodium, 1,497 mg potassium

Joslin Choices (*pebre* only): free food

Per 1-Teaspoon Serving: 16 calories (88% calories from fat), 2 g total fat (0 saturated fat), 0 protein, 0 carbohydrate, 0 dietary fiber, 0 cholesterol, 0 sodium, 8 mg potassium

Mexican Supper

Sizzling Fajita Mushrooms (page 19)

Chilean Congrio con Pebre (page 193)

Grilled Fresh Pineapple

Joslin Choices: 5 very-low-fat protein, 3½ carbohydrate (bread/starch), 2 fat, 613 calories (24% calories from fat)

Note: Items not referring to a specific recipe are not included in the nutritional analysis. Consult the Joslin Food Choices (page 287) for that information.

Broiled Halibut with Spring Mixed Beans and Spicy Thai Lemongrass Broth

Susanna Foo, SUSANNA FOO

PHILADELPHIA

Since receiving this recipe, Bonnie has made this dish no less than five times. It certainly shows off Susanna Foo's many talents. Hopefully, you will be able to find both fresh soybeans and fava beans in your market—they are several cuts above the dried beans. Frozen soybeans are readily available in Asian markets and are quite excellent. If you can't find them, use the dried; the dish will still taste great.

1½ cups Spicy Thai Lemongrass Broth
  (recipe follows)
1 teaspoon plus 1 tablespoon reduced-sodium
  soy sauce
½ teaspoon kosher salt
1 tablespoon olive oil
1 tablespoon vodka
4 4-ounce skinless halibut fillets, cut about
  1½ inches thick

½ cup fresh soybeans (see page 197)
½ cup fresh fava beans (see page 222)
½ cup Chinese long beans or French beans
  (cut about 1 inch long)
1 tablespoon soybean or corn oil
½ cup cherry tomatoes, blanched and peeled
freshly ground pepper
1 cup baby cilantro leaves, Chinese parsley leaves,
  or baby basil leaves for garnish

Make the Spicy Thai Lemongrass Broth. Set aside.

Combine the 1 teaspoon soy sauce, salt, olive oil, and vodka. Place the halibut fillets on a large shallow platter. Pour the soy-vodka mixture over the fillets. Turn the fish over until all sides are coated with the marinade. Cover and refrigerate.

Fill a medium-size pot with water and bring to a boil. Blanch the soybeans, fava beans, and Chinese long beans separately, rinse in cold water, drain well, and set aside.

Preheat the broiler.

Using a large nonstick skillet, heat the soybean or corn oil until very hot. Add the fish fillets and sear on one side for 1 minute, then turn and sear the other side for an additional minute. Place the seared fish on a broiler pan. Broil the fish until done, a total of 10 minutes per inch of fish thickness.

While the fish is broiling, heat the prepared lemongrass broth. Place ½ cup of the hot broth in a medium saucepan. Add the soybeans, fava beans, and Chinese long beans. Cook until heated through. Add the tomatoes; season to taste with pepper.

Divide the bean mixture among 4 large plates or shallow wide bowls. Place the fish fillets on top of the bean mixture and ladle on ¼ cup of the broth. Decorate with the baby cilantro leaves. Serve at once.

MAKES 4 SERVINGS

Joslin Choices: 5 very-low-fat protein, 1 carbohydrate (bread/starch), 1 fat

Per Serving: 354 calories (33% calories from fat), 13 g total fat (2 g saturated fat), 36 g protein, 21 g carbohydrate, 7 g dietary fiber, 37 mg cholesterol, 923 mg sodium, 1,110 mg potassium

Spicy Thai Lemongrass Broth

1 tablespoon soybean or corn oil
1 2-inch piece lemongrass, tender parts only, very thinly sliced
2 tablespoons minced shallots
2 tablespoons minced garlic
1 tablespoon grated fresh ginger
1 jalapeño chile pepper, seeded and coarsely chopped
1 tablespoon Thai red curry paste (optional)

¼ cup Thai fish sauce
2 tablespoons rice wine vinegar
1 tablespoon tamarind paste (optional)
6 cups Fish Stock (page 93) or Vegetable Stock (page 115)
1 medium vine-ripened tomato, blanched, peeled, cored, and diced
1 kaffir lime leaf (optional, see page 120)

In a medium stockpot, heat the oil over medium-high heat. Add the lemongrass, shallots, garlic, and ginger. Cook until soft. Add the jalapeño pepper, red curry paste (if using), fish sauce, rice vinegar, tamarind paste (if using), and stock. Turn heat to low and cook 30 to 45 minutes. Strain and discard the solids.

Pour the broth back into the pot and add the tomato and lime leaf (if using). Bring to a boil and turn off the heat. This broth can be made in advance and kept refrigerated about 3 days.

MAKES ABOUT 7 CUPS

Joslin Choices: free food

Per ¼-Cup Serving: 19 calories (44% calories from fat), 1 g total fat (0 saturated fat), 1 g carbohydrate, 0 dietary fiber, 0 cholesterol, 277 mg sodium, 99 mg potassium

Soybeans

The use of soybeans dates back to the year 2000 B.C. The United States was not inter-ested in the soybean until the twentieth century but has made up for this neglect and now produces 45 percent of the world's supply of these nutritive legumes. You can purchase frozen green soybeans at oriental food markets and some health food stores. They are low in calories and carbohydrate and high in protein. They also contain an essential fat, linoleic acid. Soybeans are very high in fiber. All of this makes them an excellent addition to soups and stir-fries and other recipes. Soy-based foods are omnipresent in many cultures, from fermented black beans in China, to miso in Japan, and to soy milk and other food products around the world.

Red Wine–Braised Halibut with Roasted Root Vegetables

Rémi Cousyn, CALORIES

SASKATOON, SASKATCHEWAN, CANADA

Braised fish—can this be? In the talented hands of Chef Cousyn of Calories, it is not only possible, it becomes a meal to prepare over and over. Try this on a cold evening, adding some crusty peasant-style French bread, and you will think you are in Provence.

2 medium carrots
1 small butternut squash
1 medium turnip
1 medium onion
5 teaspoons unsalted butter
salt (optional)
freshly ground pepper

1½ cups dry red wine
3 tablespoons balsamic vinegar
3 cloves garlic
1 bay leaf
1 sprig fresh thyme
4 5-ounce halibut steaks, cut 1 inch thick

Preheat the oven to 450°F.

Peel and cut the vegetables into ½-inch cubes. Sauté the vegetables individually in a nonstick skillet with 1 teaspoon butter, seasoning each batch with salt (if using) and pepper. Cook until tender. Cool and then mix the vegetables together.

In a large sauté pan, combine the red wine, balsamic vinegar, garlic, bay leaf, and thyme. Bring the mixture to a boil and reduce by one-third (you should have about 1 cup remaining).

Season the halibut steaks with salt (if using) and pepper. In another large sauté pan, sauté the halibut in the remaining 1 teaspoon butter. Turn over when caramelized and pour ½ of the wine reduction over the fish. Finish the cooking in the hot oven, adding more wine reduction as needed to baste the fish. When done and the fish flakes easily when tested with a fork, 5 to 8 minutes, remove the halibut steaks from the pan and keep warm. Pour the remaining wine reduction into the pan and add the mixed vegetables. Maintain on high heat until the vegetables are hot and they are coated with the wine reduction. Adjust the seasoning.

Scoop the vegetables onto a warm serving platter. Arrange the steaks on top and drizzle the remaining pan juices over all. Garnish with a twist of fresh pepper. Discard the thyme sprig and bay leaf. Serve immediately.

MAKES 4 SERVINGS

Joslin Choices: 4 very-low-fat protein, 1 carbohydrate (bread/starch), 1 fat

Per Serving: 344 calories (22% calories from fat), 8 g total fat (3 g saturated fat), 32 g protein, 22 g carbohydrate, 4 g dietary fiber, 58 mg cholesterol, 122 mg sodium, 1,239 mg potassium

An Autumn Dinner

Red Wine–Braised Halibut with Roasted Root Vegetables (page 198)

Warm Mango Soufflé with Coconut Sauce (page 273)

Joslin Choices: 4 very-low-fat protein, 2½ carbohydrate (1 bread/starch, 1½ fruit), 1 fat, 450 calories (19% calories from fat)

Maine Lobster with Sweet Corn and Fingerling Potatoes

Anne Quantrano and Clifford Harrison, FLOATAWAY CAFÉ
AND BACCHANALIA

ATLANTA

These talented chefs have been together since student days at the California Culinary Academy in San Francisco. Their list of accolades and awards is long, and includes being named the James Beard Foundation's 1991 Discovery Chefs of the Year, and the American Express "Best Chef of the Southeast" in both 2000 and 2001.

You probably have seen Chef Quantrano and Chef Harrison on the Food Network's "Great Chefs," as well as on CNN. The two pride themselves in using locally grown and seasonal organic produce, much of which comes from their own gardens at Summerland Farm. There the couple raises Jersey cows, which provide milk for their own cheese and butter. They also raise horses, free-range chickens, and pigs. As if not busy enough, Anne also travels around the States as a member of the Board of Directors for Women Chefs and Restaurateurs. Our hats are off to this talented, dedicated, and most kind duo.

3 1- to 1¼-pound Maine lobsters
1 teaspoon olive oil
1 shallot, finely minced
1 medium carrot, finely diced
1 large rib celery, finely chopped
4 medium ears sweet corn, kernels cut
 from the cob
1 pound fingerling potatoes, peeled, diced, and
 blanched

1 cup reduced Chicken Stock (reduced from 3 cups
 stock, page 31)
2 tablespoons unsalted butter
salt (optional)
freshly ground pepper
1 teaspoon freshly chopped tarragon

Poach the lobsters in boiling water for 6 minutes. Run under cold water. Crack the shells and pull out the lobster meat. Reserve the lobster in the refrigerator. Discard the shells.

In a large sauté pan, heat the olive oil over high heat. Add the shallot, carrot, and celery. Sauté until the vegetables are wilted, about 5 minutes, then add the corn and potatoes, cooking for 2 to 3 minutes until slightly golden. Add ½ cup of the reduced chicken stock. Bring to a simmer and add 1 tablespoon of the butter. Add salt (if using) and pepper to taste. Remove from the heat and season with tarragon. Keep warm.

In a large saucepan over medium-low heat, heat the lobster slowly in the remaining ½ cup chicken stock and 1 tablespoon butter. When the lobster is heated through, divide the corn mixture among 6 large soup plates and top each with an equal portion of the lobster meat. Serve hot.

MAKES 6 SERVINGS

Joslin Choices: ½ very-low-fat protein, 1½ carbohydrate, 1 fat

Per Serving: 183 calories (26% calories from fat), 5 g total fat (3 g saturated fat), 8 g protein, 28 g carbohydrate, 4 g dietary fiber, 23 mg cholesterol, 113 mg sodium, 535 mg potassium

Monkfish with Asparagus and Tomato–Wild Bear's Garlic Vinaigrette

Yochen Voss, THE MANOR

WEST ORANGE, NEW JERSEY

When you cross the George Washington Bridge into New Jersey, head for this restaurant for an evening you will remember for years to come. Look for monkfish in Italian fish markets. Italians and the French, who call it *lotte,* have long appreciated this firm, tasty fish. This restaurant has won many awards and has been called "almost too perfect to be true" by *The New York Times.*

Chef Voss wrote, "Wild Bear's Garlic is one of the oldest medicinal herbs known to man. Its healing properties have been recognized by Europeans for centuries, where it is valued for its ability to cleanse the blood of impurities. The name comes from the observation that bears awakening from their winter hibernation devoured vast quantities of the plant to restore their strength." If you cannot find Wild Bear's Garlic (we could not when we tested the recipe), substitute 3 minced garlic cloves and a few chopped fresh chives.

juice of ½ large fresh lime
4 5-ounce monkfish fillets (you may also use cod,
   catfish, haddock, or mako shark)
salt (optional)
freshly ground pepper
1 tablespoon olive oil
1¼ pounds large fresh asparagus spears

TOMATO–WILD BEAR'S GARLIC VINAIGRETTE:
1 large shallot, chopped
½ tablespoon olive oil

2 tablespoons sherry vinegar
½ cup dry white wine
3 teaspoons fresh lime juice
2 tablespoons grapeseed oil
salt (optional)
freshly ground pepper
1 bunch Wild Bear's Garlic, chopped
4 medium tomatoes, peeled, seeded, and diced

Preheat the oven to 380°F.

Sprinkle the lime juice on the monkfish. Season with salt (if using) and pepper to taste. Pan-sear the fillets in the olive oil in a heavy, ovenproof pan until the fish is lightly browned on both sides. Place the pan in the oven for 8 minutes. Remove from the oven and keep warm.

If desired, peel the asparagus. Blanch in lightly salted water to cover until asparagus is crisp-tender, about 3 to 6 minutes, depending on thickness.

TO MAKE THE TOMATO–WILD BEAR'S GARLIC VINAIGRETTE: In a sauté pan, sauté the shallot in the olive oil. Add the vinegar and reduce until only the shallot remains. Add the wine and lime juice; reduce to half. Add the grapeseed oil, salt (if using), and pepper to taste. Before serving, add the Wild Bear's Garlic and diced tomato.

Divide the asparagus among 4 large heated serving plates, making beds. Place a monkfish fillet on each bed of asparagus and drizzle the Tomato–Wild Bear's Garlic Vinaigrette over the monkfish.

MAKES 4 SERVINGS

Joslin Choices: 4 low-fat protein, 1 carbohydrate (bread/starch)

Per Serving: 318 calories (31% calories from fat), 12 g total fat (2 g saturated fat), 29 g protein, 24 g carbohydrate, 8 g dietary fiber, 35 mg cholesterol, 68 mg sodium, 1,765 mg potassium

Provençal-Style Mussels

Tamara Murphy, BRASA
SEATTLE, WASHINGTON

Tamara Murphy takes seafood preparation to new levels. Here she shares a recipe for mussels that makes you think sea breezes have found you, no matter where you live. *Gourmet* calls her cooking "sleek and sophisticated," while the *Seattle Times* restaurant editors, when awarding the Silver Platter Award to the restaurant, stated the chef ". . . comes up with combinations that thrill." Chef Murphy calls her cuisine Pan-Mediterranean; we call it divine simplicity.

60 mussels
¼ cup chopped shallots
1 teaspoon chopped garlic
2 tablespoons canola oil

¾ cup combined mixture snipped fresh chives and
   chopped flat-leaf parsley
½ cup fresh lemon juice
1 cup dry white wine

Scrub the mussels well and rinse in several changes of cold water. Remove the beards just before cooking.

In a large heavy pot, heat the shallots and garlic in the canola oil until they turn golden, stirring often, about 5 minutes. Set aside 2 tablespoons of the herb mixture. Add the mussels, remaining herb mixture, lemon juice, and wine to the pot. Cover and cook over medium-high heat for about 15 minutes, until the mussels open. Shake the pan often for even cooking. Discard any unopened mussels.

Spoon the mussels into 4 shallow soup bowls and ladle over equal amounts of the herb-broth mixture. Sprinkle with the reserved herbs and serve immediately.

MAKES 4 SERVINGS

Joslin Choices: 3½ low-fat protein, 1 carbohydrate (1 bread/starch)

Per Serving: 315 calories (34% calories from fat), 11 g total fat (1 g saturated fat), 28 g protein, 14 g carbohydrate, 0 dietary fiber, 67 mg cholesterol, 474 mg sodium, 427 mg potassium

Seaside at Home Supper

Provençal-Style Mussels (page 204)

Crusty Country Whole-Wheat Bread

Cheese and Fruit

Joslin Choices: 3½ low-fat protein, 1 carbohydrate (bread/starch), 315 calories (34% calories from fat)

Note: Items not referring to a specific recipe are not included in the nutritional analysis. Consult the Joslin Food Choices (page 287) for that information.

Rouget de Roche and Grilled Fresh Market Vegetables with Anchovy Sauce

Stéphane Raimbault, L'OASIS
LA NAPOULE, FRANCE

Chef Raimbault brings the South of France to your table with this recipe. His ability to take the freshest of ingredients, layer them, and then work his magic is why L'Oasis truly is a gem. You will swear that you can hear the Mediterranean when you serve this entrée.

ANCHOVY SAUCE:
2 tablespoons anchovy paste
about 3 tablespoons aged balsamic vinegar

1¼ pounds fish (such as red mullet, porgy, red
   snapper, flounder, grouper, sea bass, or any firm,
   flaky whitefish)
4 small zucchini
2 small fennel bulbs, about ¾ pound total
1 pound small red potatoes
5 ounces cherry tomatoes
4 water-packed canned artichoke hearts, quartered
¼ ounce fresh chives

1 large tomato, diced
4 sun-dried tomatoes, reconstituted in warm water
   for 10 minutes, drained and chopped
8 Niçoise olives, diced
1 medium rib celery, diced
1 tablespoon small capers
3 tablespoons flat-leaf parsley leaves
2 tablespoons celery leaves
sea salt (optional)
freshly ground pepper
fresh-snipped chives for garnish
fresh coriander flowers (optional)
1 tablespoon olive oil for garnish

Preheat the oven to 400°F. Light a grill or preheat a broiler. If you are broiling and only have one oven, you'll need to broil the vegetables, then bake them before broiling the fish.

TO PREPARE THE ANCHOVY SAUCE: Mix the anchovy paste with sufficient balsamic vinegar to make a nice smooth consistency. Set aside.

Clean the fish, removing any skin and bones. Cut into 4 equal portions. Wrap tightly in plastic wrap and set in the refrigerator atop a shallow dish of ice cubes until ready to cook.

TO PREPARE THE VEGETABLES: Clean and remove the stem and blossom ends of the zucchini. Slice in half lengthwise. Trim the fennel bulbs and cut in half. If desired, reserve some of the feathery leaves to use as garnish. Peel the potatoes and clean the tomatoes. Broil or grill the vegetables over hot coals until nicely browned on all sides. Transfer to a baking dish to finish cooking in the oven, until done to your likeness, another 20 to 25 minutes. (If working without a grill and with only one oven, remove the vegetables and keep warm. Reset the broiler.)

Grill or broil the fish until golden on both sides and the fish just begins to flake when prodded with the tines of a fork. Set aside.

When the vegetables are tender, scatter the artichoke hearts, chives, diced tomato, sun-dried tomatoes, olives, celery, capers, parsley leaves, and celery leaves on a large, heated serving platter. Top with grilled fish and grilled vegetables. Season with salt (if using) and pepper to taste. Decorate with snipped chives and coriander flowers (if using) and reserved fennel leaves (if using). Drizzle with 2 teaspoons of the prepared Anchovy Sauce and some of the olive oil.

MAKES 4 SERVINGS

Joslin Choices: 4 very-low-fat protein, 2 carbohydrate (bread/starch), 1 vegetable

Per Serving: 368 calories (16% calories from fat), 7 g total fat (1 g saturated fat), 36 g protein, 44 g carbohydrate, 9 g dietary fiber, 57 mg cholesterol, 1,650 mg sodium, 2,376 mg potassium

Herb-Roasted Salmon

Waldy Malouf, BEACON

NEW YORK CITY AND STAMFORD, CONNECTICUT

Waldy Malouf is known for grilling and roasting at high temperatures to lock in the natural flavors of the food. At his very popular restaurants, this is done over wood to impart another level of flavors. Fran asked a family member to try this with some salmon he had just caught fishing at Westport off the coast of Washington. He did and opined the dish was "mighty fine."

HERB CRUST:

2½ tablespoons finely chopped fresh basil

2 tablespoons finely chopped fresh tarragon

2½ tablespoons finely chopped fennel fronds

1½ tablespoons finely chopped fresh mint

1 tablespoon extra-virgin olive oil

2 tablespoons horseradish, fresh or prepared

¼ teaspoon fine sea salt

¾ teaspoon freshly ground pepper

HORSERADISH BREAD SAUCE:

2 tablespoons fresh white bread crumbs

3 tablespoons prepared horseradish

4 tablespoons extra-virgin olive oil

1½ tablespoons water

½ teaspoon ground white pepper

8 2½-ounce pieces salmon, cut into squares

TO MAKE THE HERB CRUST: Combine the herbs; measure out 4 teaspoons of the herb mixture and reserve. Combine the remaining herbs with the olive oil, horseradish, sea salt, and pepper. Set aside.

TO PREPARE THE BREAD SAUCE: Combine the bread crumbs and horseradish in a small food processor and gradually add the oil in a steady stream through the feed tube. Thin with water and season with the white pepper. Set aside.

Preheat the oven to 500°F.

Season the fish lightly with salt (if using) and fresh pepper, and place on a greased cooking pan. Spread 1 tablespoon of the Herb Crust on top of each portion of fish. Bake the salmon for 6 to 8 minutes.

TO SERVE: Drizzle about 1½ tablespoons of the Horseradish Bread Sauce on a plate. Place 2 salmon pieces overlapping on the sauce. Finish with a drizzle of the remaining Herb Crust and a sprinkle of the reserved chopped herbs.

MAKES 4 SERVINGS

Joslin Choices: 4 low-fat protein, 1 vegetable, 2 fat

Per Serving: 352 calories (60% calories from fat), 23 g total fat (4 g saturated fat), 29 g protein, 5 g carbohydrate, 1 g dietary fiber, 66 mg cholesterol, 304 mg sodium, 608 mg potassium

Grilled Salmon Fillet on White Asparagus with Crispy Potatoes and Herbed Crème Fraîche

Jürgen Bemmerl, THE RITZ CARLTON
HONG KONG

Chef Bemmerl designed this dish specifically for this cookbook, but he stated that it is indicative of the delicious and healthy cuisine to be found in any of the many elegant restaurants at his hotel. At the Ritz, he grows herbs in a special garden to ensure a never-ending supply for the needs of the kitchens. He even sent a photo of this gorgeous dish. We can confirm that the dish is as lovely to the taste as it is to the eye. When we tested the recipe, we did have to substitute green asparagus for the white asparagus, which is difficult to find where we live. We plan to use the Herbed Crème Fraîche recipe again and again. It is marvelous.

1¼ pounds salmon fillets, skin removed and cut into 4 portions
1 teaspoon fresh lemon juice
2 teaspoons extra-virgin olive oil

ASPARAGUS:
2¼ pounds fresh white asparagus or large green asparagus spears
2 quarts water
2 tablespoons fresh lemon juice
salt (optional)

HERBED CRÈME FRAÎCHE:
asparagus cooking liquid
1 tablespoon plus 1 teaspoon dry white wine

2½ tablespoons heavy cream
1 cup crème fraîche (page 37) or low-fat sour cream
3 tablespoons chopped fresh chives
3 tablespoons chopped fresh chervil
3 tablespoons chopped flat-leaf parsley
1½ tablespoons chopped fresh basil

salt (optional)
freshly ground pepper
7 ounces small new potatoes, cooked with skin on and quartered
additional fresh herbs for garnish

Marinate the salmon in the lemon juice and olive oil. Set aside.

If desired, using a vegetable peeler, peel the asparagus lengthwise starting about 1½ inches from the tip. Wash under running cold water. Bring the water to a boil in a pot. Add the lemon juice and salt (if using). Place the asparagus in the pot and boil for about 2 to 4 minutes, or until crisp-tender, depending on the thickness of the asparagus. Drain, reserving ¾ cup of the cooking liquid. Keep the asparagus warm.

Transfer the reserved cooking liquid to a saucepan and boil until reduced by half. Lower the heat and whisk in the wine, cream, and crème fraîche. Simmer until smooth and slightly thickened. Stir in the herbs and simmer for 1 minute. Transfer the mixture to a food processor or blender and pulse until a smooth consistency is produced.

Place a grill pan or heavy nonstick skillet over medium-high heat. Season the salmon with salt (if using) and pepper to taste. Pan-grill the salmon for 4 to 5 minutes per side, turning once. At the same time, pan-grill the potatoes until lightly browned and crispy.

Divide the asparagus among 4 large plates and top with the grilled salmon. Surround with the grilled potatoes. Nap with some of the sauce and garnish with additional fresh herbs. Serve at once.

MAKES 4 SERVINGS

Joslin Choices: 4½ low-fat protein, 2 carbohydrate (bread/starch)

Per Serving: 399 calories (34% calories from fat), 16 g total fat (7 g saturated fat), 38 g protein, 30 g carbohydrate, 5 g dietary fiber, 99 mg cholesterol, 183 mg sodium, 1,000 mg potassium

Miso Salmon with English Pea Sauce

Michel Nischan, HEARTBEAT
NEW YORK CITY

Nation's Restaurant News has described Heartbeat as "pulsing with the essence of healthful dining." That is how we felt the time we dined at this popular restaurant on Lexington Avenue in Manhattan. Here, Chef Nischan infuses natural flavors from organic ingredients without the addition of butter or cream. This recipe for salmon is a prime example of his talent for cooking with gusto and inspiration. By the way, English peas are just common garden peas. You can use fresh or frozen—your choice. If you do not own a juicer, take your peas to a neighbor or friend who does and ask him or her to make the juice for you. You can also use the plastic paddle of your food processor and then strain through a sieve.

1 tablespoon dark miso
2 tablespoons reduced-sodium soy sauce
4 4-ounce salmon fillets
6 cups raw English peas

salt (optional)
freshly ground pepper
2 teaspoons grapeseed oil

Place the dark miso and soy sauce in a small mixing bowl and whisk until well blended. Smear the mixture onto both sides of each salmon fillet, cover, and refrigerate for 1 hour.

Meanwhile, run the peas through a vegetable juicer (you should get 1 cup pea juice). Place the pea juice in a small, heavy-bottomed saucepan over a low heat. Heat the juice, stirring slowly and constantly until the juice begins to thicken and form a sauce. Remove from the heat and continue to stir until the sauce stops cooking, about 3 minutes. Season the sauce with salt (if using) and pepper to taste. Set aside and keep warm.

Preheat the oven to 375°F.

Heat a medium nonstick ovenproof skillet over medium-high heat. Swirl in the grapeseed oil and add the salmon fillets. Cook until well browned, about 3 to 4 minutes, then turn over. Place in the oven to cook 3 to 4 minutes more.

Spoon the pea sauce into the center of each of 4 warm soup plates. Serve the salmon fillets on the sauce.

MAKES 4 SERVINGS

Joslin Choices: 3 low-fat protein, ½ carbohydrate (bread/starch)

Per Serving: 247 calories (42% calories from fat), 11 g total fat (2 g saturated fat), 25 g protein, 9 g carbohydrate, 0 dietary fiber, 68 mg cholesterol, 408 mg sodium, 513 mg potassium

Moroccan-Spiced Salmon over Vegetable Couscous with Preserved Lemon and Coriander Vinaigrette

Michael Leviton, LUMIÈRE

WEST NEWTON, MASSACHUSETTS

Chef Leviton and his wife make magic in their restaurant Lumière on a nightly basis, as shown on Food Network's *The Best of Show*. This recipe is indicative of how Chef Leviton melds flavors from around the world into perfection. Preparing his recipes will give you the skills and pride for any preparation. Do your chopping early in the day. Prepare the lemons, marinades, and vinaigrette beforehand and then enjoy having your friends watch you make history in your kitchen.

COUSCOUS:

3 plum tomatoes, peeled, seeded, and halved lengthwise

1 teaspoon extra-virgin olive oil

salt (optional)

freshly ground pepper

$\frac{1}{8}$ teaspoon sugar

1 small red onion, cut into $\frac{1}{4}$-inch dice

1 carrot, cut into $\frac{1}{4}$-inch dice

1 medium fennel bulb, trimmed and cut into $\frac{1}{4}$-inch dice

1 small celery root, peeled and cut into $\frac{1}{4}$-inch dice

2 teaspoons canola oil

1 cup quick-cooking couscous

1 tablespoon extra-virgin olive oil

7 fluid ounces water

1 teaspoon Moroccan Seasoning (recipe follows)

1 teaspoon salt (optional)

4 5-ounce salmon fillets, skin on

salt (optional)

2 teaspoons Moroccan Seasoning (recipe follows)

2 tablespoons canola oil

4 tablespoons Preserved Lemon and Coriander Vinaigrette (recipe follows)

fresh chives for garnish

Preheat the oven to 200°F.

Toss the tomatoes with the olive oil, salt (if using), pepper, and sugar. Place the tomatoes on a greased rack, cut side up. Place the rack on a cookie sheet and bake for 2 hours. Flip the tomatoes and bake for another 30 minutes. Remove the tomatoes from the oven. Let cool, then dice.

In a sauté pan, sauté the onion, carrot, fennel, and celery root separately, each with $\frac{1}{2}$ teaspoon of the canola oil. Cook the onion until tender and the carrot, fennel, and celery root until the crunch is barely gone. Drain. Season with salt (if using) and pepper. Gently combine the vegetables and set aside.

In a large bowl, combine the couscous and olive oil. In a saucepan, combine the water, 1 teaspoon of the Moroccan Seasoning, and salt (if using). Bring to a boil. Pour the boiling water mixture over the couscous mixture and mix well. Cover with plastic wrap and set in a warm area. After 10 minutes, gently fluff the couscous with a fork to separate the grains. Cover and return to the warm area for another 20 minutes. Repeat the fluffing process. Gently fold in the vegetables. Keep warm.

Preheat the oven to 500°F.

Place an ovenproof heavy-bottomed sauté pan large enough to comfortably hold 4 pieces of salmon over high heat. Rinse the salmon and pat dry. Season each salmon fillet with salt (if using) and ¼ teaspoon of the Moroccan Seasoning on both sides. Drizzle the hot pan with the canola oil and add the salmon, skin side down. The skin will seize and the fish will curl—with continued cooking, the fish will relax and flatten out. When the skin releases from the pan and the fish slides around the pan easily, place the pan in the oven for 4 minutes. Remove from the oven and flip the fillets over so the skin is now facing up. Return to the oven for 1 minute more and remove. Keep warm.

TO SERVE: Portion out the couscous on 4 large plates and top with the salmon. Drizzle each salmon fillet with 1 tablespoon of the vinaigrette and garnish with the chives.

MAKES 4 SERVINGS

Joslin Choices: 4 medium-fat protein, 2½ carbohydrate, 2 fat

Per Serving: 632 calories (50% calories from fat), 35 g total fat (4 g saturated fat), 34 g protein, 45 g carbohydrate, 6 g dietary fiber, 85 mg cholesterol, 150 mg sodium, 909 mg potassium

Joslin Choices (couscous only): 2½ carbohydrate, 1 fat

Per Serving: 273 calories (25% calories from fat), 8 g total fat (1 g saturated fat), 7 g protein, 45 g carbohydrate, 5 g dietary fiber, 0 cholesterol, 53 mg sodium, 524 mg potassium

Moroccan Seasoning

2 tablespoons cumin seeds, toasted and ground
2 tablespoons coriander seeds, toasted and ground
1 tablespoon paprika

1 tablespoon ground cinnamon
½ teaspoon cayenne pepper

TO MAKE THE MOROCCAN SEASONING: Combine the cumin, coriander, paprika, cinnamon, and cayenne. Transfer to an airtight jar. Use as directed in the couscous recipe, reserving the rest for seasoning chicken, pork, lamb, or vegetables. (Makes about 6 tablespoons.)

Preserved Lemon and Coriander Vinaigrette

1 cup champagne vinegar
½ cup Dijon mustard
2 cups canola oil
2 cups extra-virgin olive oil
salt (optional)

freshly ground pepper
2 preserved lemons, drained and finely minced
  (see Box below)
2 shallots, finely diced
3 sprigs cilantro, finely chopped

Whisk together the champagne vinegar and Dijon mustard. While whisking, slowly add the canola and olive oils until the mixture makes an emulsified vinaigrette. Season with salt (if using) and pepper.

Mix the vinaigrette with the preserved lemons, shallots, and cilantro. Place in a covered container and use as directed. Will keep, refrigerated, for up to 1 week. Bring to room temperature and whisk before each use. (Makes about 6 cups.)

*P*reserved lemons can be purchased at some specialty food stores and Mediterranean markets. To make the preserved lemons at home, place 2 lemons in a crockery bowl. Add ⅓ cup kosher salt and ½ cup lemon juice. Cover the bowl and let sit in a cool place for 1 week. Drain and cover with extra-virgin olive oil. Cover and refrigerate. Drain before using as directed or for seasoning a tagine or other Mediterranean stew. Will keep, refrigerated, for up to 1 week.

A Night at the Casbah

Moroccan-Spiced Salmon over Vegetable Couscous with Preserved Lemon
and Coriander Vinaigrette (page 212)

Sliced Papaya with Lime Juice

Joslin Choices: 4 medium-fat protein, 2½ carbohydrate (bread/starch), 2 fat, 632 calories, (50% calories from fat)

Note: Items not referring to a specific recipe are not included in the nutritional analysis. Consult the Joslin Food Choices (page 287) for that information.

Pan-Seared Salmon with Wilted Leek and Cucumber Salad

Anne Quantrano and Clifford Harrison, FLOATAWAY CAFÉ
AND BACCHANALIA

ATLANTA

Connecticut and Hawaii lost these two chefs to Atlanta. They were named American Express "Best Chef of the Southeast" in 2000 and 2001 and included in *Food & Wine*'s "10 Best New Chefs" Award in 1996. In 1998, they were chosen to represent Atlanta at the James Beard Olympic Preview and in the same year, Bacchanalia was inducted into the Fine Dining Hall of Fame of the National Restaurant Association.

WILTED LEEK AND CUCUMBER SALAD:

2 English cucumbers, peeled, any seeds removed, and diced

¼ teaspoon salt

4 leeks, trimmed

4 shallots, minced

1 tablespoon chopped fresh chervil

1 cup champagne vinegar

1 tablespoon Dijon mustard

4 tablespoons sugar

2 tablespoons extra-virgin olive oil

salt (optional)

freshly ground pepper to taste

SALMON:

6 5-ounce salmon fillets

1 teaspoon extra-virgin olive oil

sea salt (optional)

freshly ground pepper

1 large lemon, cut in half

1 tablespoon chopped fresh chives

some whole springs chervil for garnish

Lightly salt the cucumbers after they are diced and set aside for about 1 hour.

Slice the leeks lengthwise, then lay on a work surface, flat side down, and thinly slice across. Rinse in cool water; drain well. In a pot of boiling water, blanch the leeks for 1 minute, drain, refresh in ice water, and drain again. Cool in the refrigerator.

Combine the shallots, chopped chervil, vinegar, mustard, and sugar in a bowl. Whisk together slowly, drizzling on the olive oil until emulsified. Season with salt (if using) and pepper. Squeeze out the excess liquid in the leeks and cucumbers by draining in a sieve and pressing slightly with the back of a spoon. Combine the leeks and cucumbers with the vinaigrette.

TO COOK THE SALMON: Heat the olive oil in a nonstick pan until almost smoking. Season the salmon on both sides with sea salt (if using) and pepper. Sear the salmon in the hot pan about 1 to 2 minutes per side, until crispy. (If the fillets are thick, place in a 400°F oven for about 5 to 7 minutes to finish.) Squeeze the lemon halves over the salmon.

TO SERVE: Place a bed of the Wilted Leek and Cucumber Salad on each of 6 large plates. Top with a salmon fillet and garnish with the chives and chervil sprigs. Serve hot.

MAKES 6 SERVINGS

Joslin Choices: 3½ very-low-fat protein, 2 carbohydrate (bread/starch), 1 fat

Per Serving: 323 calories (31% calories from fat), 11 g total fat (2 g saturated fat), 30 g protein, 26 g carbohydrate, 2 g dietary fiber, 66 mg cholesterol, 150 mg sodium, 800 mg potassium

Note: The Wilted Leek and Cucumber Salad may also be made without oil, with a reduction of 42 calories and 1 fat choice per serving.

Poached Wild King Salmon with Basil Orzo and Red Wine–Niçoise Olive Vinaigrette

Todd Davies, BERTRAND a MISTER A'S
SAN DIEGO, CALIFORNIA

When we asked Chef Davies for a recipe, he researched low-fat and more healthy cooking on his own and came up with this most exciting recipe for wild salmon. We can purchase wild salmon here in Middle America, so look for it. It has a different texture than farm-raised salmon. You can learn a lot from great chefs, and just reading this recipe is an education. The results are a meal to remember. Chef Davies very proudly told us that he has added healthier recipes to his menu and his restaurant patrons love the change.

POACHING BROTH:
1 cup chopped onion
½ cup chopped carrot
½ cup chopped celery
2 bay leaves
2 large lemons, cut in half
1 cup white wine
2 cups water
2 tablespoons kosher salt (optional)
1 tablespoon freshly ground black pepper
3 sprigs fresh lemon thyme or thyme

4 fillets wild King salmon, about 4 ounces each, deboned and skinned

VINAIGRETTE:
2 cups good-quality cabernet sauvignon
½ cup minced red onion

¼ cup coarsely chopped Niçoise olives
¼ teaspoon kosher salt
½ teaspoon cracked black pepper
1 tablespoon extra-virgin olive oil

ORZO:
1 bunch fresh basil, leaves picked
½ cup minced red onion
1 teaspoon olive oil
1 cup dry orzo pasta
2 tablespoons grated Parmigiano-Reggiano cheese or fresh Parmesan cheese
kosher salt (optional)
freshly ground black pepper

1½ pints assorted red and yellow cherry, teardrop, and currant tomatoes for garnish

Add all the ingredients for the poaching broth to a medium stainless pan (including salt if using), squeezing the lemons before adding the halves to the pan. Bring to a boil for 5 minutes. Turn off the heat and let cool.

Preheat the oven to 350°F.

Lay the salmon fillets in a shallow poaching vessel. In the meantime, continue with the rest of the recipe.

FOR THE VINAIGRETTE: Combine the cabernet and red onion in a small saucepan and reduce to about ¾ cup. Let cool. Add the rest of the ingredients and stir to incorporate.

FOR THE ORZO: Set aside 10 of the largest basil leaves for later use. In a pot of boiling water, blanch the remaining basil leaves for 5 seconds and immediately shock in ice water and squeeze dry. Reserve the blanching water. Puree the basil in a food processor or blender, adding a few drops of cold water if necessary to puree it thoroughly. Do not overprocess in the machine, as the friction of the blades will heat up the basil.

In a medium saucepan, cook the onion in the oil until limp, about 4 minutes. Add the orzo, cook for a minute while stirring with a wooden spoon, and add 1¼ cups of the reserved water that the basil was blanched in. Stir continuously until the pasta is cooked al dente, about 8 to 10 minutes. Add the cheese and set aside.

Strain the poaching broth, heat back to a boil, and pour over the salmon fillets. Place in the oven for 5 to 7 minutes. Do not overcook; wild King salmon has less natural oil than farmed salmon and cooks more quickly.

Stir the basil puree into the orzo and reheat if necessary. Adjust the seasoning, adding salt (if using) and pepper to taste. Using a ring mold (see page 135), spoon one quarter of the orzo into the centers of 4 large plates. Remove the ring molds. Spoon the vinaigrette around the orzo, reserving some of the olives and onion. Place a fillet of salmon on top of the orzo. Garnish the plates with the tomatoes, after slicing them in half and being careful not to squeeze out too many seeds. Spoon the reserved olives and onions from the vinaigrette over the salmon. Cut the reserved basil leaves into a chiffonade and sprinkle over all. Serve at once.

MAKES 4 SERVINGS

Joslin Choices: 3 low-fat protein, 3 carbohydrate (bread/starch)

Per Serving: 456 calories (23% calories from fat), 12 g total fat (3 g saturated fat), 31 g protein, 44 g carbohydrate, 4 g dietary fiber, 55 mg cholesterol, 330 mg sodium, 923 mg potassium

Day Boat Scallops with Summer Succotash and Corn-Tarragon Broth

Tim Kelly, THE PAINTED TABLE

SEATTLE, WASHINGTON

When we first approached this talented chef, he said he was very familiar with cooking for people with diabetes; his mother has type 2 diabetes and loves to come to his restaurant to eat. The Painted Table serves elegantly presented Northwest cuisine in an intimate saloon setting in the heart of downtown Seattle. Chef Kelly scours the nearby Pike Place Market for the best produce, then decides what fish or meat will go best with his finds.

Day boat scallops are scallops that arrive at the market the same day they are pulled out of the sea. We cannot get them here in the Heartland, but if you live near fishing ports, be sure to ask for them because they are so fresh and delicious. Always ask for scallops that are dry-packed as opposed to swimming in a liquid. They will have a better flavor in recipes.

8 medium ears corn

1 cup fresh shallots, sliced

2 teaspoons olive oil

1 cup dry white wine

4 sprigs fresh thyme

½ bunch fresh tarragon, leaves picked
and reserved

2 tablespoons unsalted butter

4 clusters oyster mushrooms, about 7 ounces
total, cleaned

½ cup fresh fava beans, peeled and blanched
(see page 222)

1 bunch baby carrots, about 6, peeled, quartered,
and blanched

1 bunch small turnips, about 3, peeled, quartered,
and blanched

¾ cup fresh or frozen peas

salt (optional)

freshly ground pepper

1 pound day boat scallops (dry pack)

4 sprigs fresh chervil for garnish

TO PREPARE THE BROTH: Remove the corn kernels from the cobs. Reserve. Place the cobs in a stock pot and cover with water. Simmer for 1 hour. Strain and reserve the liquid.

In another saucepot, cook the shallots over low heat in the olive oil for 2 to 3 minutes, until limp. Add the corn and continue to cook for 2 more minutes. Deglaze the pan with ¾ cup of the white wine, and then add the corncob stock, thyme sprigs, and tarragon stems. Simmer for 20 minutes; remove the thyme sprigs and tarragon stems. Puree the corn mixture in a blender or food processor. Pass the puree through a strainer and set aside.

In a large nonstick skillet, melt 1 tablespoon of the butter over medium heat. Add the mushrooms, fava beans, carrots, turnips, and remaining ¼ cup white wine. Sauté, tossing the vegetables occasionally for even cooking, until crisp-tender, about 5 minutes. Add the peas and cook, tossing, for another minute or two until the vegetables are done to your liking. Add the reserved tarragon leaves and season with salt (if using) and pepper to taste. Set aside and keep warm.

Melt the remaining 1 tablespoon butter in a heavy sauté pan over high heat. Add the scallops and cook until well browned on one side, 2 to 3 minutes, then turn and cook another 2 to 3 minutes on the other side, until opaque throughout (cut a scallop to test).

TO SERVE: Spoon the hot vegetables into the center of 4 shallow soup plates. Place the scallops on top. Reheat the corn broth and spoon around the vegetables and scallops. Garnish with the chervil and serve.

MAKES 4 SERVINGS

Joslin Choices: 5 very-low-fat protein, 3 carbohydrate (bread/starch), 2 fat

Per Serving: 539 calories (19% calories from fat), 12 g total fat (4 g saturated fat), 42 g protein, 59 g carbohydrate, 10 g dietary fiber, 90 mg cholesterol, 424 mg sodium, 1,305 mg potassium

Fava Beans

Fava beans are very popular in Mediterranean cookery and are called for in several of our chefs' recipes. The first fresh fava beans that appear in our markets in early spring are the most tender. As the season progresses into late spring and early summer, their outer pods get tougher and are sometimes splotched with black. Also known as broad beans or horse beans, fava beans have a kidney-shaped appearance once their outer pod has been removed. Removing the beans from the pod is much like shelling peas. Once they are out of the pod, drop the favas into a pot of boiling water for 30 seconds. Drain and refresh under running cold water. The skins should slip off easily, ready for you to use them raw as a snack or in salads or to use in recipes. You will get 1 pound of shelled fresh fava beans from 3 pounds of the beans still in their pods.

In many parts of the country, finding fresh fava beans can be difficult, so we keep dried beans in our pantry for recipes with a Mediterranean flair. Dried fava beans must also be peeled before using. To peel dried beans, blanch the beans in boiling water for 10 minutes. Do not soak the beans. Drain and slip off the outer skin. You are now ready to add to your recipe for the final cooking. It will take them about 45 minutes to become tender in a simmering liquid.

Seared Scallops and Cannellini Beans

Ricardo Ullio, SOTTO SOTTO

ATLANTA

One review about Chef Ullio and his restaurant Sotto Sotto reads, "You'll rejoice, too, when you try any dish on the stunning menu." Here the chef shares one of his signature dishes.

Chef Ullio took his task of developing recipes for this book so seriously that he called many times as he was preparing them, to make sure he was on target. And after you prepare this dish, you, too, will answer with a resounding, "You surely are."

1 cup dried cannellini beans
1 tablespoon diced carrots
1 tablespoon diced celery
1 tablespoon diced onion
½ teaspoon olive oil
cheesecloth square filled with 1 sprig fresh thyme,
   1 bay leaf, and several black peppercorns to
   form an herb packet

salt (optional)
1 pound dry-packed jumbo sea scallops
¼ cup diced fresh tomato
½ cup coarsely chopped arugula leaves
2 teaspoons truffle oil

Wash and pick over the beans, discarding any small stones or discolored beans. Place the beans in a bowl and cover with cold water to soak overnight. Drain, discarding the soaking liquid, and set aside. Or use the quick-soak method.

In a pot over low heat, sauté the carrots, celery, and onion in olive oil until wilted, about 4 minutes. Add the drained beans and the herb packet. Cover with fresh water, bring to a boil, reduce the heat, cover the pot, and gently simmer for 1 to 1½ hours, until the beans are tender but not mushy. Cooking time depends on the age of the beans, which is hard to assess. At the end of 1 hour, start testing the beans to determine how tender they are and add salt (if using). Continue testing periodically so that they do not overcook. When the beans are done, remove from heat and let sit in the liquid.

Sear the scallops in a large nonstick pan with very high heat until they are brown on both sides, allowing about 2 minutes per side. Arrange the scallops on a hot large serving platter.

TO SERVE: Reheat the beans with a small amount of the liquid, adding the fresh tomato, arugula, and truffle oil. Spoon the bean mixture over and around the seared scallops. Serve at once.

MAKES 4 SERVINGS

Joslin Choices; 3½ very-low-fat protein, 2 carbohydrate (bread/starch)

Per Serving: 302 calories (13% calories from fat), 4 g total fat (1 g saturated fat), 31 g protein, 35 g carbohydrate, 8 g dietary fiber, 37 mg cholesterol, 196 mg sodium, 1,331 mg potassium

Chilled Shrimp and Chicken Spring Roll with Fresh Mint, Basil, and Chives and Spicy Peanut Vinaigrette

Brian Partelow, EMERSON INN BY THE SEA
ROCKPORT, MASSACHUSETTS

When Fran visited the Emerson Inn, the menu was changing for the summer, and this stunning spring roll was available. It is very special. When the *Boston Globe* reviewed the restaurant, it said, "A restaurant that lives up to its unparalleled ambiance." Dining here, one looks out onto rocky cliffs and the Atlantic Ocean just beyond. Indeed, both the food and the setting are spectacular.

1 pound cellophane noodles
4 8-ounce boneless, skinless chicken breasts, grilled
1 pound tiger shrimp, cooked
8 12-inch rice paper wrappers

16 sprigs fresh mint, washed and dried
16 sprigs fresh basil, washed and dried
16 fresh chives
8 tablespoons Spicy Peanut Vinaigrette (recipe follows)

Cook the cellophane noodles according to package directions. Drain and place in a rectangular mold to cool. When cooled, the cellophane noodles will be sticky. Invert and slice into 8 blocks.

Meanwhile, slice the chicken breasts on the bias, lengthwise, each into 4 strips. Halve the shrimp.

TO ASSEMBLE: Place a rice paper wrapper in lukewarm water to rehydrate. Remove the wrapper from the water and put on a work surface. Lay a block of noodles along the bottom of the wrapper. Top with a 2 sprigs of mint, 2 sprigs of basil, 2 chives, 2 strips of chicken, and 4 to 5 of the shrimp halves. Roll the rice paper, tucking in the sides, and making as tight a roll as possible without tearing the rice paper wrapper. Wrap the filled spring roll in a moist linen napkin. Repeat until all the rice paper wrappers are filled, wrapping each spring roll in a moist linen napkin. Chill for at least 1 hour.

TO SERVE: Drizzle 1 tablespoon of the Spicy Peanut Vinaigrette in a decorative pattern on each of 8 large plates. Unwrap the spring rolls and cut in half on the diagonal. Place the 2 halves of each spring roll on the plate and serve cold.

MAKES 8 SERVINGS

Joslin Choices: 4 low-fat protein, 4 carbohydrate (bread/starch)

Per Serving: 535 calories (27% calories from fat), 16 g total fat (3 g saturated fat), 38 g protein, 57 g carbohydrate, 0 dietary fiber, 179 mg cholesterol, 215 mg sodium, 343 mg potassium

Spicy Peanut Vinaigrette

¼ cup rice wine vinegar

2 tablespoons red wine vinegar

½ tablespoon honey

½ tablespoon Thai chili paste

¾ cup canola oil

½ tablespoon dark sesame oil

2 tablespoons natural peanut butter

salt (optional)

freshly ground pepper

Place the vinegars, honey, and chili paste in a food processor. Pulse until well blended. Through the feed tube, with the motor running, slowly add the canola oil, then the sesame oil. Add the peanut butter and blend until smooth.

Taste and add salt (if using) and pepper to taste. Use as directed, refrigerating any leftover vinaigrette for another use. Use within 2 days.

MAKES ABOUT 1⅓ CUPS

Joslin Choices: 2 fat

Per 1-Tablespoon Serving: 84 calories (92% calories from fat), 9 g total fat (1 g saturated fat), 0 protein, 1 g carbohydrate, 0 dietary fiber, 0 cholesterol, 19 mg sodium, 11 mg potassium

Picnic Before the Concert

Spicy Lobster Gazpacho with Avocado Crème Fraîche *(page 35)*

Chilled Shrimp and Chicken Spring Roll with Fresh Mint, Basil, and
Chives and Spicy Peanut Vinaigrette *(page 225)*

Fresh Strawberries

Joslin Choices: 4 low-fat protein, 5 carbohydrate (bread/starch), 2 fat, 731 calories
(36% calories from fat)

Note: Items not referring to a specific recipe are not included in the nutritional analysis. Consult
the Joslin Food Choices (page 287) for that information.

Mixed Seafood Risotto with Roasted Tomato Broth

Terry Conlan, LAKE AUSTIN SPA AND RESORT
AUSTIN, TEXAS

The very first spa Bonnie's exercise group went to was Lake Austin; they have continued to return for camaraderie, excellent classes and instructors, beauty, quiet, and great water sports. All of that work and play make one hungry even if you are there to lose a pound or two, and meals overseen by Chef Conlan are a treat. His recipes, which include the freshest ingredients from the spa's gardens, have been hailed by *Cooking Light* and *Travel + Leisure* as taking low-fat cooking to a high art form. We thank him for sharing this recipe.

ROASTED TOMATO BROTH:
2 large cloves garlic, peeled
olive oil
2 large Roma (plum) tomatoes, stem end removed
salt (optional)
cayenne pepper

RISOTTO:
4 cups Fish Stock (page 93) or bottled clam juice
4 cups canned low-fat, low-sodium chicken broth
1 medium carrot, coarsely chopped
1/2 medium onion, cut into 4 pieces
1 large rib celery, coarsely chopped
1 bay leaf
1/2 teaspoon fennel seeds
5 sprigs parsley

12 large shrimp, peeled and deveined,
  and their shells
4 ounces salmon fillet
4 ounces red snapper fillet, or other
  white-fleshed fish
12 mussels or clams
1/2 cup dry white wine
1/4 cup minced onion
2 teaspoons olive oil
1 cup Arborio (Italian short-grain) rice
2 large cloves garlic, minced
1/4 teaspoon saffron threads, crushed
3 tablespoons grated Parmesan cheese
chopped flat-leaf parsley for garnish
1/4 cup frozen baby peas, thawed,
  for garnish

Preheat the oven to 400°F.

TO MAKE THE ROASTED TOMATO BROTH: Rub the garlic cloves with a drop of olive oil and loosely wrap in aluminum foil. Place on a baking sheet along with the tomatoes. Roast until the tomatoes are soft and mottled brown, about 20 minutes.

Place the tomatoes and garlic in a food processor fitted with the metal chopping blade. Puree, adding salt (if using) and cayenne pepper to taste. Transfer to a saucepan and set aside.

TO MAKE THE RISOTTO: In a large pot, combine the Fish Stock and chicken broth with the carrot, onion, celery, bay leaf, fennel seeds, parsley, and shrimp shells. Simmer for 20 minutes. Strain, discarding the vegetables, bay leaf, and shrimp shells.

Cut the fish fillets into ½-inch cubes. Poach the fish pieces in the stock mixture until opaque throughout (cut to test), about 2 minutes. Remove the fish and set aside. Keep the stock at a lively simmer.

Scrub the mussels and remove the beards. Set aside. Measure out ½ cup of the stock mixture and combine with the white wine. Place the mixture in a heavy deep skillet with a lid. Set aside.

In a large pot, sauté the minced onion in the olive oil over medium heat until the onion is soft. Add the rice, garlic, and saffron; sauté for another minute, stirring constantly. Add 1 cup of the stock to the rice and cook at a simmer, stirring, until most of the stock has been absorbed. Add a second cup of the stock and cook, stirring, until most of the stock has been absorbed. Test the texture of the rice by eating a tiny bite, then add as much as ⅓ cup of the stock as needed to complete the cooking. When the final liquid installment has been absorbed, cool the rice slightly; then fold in the fish and Parmesan cheese.

Place the mussels or clams, the shrimp, and the reserved stock-and-wine mixture in a large skillet with a lid. Put the pan on the stove and bring to a boil. Cover and cook over high heat, shaking the skillet occasionally, until the mussels or clams have all opened, about 3 minutes, and the shrimp are cooked and have turned pink. Remove the mussels and shrimp from the cooking liquid and set aside. Use the cooking liquid to thin the Roasted Tomato Broth to the desired consistency. Keep warm. Discard any unused cooking liquid.

Divide the rice mixture into 4 equal portions and press each portion into a lightly buttered 1-cup mold. Invert each mold into individual wide, shallow soup plates. Ladle the Roasted Tomato Broth around the rice and arrange 3 shrimp and 3 mussels around each serving. Garnish with chopped flat-leaf parsley and a few thawed green peas. Serve at once.

MAKES 4 SERVINGS

Joslin Choices: 4 low-fat protein, 3 carbohydrate (bread/starch)

Per Serving: 485 calories, (22% calories from fat), 12 g total fat (3 g saturated fat), 37 g protein, 52 g carbohydrate, 3 g dietary fiber, 81 mg cholesterol, 804 mg sodium, 1,132 mg potassium

Crispy Snapper with Peruvian Potatoes and Baby Clam Vinaigrette

Tim Andriola, MARK'S SOUTH BEACH

MIAMI

Acclaimed by *Esquire* magazine as a "chef to watch," Tim Andriola cooks for an eclectic crowd of serious gourmets, South Beach trendsetters, and celebrities. This chic restaurant is located in the historic Hotel Nash. His recipe for snapper explodes with flavor and is a fine example of why Mark's South Beach has put Miami on the nation's culinary map.

POTATOES:

6 ounces Peruvian purple or small white
   potatoes, scrubbed
1 tablespoon blended olive oil and canola oil
salt (optional)
2 teaspoons extra-virgin olive oil
freshly ground pepper

SNAPPER:

1 3-pound red snapper, scaled and filleted,
   reserving bones for broth salt (optional)
salt (optional)
freshly ground pepper
2 tablespoons unbleached all-purpose flour
   for dredging
1 tablespoon olive oil

FISH BROTH:

reserved snapper bones
½ small white sweet onion, coarsely chopped
1 small carrot, cut into 3 pieces
2 medium ribs celery, each cut into 3 pieces

2 cups water
1 bay leaf
a few fronds fresh fennel
juice of 1 large lemon
4 stems parsley
1 cup dry white wine
2 black peppercorns

VINAIGRETTE:

1 tablespoon extra-virgin olive oil
½ anchovy fillet
8 cloves garlic, minced
1 tablespoon diced fresh fennel bulb
12 small clams, such as littleneck, scrubbed
2 tablespoons dry white wine
¼ cup reserved fish broth (see above)
2 tablespoons chopped Picholine olives
   (see page 177)
1 tablespoon finely diced peeled and
   seeded tomato
½ tablespoon chopped flat-leaf parsley

Preheat the oven to 375°F.

Lightly season the potatoes with the blended oil and salt (if using). Place in a roasting pan and roast until tender, about 30 minutes. Peel when hot and immediately rice through a food mill, or mash with a potato masher. Season with the extra-virgin olive oil, salt (if using), and pepper to taste. Keep warm.

Meanwhile, place a heavy sauté pan over high heat. Season both sides of the fish with salt (if using) and pepper. Dredge the skin side lightly in the flour and pat off the excess. Place the olive oil in the hot sauté pan. Place the fish, skin side down, in the pan and gently press with the back of a spatula to prevent the skin from curling and not allowing an even searing. Cook over medium-high heat until the flesh is almost cooked through. Flip the fish and finish cooking on the other side, until the fish flakes when prodded with a fork. The total cooking time is about 10 minutes per inch of the thickness of the fish. Remove the fish from the sauté pan and drain on a paper towel to absorb the excess oil. Keep warm.

TO MAKE THE BROTH: Place the reserved fish bones in boiling water for a minute to remove any impurities. Drain and put the bones and the remaining broth ingredients in a pot. Bring to a simmer and cook, uncovered, for 15 minutes. Strain and reserve ¼ cup, discarding the solids.

FOR THE VINAIGRETTE: Heat the oil, anchovy, and garlic in a sauté pan over medium heat until the garlic is golden brown, about 6 to 7 minutes. Add the diced fennel and cook for 1 minute. Then add the clams, white wine, reserved ¼ cup broth, and olives. Bring to a boil and cover tightly until the clams open (3 or 4 minutes). Add the diced tomato and parsley to the hot vinaigrette. Adjust the seasoning with salt (if using) and pepper.

Arrange the hot potatoes in the center of a large serving platter. Transfer the clams to the platter, ringing the potatoes. Drizzle the vinaigrette around the potatoes and place the fish on top. Serve hot.

MAKES 6 SERVINGS

Joslin Choices: 5 very-low-fat protein, 1 carbohydrate (bread/starch), 1 fat

Per Serving: 309 calories (35% calories from fat), 12 g total fat (2 g saturated fat), 38 g protein, 10 g carbohydrate, 1 g dietary fiber, 70 mg cholesterol, 180 mg sodium, 921 mg potassium

Basil-Rubbed Tuna with Heirloom Tomato and Cranberry Bean Salad

Jeremy Sewall, LARK CREEK INN

LARKSPUR, CALIFORNIA

Lark Creek Inn is known for featuring seasonal fresh ingredients on its menu, so it makes sense that the chef now in charge comes from a long line of farmers and fishermen. First working as a dishwasher at his parents' New York restaurant where his mother and sisters cooked, Chef Sewall trained at the Culinary Institute of America. He cooked on the East Coast of the United States and in London and Amsterdam before heading West to find his niche in Marin County just north of San Francisco. Here he dishes up specialties using what's fresh from the land and the sea. Cranberry beans are one of the few types of beans regularly found fresh; these white beans have purplish streaks that fade when the beans are cooked. Chef Sewall also uses heirloom tomatoes, an umbrella name for old varieties. These tomatoes are known for their odd shapes and intense flavors.

BASIL RUB:
1 cup loosely packed fresh basil leaves
1 small shallot, peeled
2 scallions, white part and 2 inches green
1 large clove garlic, peeled
3 tablespoons extra-virgin olive oil
salt (optional)
1 teaspoon freshly ground white pepper
3 tablespoons fresh lemon juice
2 tablespoons rice wine vinegar

CRANBERRY BEAN SALAD:
1 tablespoon olive oil
1 small white onion, minced
$1\frac{1}{3}$ cups shelled fresh cranberry beans
6 cups Vegetable Stock (page 115)
1 sprig fresh rosemary
3 large ripe heirloom tomatoes

2 tablespoons chopped chives for garnish

4 5-ounce tuna steaks, cut 1 inch thick

In a food processor or blender, place the basil, shallot, scallions, garlic, olive oil, salt (if using), white pepper, lemon juice, and vinegar. Pulse until smooth. Rub onto the tuna steaks, cover, and refrigerate for 1 to 2 hours.

MEANWHILE, PREPARE THE BEAN SALAD: In a large saucepan heat the olive oil and add the onion. Cook over medium heat until the onion is limp, about 5 minutes. Add the beans, stock, and rosemary sprig. Simmer until the beans are tender, about 25 to 35 minutes. Transfer to a flat pan and let cool. Discard the rosemary sprig.

While the beans are cooking, dice the tomatoes into 1-inch pieces. Place in a mixing bowl with the liquid that comes from dicing the tomatoes. Add the beans and gently mix. Add salt (if using) and pepper to taste.

Place a large nonstick sauté pan over high heat. When the pan is good and hot (a drop of water will skip and evaporate), add the tuna steaks and sear for 2 minutes on each side, turning once and making sure to caramelize the Basil Rub. Slightly warm the bean salad and pile the salad into the middle of 4 large shallow soup plates, letting the liquid run off the side into the bowl. Place the seared tuna on top and sprinkle with the chives. Serve at once.

MAKES 4 SERVINGS

Joslin Choices: 5 low-fat protein, 2½ carbohydrate (bread/starch)

Per Serving: 529 calories (26% calories from fat), 15 g total fat (3 g saturated fat), 45 g protein, 56 g carbohydrate, 20 g dietary fiber, 43 mg cholesterol, 111 mg sodium, 1,870 mg potassium

Charred Yellowfin Tuna with Crispy Leeks, Shiitake Mushroom Pot Stickers, and Pineapple Salsa

Mark McEwan, NORTH 44°

TORONTO

No wonder the culinary elite loves this glitzy Toronto restaurant. Presentation is very important to Chef McEwan; here he presents an entrée whose beauty is surpassed only by the combination of ingredients to give us tastes and textures you will not soon forget. Once again, his ingredients take center stage and we stand to say "Encore!"

The soy glaze will keep indefinitely if refrigerated.

SOY GLAZE (SEE HEADNOTE ABOVE):
1 sliver fresh garlic
6 tablespoons reduced-sodium soy sauce
2 tablespoons sugar
4 thin medallions peeled fresh ginger
1 small chile pepper, seeded
2 2-inch pieces orange peel

4 teaspoons wasabi powder

POT STICKERS:
¼ cup finely diced leek
4 shiitake mushrooms, sliced
1 teaspoon chopped fresh ginger
1 tablespoon bias-cut scallion
pinch chili powder
pinch salt
pinch freshly ground pepper
½ teaspoon canola oil
1 teaspoon mirin
½ teaspoon reduced-sodium soy sauce

1 teaspoon soy glaze (see above)
6 wonton wrappers
1 egg white, lightly beaten

TUNA DRY RUB:
1 teaspoon freshly ground pepper
1 tablespoon toasted sesame seeds
1 tablespoon toasted crushed coriander seeds
1 tablespoon finely cut chives
1 teaspoon grated lemon zest
pinch salt

2 4-ounce center-cut yellowfin tuna steaks
1 tablespoon plus 1 teaspoon canola oil

PINEAPPLE SALSA:
1 cup finely diced fresh pineapple
1 tablespoon finely diced red bell pepper
1 tablespoon finely cut chives or scallion
½ teaspoon canola oil
freshly ground pepper to taste

Put all the ingredients for the soy glaze in a small saucepan and place over high heat. Bring the temperature up to about 180°F on a candy thermometer. Remove from the stove and allow to infuse. After 6 hours, strain and reserve, discarding the solids.

Mix the wasabi powder with water to form a paste with the consistency of cream. Set aside.

TO MAKE THE POT STICKERS: Sauté the leek, mushrooms, ginger, scallion, chili powder, salt, and pepper in the canola oil over medium heat. Once the vegetables are tender, add the mirin and soy sauce, and sauté for 1 minute more. Remove and cool. Once cool, if any liquid remains, reduce over the heat. Add 1 teaspoon of the soy glaze to the leek-mushroom mixture.

TO STUFF THE POT STICKERS: Place a wonton wrapper flat on a work surface. Lightly brush the entire surface with the egg white. Place a scant teaspoon of the mushroom-leek mixture in the center of the wonton and fold into a triangle, making sure all the edges are sealed. Repeat until all the pot stickers have been filled. Set aside.

Mix all the ingredients for the dry rub together, and roll the tuna in the mixture to coat evenly. Place a heavy cast-iron pan on the stove and allow to heat until very hot. Add 1 tablespoon of the canola oil to the pan. Add the tuna and allow to char for about 2 minutes per side, turning once. The center should remain pink. Remove from the pan and cut in ¼-inch-thick slices.

TO FINISH THE POT STICKERS: Blanch them in simmering water to cover for 1 minute. Drain. Put the remaining 1 teaspoon canola oil in a heavy nonstick skillet and place over medium heat. Add the blanched pot stickers to the skillet and sauté gently, allowing the edges to become golden brown and crispy.

Combine all the ingredients for the salsa and set aside.

TO SERVE: Place the sliced charred tuna (room temperature) on a serving platter. Place the pot stickers by the tuna with some of the wasabi, soy glaze, and Pineapple Salsa on each plate.

MAKES 2 SERVINGS

Joslin Choices: 4 low-fat protein, 2½ carbohydrate (1½ bread/starch, 1 fruit), 1 fat

Per Serving: 464 calories (34% calories from fat), 18 g total fat (2 g saturated fat), 35 g protein, 43 g carbohydrate, 7 g dietary fiber, 53 mg cholesterol, 796 mg sodium, 956 mg potassium

235

Seared Tuna with Israeli Couscous

Donna Nordin, CAFÉ TERRA COTTA
SCOTTSDALE AND TUCSON, ARIZONA

Having been around many chefs over the years, we wonder how they have any time for a personal life, let alone time to devote to community service. While spreading her time between two restaurants 120 miles apart, Chef Nordin has been cited frequently for her outstanding work in the community.

For example, this very popular item from the Café Terra Cotta menu is frequently demonstrated in the periodical classes she teaches on heart-healthy cooking at the nearby Arizona Heart Institute in Phoenix. She is another chef who has proven that healthy, low-fat food (there are only 4 grams of fat in the entire whole-meal dish) can be absolutely delicious.

4 large cloves garlic, crushed
8 sprigs cilantro
1 cup fresh orange juice
2 pounds Ahi tuna (sushi grade)
2 cups Israeli couscous (or instant)
2 cups plus ¼ cup Chicken Stock (page 31) or
    Fish Stock (page 93)
¼ cup diced eggplant

¼ cup diced onion
¼ cup diced red bell pepper
¼ cup diced yellow squash
¼ cup diced zucchini
1 serrano or jalapeño chile pepper (see page 78),
    seeded and minced (optional)
salt (optional)
freshly ground pepper

In a shallow dish, combine the garlic, cilantro, and orange juice. Add the tuna and turn to coat evenly. Cover and refrigerate for 1 hour.

Bring the couscous and 2 cups of the Chicken Stock to a boil. Remove from the heat and cover for about 5 minutes. Place the vegetables and chile pepper (if using) in a small saucepan with the remaining ¼ cup Chicken Stock and cook until the vegetables are crisp-tender, about 4 minutes. Season with salt (if using) and pepper to taste.

Fluff the couscous with a fork and gently stir in the cooked vegetables. Set aside to reheat when ready to serve.

Sear the tuna in a hot nonstick skillet or grill it for about 2 to 3 minutes per side, turning once, or to desired doneness.

When ready to serve, reheat the couscous mixture and mound onto a large heated serving platter. Slice the tuna thinly and fan onto the platter. Serve at once.

MAKES 8 SERVINGS

Joslin Choices: 4 very-low-fat protein, 2 carbohydrate (bread/starch) 1 vegetable

Per Serving: 357 calories (12% calories from fat), 4 g total fat (0 saturated fat), 37 g protein, 38 g carbohydrate, 3 g dietary fiber, 2 mg cholesterol, 245 mg sodium, 403 mg potassium

Warm Peppered Tuna with Potato Gratin, Haricots Verts, and Pine Nut Currant Dressing

Mark Filippo, CAFÉ MEZE
HARTSDALE, NEW YORK

The dish presented here is a popular entrée at this busy Westchester County Mediterranean restaurant, where Chef Filippo focuses on the cuisines of France and Italy with touches of Greece, Turkey, Spain, and Morocco. Fran first enjoyed his culinary talents years ago at the Quilted Giraffe in Manhattan. Now he has mastered the sultry flavors of the Mediterranean and brought them into use. Notice how he makes a savory Potato Gratin without a drop of cream.

HARICOTS VERTS:
1 pound haricots verts (young green
   beans), trimmed
salt (optional)
1 tablespoon olive oil
2 tablespoons diced red onion
1 tablespoon chopped flat-leaf parsley
1 tablespoon snipped fresh chives

POTATO GRATIN:
1 teaspoon unsalted butter
1 teaspoon minced garlic
3 large Idaho potatoes, about 1½ pounds total,
   peeled and thinly sliced
salt (optional)
freshly ground pepper
about 3 cups Chicken Stock (page 31)

TUNA:
1½-pounds fresh sushi-quality tuna steak,
   cut about ¾ to 1 inch thick
kosher salt (optional)
4 ounces (about ½ cup) freshly ground pepper
1 tablespoon canola oil

PINE NUT CURRANT DRESSING:
3 ounces (about ½ cup) pine nuts, toasted
2 ounces (about ½ cup) currants, plumped in
   warm water and drained
½ cup extra-virgin olive oil
¼ cup canola oil
2 tablespoons sherry vinegar
1 tablespoon honey
salt (optional)
freshly ground pepper

Blanch the haricots verts in lightly salted boiling water for 1 minute. Drain and plunge the beans into ice water to stop the cooking. Drain again and refrigerate. Place the olive oil and red onion in a large sauté pan. Combine the parsley and chives, and set aside.

Preheat the oven to 500°F. Butter a 6 x 8½-inch baking dish.

Sprinkle the prepared dish with some of the garlic and add 1 layer of the potatoes. Season with salt (if using) and pepper. Continue to alternate a layer of potatoes, garlic, salt (if using), and pepper, until all the potatoes are layered. Add enough stock to reach the top layer of potatoes. Do not cover.

Bake for 20 minutes, lower the oven temperature to 350°F, and continue baking for another 30 minutes, until the liquid has been absorbed and the potatoes are tender. Remove the potatoes from the oven and allow to set for 30 minutes. Cut into 2-inch squares and keep warm.

TO PREPARE THE TUNA: Clean the tuna, discarding all the skin. Cut the tuna so that it is in 6 pieces about 2½ inches across. Season with salt (if using) and roll in pepper to coat. Heat the canola oil in a large nonstick skillet over high heat. Add the tuna and sear on all sides for no longer than 2 to 3 minutes per side, turning once, or cook to desired doneness. Set the tuna on a plate and keep warm.

TO MAKE THE DRESSING: Mix all the ingredients together, adding salt (if using) and pepper to taste. Set aside.

TO ASSEMBLE: Place a stack of potatoes in the center of each of 6 large dinner plates. Slice each piece of tuna into 3 slices and fan out around the potatoes. Spoon 2 tablespoons of the dressing onto the plate around the tuna.

Heat the olive oil–red onion mixture over medium-high heat. Stir in the haricots verts. When the haricots verts are heated, remove the pan from the stove and add the parsley-chive mixture. Divide the haricots verts among the plates, placing them between the tuna slices. Serve at once.

MAKES 6 SERVINGS

Joslin Choices: 5 low-fat protein, 1½ carbohydrate (bread/starch), 1 fat

Per Serving: 426 calories (42% calories from fat), 20 g total fat (3 g saturated fat), 37 g protein, 24 g carbohydrate, 3 g dietary fiber, 55 mg cholesterol, 424 mg sodium, 930 mg potassium

Joslin Choices (dressing only): 2½ fat

Per 2-Tablespoon Serving: 129 calories (88% calories from fat), 13 g total fat (2 g saturated fat), 1 g protein, 2 g carbohydrate, 0 dietary fiber, 0 cholesterol, 0 sodium, 44 mg potassium

Aubergine (Eggplant) and Courgette (Zucchini) Lasagne

Josef Gander, EL QUIJOTE AT THE SAN CRISTOBAL TOWER HOTEL
SANTIAGO, CHILE

Lush gardens and the snowy summits of the Andes provide a backdrop for this luxury hotel. Here Chef Gander practices his trade near the hub of one of Chile's primary financial and commercial centers. From his homeland in the Italian part of the Tyrol, his career took him to Switzerland, the Caribbean, Australia, and Asia before he brought his talents to Chile. This vegetarian lasagne shows his expertise is making something special out of everyday ingredients.

2 small Japanese eggplant (aubergine), trimmed
   and each sliced lengthwise into 3 slices
2 small zucchini (courgette), trimmed and each
   sliced lengthwise into 4 slices
1 tablespoon olive oil
⅓ cup fresh bread crumbs
olive oil cooking spray
2 medium tomatoes, cored and each sliced into
   4 crosswise slices
3 ounces low-fat mozzarella cheese

PESTO SAUCE:
2 tablespoons chopped fresh basil leaves
2 teaspoons chopped flat-leaf parsley
1 tablespoon chopped pine nuts
1 tablespoon freshly grated Parmesan cheese
1½ tablespoons olive oil
1½ tablespoons canned low-fat,
   low-salt chicken broth

Light a grill or preheat the broiler. Grill the eggplant slices for 5 minutes per side, turning once. Remove from the grill and keep warm.

Brush the zucchini slices with ½ tablespoon of the olive oil. Sprinkle with the bread crumbs, and sauté in a nonstick skillet lightly coated with cooking spray until nicely browned on both sides, turning once. Remove from the pan and keep warm. Wipe out the skillet.

Brush the tomato slices with the remaining ½ tablespoon olive oil and lightly sauté in the same skillet over medium-high heat for about 30 seconds per side, turning once. Set aside and keep warm.

Cut the mozzarella cheese into 6 round slices. Set aside.

TO MAKE THE PESTO SAUCE: In a blender, pulse the basil, parsley, pine nuts, and Parmesan cheese until finely chopped and well mixed. With the motor running, drizzle the olive oil and chicken broth through the lid hole until the mixture forms a smooth sauce.

Preheat the oven to 300°F.

TO ASSEMBLE THE LASAGNE: Place an eggplant slice in the center of each of 2 large oven-proof plates. Following the shape of the eggplant, layer 2 zucchini slices, then 2 tomato slices on top of each eggplant slice. Top with 3 of the cheese slices. Spread 2 teaspoons of the Pesto Sauce over the cheese. Top each with another eggplant slice, 2 zucchini slices, 2 tomato slices, and the final eggplant slices. Place the plate in the oven until the lasagne is quite warm and the cheese is starting to melt, about 4 to 5 minutes. Remove from the oven and serve.

MAKES 2 SERVINGS

Joslin Choices: 2 low-fat protein, 2 carbohydrate (bread/starch), 3 fat

Per Serving: 459 calories (44% calories from fat), 23 g total fat (4 g saturated fat), 21 g protein, 47 g carbohydrate, 12 g dietary fiber, 8 mg cholesterol, 520 mg sodium, 1,365 mg potassium

Insalata de Farro (Farro Salad)

Maristella Innocenti, I COPPI
NEW YORK CITY

This interesting dish uses a grain that we knew very little about before writing this book. We have since come to love its nutty flavor, which in this recipe is complemented by the herbs and the tangy mâche, or lamb's lettuce. Chef Innocenti sent us a picture of the dish, and we could not wait to try it. Farro, a variety of wheat, is found in Italian grocery stores. It is also available via the Internet (see Sources, page 296).

2 cups farro
1½ medium cucumbers, seeded and finely chopped
2 small Belgian endives, trimmed and
   finely chopped
2 small leeks, white part only, well washed and
   finely chopped
15 cornichons, finely chopped
2 tablespoons chopped fresh basil

2 tablespoons chopped flat-leaf parsley
1 tablespoon chopped fresh chives
2 tablespoons extra-virgin olive oil
salt (optional)
freshly ground pepper
2 cups mâche, rinsed and dried
2 medium tomatoes, thinly sliced into wedges

In a medium saucepan, cook the farro in lightly salted water for 10 minutes. Drain, rinse with cold water, and drain again. Stir in the cucumbers, endives, leeks, cornichons, basil, parsley, and chives. Drizzle with 1½ tablespoons of the olive oil and toss to coat evenly. Season to taste with salt (if using) and pepper.

Arrange the farro mixture in the middle of a large serving plate. Decorate one side of the plate with the mâche and the opposite side of the plate with the tomatoes. Drizzle with the remaining ½ tablespoon olive oil and serve.

MAKES 4 SERVINGS

Joslin Choices: 1 medium-fat protein, 3½ carbohydrate (bread/starch)

Per Serving: 414 calories (18% calories from fat), 9 g total fat (1 g saturated fat), 15 g protein, 76 g carbohydrate, 24 g dietary fiber, 0 cholesterol, 309 mg sodium, 1,589 mg potassium

Picnic in the Country

*Insalata de Farro (Farro Salad) (page 242)
in Red or Green Leaf Lettuce Wrappers* •

Fresh Fruit •

Joslin Choices: 1 medium-fat protein, 3½ carbohydrate (bread/starch), 414 calories (18% calories from fat) •

Note: Items not referring to a specific recipe are not included in the nutritional analysis. Consult the Joslin Food Choices (page 287) for that information. •

Oregon Black Morel Risotto with Chèvre and Fiddlehead Fern Relish

Greg Higgins, HIGGINS
PORTLAND, OREGON

This risotto makes a fine meal, needing only a green salad and maybe a pear and some fat-free or low-fat Cheddar cheese for dessert. Fiddlehead ferns are only in season from April through July, depending on where you live. If you cannot find them, you could use fresh asparagus with little difference in taste and texture.

FIDDLEHEAD FERN RELISH:
½ pound fresh fiddlehead ferns
1 tablespoon extra-virgin olive oil
1 teaspoon Sambal Oelek (page 144)
1 tablespoon minced garlic
2 tablespoons chiffonade-cut fresh mint
chopped zest and juice of 1 large lemon
salt (optional)
freshly ground pepper

RISOTTO:
1 medium onion, diced
¼ cup minced shallots

1 teaspoon Sambal Oelek (page 144)
3 tablespoons minced garlic
1 tablespoon extra-virgin olive oil
1½ cups Arborio (Italian short-grain) rice
1½ quarts Vegetable Stock (page 115),
   heated to a lively simmer
salt (optional)
freshly ground pepper
8 ounces fresh morel mushrooms, cleaned
4 ounces chèvre

2 tablespoons chiffonade-cut fresh mint

Poach the fiddlehead ferns until al dente in lightly salted water, 1 to 2 minutes. Refresh in cold water and drain. Toss them in the olive oil, Sambal Oelek, garlic, 2 tablespoons mint chiffonade, and the lemon zest and juice. Season to taste with salt (if using) and pepper. Set aside.

In a heavy saucepan over medium heat, sauté the onion, shallots, Sambal Oelek, and garlic in ½ tablespoon of the olive oil. Cook, stirring occasionally for 3 to 5 minutes, until the onions are translucent. Add the rice and continue cooking and gently stirring for 5 minutes. Add the hot Vegetable Stock in 3 to 4 batches, taking care not to stir too much and only adding more hot stock after all of the previous batch has been absorbed.

Before the final addition of stock, sauté the morels in a hot heavy skillet with the remaining ½ tablespoon olive oil. Season with salt (if using) and pepper to taste. Add half of the cooked morels and the chèvre to the risotto along with the remaining stock and continue cooking. Adjust the seasoning with salt (if using) and pepper.

Portion the finished risotto into 6 soup plates. Top each portion with the Fiddlehead Fern Relish, the remaining cooked morels, and a sprinkle of the mint chiffonade.

MAKES 6 SERVINGS

Joslin Choices: 3½ carbohydrate (bread/starch), 1 fat

Per Serving: 333 calories (25% calories from fat), 9 g total fat (3 g saturated fat), 12 g protein, 52 g carbohydrate, 2 g dietary fiber, 9 mg cholesterol, 227 mg sodium, 604 mg potassium

Curry Hot Pot

Troy N. Thompson, JER-NE AT THE RITZ CARLTON

MARINA DEL REY, CALIFORNIA

A phonetic spelling of *journey,* Jer-ne is setting trends, not following them, at this strikingly scenic California city that contains more restaurants per square mile than any place outside New York City. With Chef Thompson in the kitchen, one is assured that, although prepared with traditional cooking techniques and the freshest ingredients, the dish will come out of the kitchen with a modern twist. Never has tofu tasted so good!

CURRY:

2 tablespoons grapeseed or canola oil

1½ teaspoons cumin seeds

1½ teaspoons coriander seeds

½ teaspoon ground turmeric

½ teaspoon ground ginger

1 large onion, cut into 8 pieces

2 cloves garlic, crushed

1 medium carrot, chopped

1 medium tomato, cut into quarters

1 medium Granny Smith apple,
   peeled and sliced

3 cups Vegetable Stock (page 115)

¼ teaspoon cayenne pepper or to taste

salt (optional)

freshly ground pepper

VEGETABLES:

1 onion, cut into 8 pieces

1 medium red bell pepper, cut into 8 pieces

1 medium carrot, sliced on a diagonal

1 2-inch piece fresh ginger, peeled and julienned

1 small Japanese eggplant, cut into 4 pieces

10 green beans, trimmed and cut in half

4 small creamer potatoes, scrubbed and precooked
   until almost tender

1 pound firm tofu, pressed, drained, and cubed
   (see page 247)

6 shiitake mushrooms, cleaned and cut in half

4 leaves Napa cabbage cut into 3-inch pieces

1 bunch watercress

2 cups hot cooked rice

To a smoking hot sauté pan, add the oil, cumin, coriander, turmeric, and ginger. Sauté, stirring constantly, until the spices are fragrant and begin to darken. Add the onion, garlic, carrot, tomato, and apple. Cook over low heat until the onion is limp, about 5 minutes. Stir in the stock and cayenne pepper. Gently simmer until the vegetables are very tender, about 15 to 20 minutes.

Transfer the curry mixture to a food processor or a blender. Puree until smooth. Strain the puree through a sieve and season with salt (if using) and pepper to taste.

Using a stove-to-table pot, bring the curry mixture back to a simmer. Add the onion, bell pepper, carrot, ginger, eggplant, green beans, and potatoes. Simmer for 10 to 15 minutes, until the vegetables are tender. Add the remaining vegetables and simmer for another 3 minutes.

Press the hot rice into ½-cup molds. Unmold in the center of 4 hot shallow soup plates. At the table, ladle the curry around the rice molds and serve.

MAKES 4 SERVINGS

Joslin Choices: 1½ medium-fat protein, 2½ carbohydrate (bread/starch), ½ fat

Per Serving: 336 calories (30% calories from fat), 12 g total fat (1 g saturated fat), 17 g protein, 46 g carbohydrate, 8 g dietary fiber, 0 cholesterol, 50 mg sodium, 846 mg potassium

Preparing Tofu for Cooking

When you purchase tofu, it will be sealed in liquid. Most cooks will drain off the water and press the tofu under weight for about 30 to 60 minutes, depending on the firmness desired. Pressed tofu will become more dense and will hold together better when sliced or cubed. There are different ways to press tofu. An easy way is to wrap the tofu in paper towels on a plate and press with a second plate topped with an unopened 28-ounce can or heavy pot.

The sides of the tofu should bulge under the pressure but not break. Lift off the weight after about 15 minutes; remove the wet towels and replace with dry paper towels, discarding any liquid in the dish. You can turn the tofu when you change the paper towels. Another method of pressing tofu is to place it on a tilted board, cover with aluminum foil, and press, using another board on top with a weight. Allow to drain into a pan or sink. Refrigerate the pressed tofu in water when you are satisfied that all of the original liquid is pressed out. The tofu will not reabsorb this water and will remain fresh for 2 to 3 days.

247

Red Risotto with Tofu

Umberto Vezzoli, VIVENDO AT THE ST. REGIS GRAND
ROME

The elegantly renovated St. Regis Grand was originally built as the first luxury hotel in Rome in 1894. Each guest room bears the name of the unique hand-painted fresco hanging in it, depicting a scene of Rome. The hotel, located in the heart of Rome near the Spanish Steps and Via Condotti, was named a gem by *Bon Appétit* in 2000. Vivendo is one of the most beautiful restaurants in Rome and has a distinguished history; it was founded by none other than Escoffier himself. Today, it offers a superb selection of Mediterranean dishes from a variety of countries, including fusion cuisine with Asian seasonings and ingredients. Chef Vezzoli kindly joined us in this book with this risotto dish made with tofu that is the best we have ever tasted. Another time, substitute 1 pound of shellfish for the tofu.

1 tablespoon margarine

1 cup Arborio (Italian short-grain) rice

1 medium onion, finely chopped

½ cup dry light red wine, plus 2 tablespoons

3 cups Vegetable Stock (page 115)

8 ounces low-sodium tomato sauce

⅔ cup fresh or frozen green peas

½ cup canned cannellini beans, drained, rinsed well, and drained again

4 ounces firm tofu, pressed and diced into ⅓-inch cubes (see page 247)

1 tablespoon light cream

¼ cup grated Parmesan cheese

Melt the margarine in a heavy saucepan; add the rice, onion, and ½ cup of the red wine. Simmer until the wine is absorbed. Heat the stock and keep at a lively simmer.

Add ⅔ cup of the stock to the rice mixture, stirring until the liquid is absorbed. Add the tomato sauce with another ⅔ cup of the stock. Cook, stirring, until the liquid is absorbed. Continue adding the stock, ⅔ cup at a time, cooking and stirring until all the stock has been added, allowing the liquid to be absorbed after each addition. Stir in the peas and beans. Cook, stirring, for another 2 to 3 minutes until the rice is of the desired creamy texture.

Sauté the tofu in a hot nonstick skillet for 2 minutes, until it begins to brown on all sides. Stir into the rice. The rice should be cooked al dente; add more stock only if needed.

Before serving, stir in the cream, Parmesan cheese, and remaining 2 tablespoons red wine. Serve at once in shallow soup plates.

MAKES 4 SERVINGS

Joslin Choices: ½ high-fat protein, 3½ carbohydrate (bread/starch)

Per Serving: 389 calories (20% calories from fat), 9 g total fat (3 g saturated fat), 15 g protein, 58 g carbohydrate, 5 g dietary fiber, 7 mg cholesterol, 256 mg sodium, 614 mg potassium

Italian Vegetarian Dinner

Red Risotto with Tofu *(page 248)*

Tossed Green Salad with Aged Balsamic Vinegar

Bowl of Chilled Grapes

Joslin Choices: ½ high-fat protein, 3½ carbohydrate, 389 calories (20% calories from fat)

Note: Items not referring to a specific recipe are not included in the nutritional analysis. Consult the Joslin Food Choices (page 287) for that information.

Tofu and Vegetable Nabe

Troy N. Thompson, JER-NE AT THE RITZ CARLTON
MARINA DEL REY, CALIFORNIA

Another superb way to serve tofu comes from this talented California chef, this time in "nabemono style," a Japanese term that translates to "things-in-a-pot." Chef Thompson's experience with Japanese cuisine comes from owning a restaurant (albeit one serving American cuisine) in Osaka, Japan, prior to coming to Jer-ne. One can see the Japanese influence on the menu of this waterside restaurant. Hot Pots, Kobe Beef, Woked Long Beans, and the Bento Box (five unique appetizers served in a traditional Japanese box) are featured items.

1 large onion, cut into large dice
4 small creamer potatoes, scrubbed and precooked
  until almost tender
1 medium carrot, peeled and thinly sliced
1 head Napa cabbage, cut into 2-inch pieces
1 small Japanese eggplant, cut into 4 pieces
1 2-inch piece fresh ginger, peeled and
  thinly sliced
6 large shiitake mushrooms, cleaned and halved
  lengthwise

4 scallions, white part and 1 inch green,
  cut into thirds
1 cup cooked rye or wheat berries
1 pound firm tofu, pressed, drained, and cubed
  (see page 247)
about 4 cups Vegetable Stock (page 115)
2 tablespoons white miso
reduced-sodium soy sauce for sprinkling

In a stove-to-table pot, arrange the onion, potatoes, and carrot. Add the cabbage, eggplant, ginger, mushrooms, and scallions. Place the grain and tofu on top. Pour in sufficient stock to cover the vegetables by at least 2 inches.

Slowly bring the pot to a boil and continue to simmer until the vegetables are tender, about 6 minutes. Add the miso and bring to the table to serve family-style, ladling the vegetables and broth into 4 heated shallow soup plates.

Pass the soy sauce separately to lightly sprinkle over each serving.

MAKES 4 SERVINGS

Joslin Choices: 3 low-fat protein, 2 carbohydrate (bread/starch)

Per Serving: 333 calories (28% calories from fat), 11 g total fat (2 g saturated fat), 26 g protein, 40 g carbohydrate, 9 g dietary fiber, 0 cholesterol, 437 mg sodium, 1,168 mg potassium

Kula Vegetable and Legume Ragout with Wild Mushrooms

David Paul Johnson, DAVID PAUL'S LAHAINA GRILL
LAHAINA, MAUI, HAWAII

Kula is located in Maui's up-country. In fact, one has to drive partway up the dormant Haleakala volcano to reach Kula, where farmers take advantage of the ultra-rich volcanic soil to grow sweet onions and other vegetables. Hawaiian chefs use Kula greens and a variety of fresh herbs to grace the salads of many fine Maui restaurants.

Chef Johnson will feature this dish on his television series on Hawaiian cooking. This delicious recipe shows yet another facet of his culinary talent.

1 cup each washed, peeled, and ½-inch diced carrots, celery, leeks, onion, sweet potatoes, winter squash (such as acorn, butternut, golden nugget, pumpkin, or turban), and zucchini

4 large cloves garlic, chopped

2 shallots, peeled and chopped

2 tablespoons olive oil

salt (optional)

freshly ground pepper

1 cup dry vermouth

2 pounds assorted mushrooms, such as shiitake, cremini, morels, porcini (cèpes), or oyster, washed and quartered

1 cup quinoa

½ cup shucked fresh or frozen peas

1 cup shucked fresh or frozen lima beans

3½ tablespoons mixed dried herbs

4 cups Vegetable Stock (page 115) or Chicken Stock (page 31)

2 tablespoons unsalted butter

¼ cup finely chopped parsley

In a large pot, over high heat sauté all of the vegetables, the garlic, and shallots in oil until lightly browned, about 10 minutes. Add salt (if using) and pepper to taste. Stir in the vermouth and simmer on low heat until most of the liquid is evaporated.

Add the mushrooms, quinoa, peas, lima beans, and mixed dried herbs, along with your choice of stock and the butter. Simmer over medium-low heat, uncovered, for about 45 minutes or until the liquid has begun to cloud and thicken from the starch in the potatoes. Taste and correct the seasoning if necessary.

TO SERVE: Ladle into 8 large soup bowls. Sprinkle with the parsley and serve.

MAKES 8 SERVINGS

Joslin Choices: 1 low-fat protein, 2 carbohydrate (bread/starch), 1 fat

Per Serving: 305 calories (25% calories from fat), 9 g total fat (3 g saturated fat), 11 g protein, 40 g carbohydrate, 7 g dietary fiber, 10 mg cholesterol, 141mg sodium, 594 mg potassium

Extra Touches:
Vegetable Sides, Breads, and Condiments

Beet Terrine

James Boyce, MARY ELAINE'S AT THE PHOENICIAN
SCOTTSDALE, ARIZONA

We love beets and this is one of the most interesting ways to prepare them that we have come across. Gelatin sheets may not be familiar to you. You can buy them at specialty food stores, or use the more common envelopes of unflavored gelatin. A ¼-ounce envelope (scant tablespoon) is equal to 5 sheets of gelatin.

When we called Mary Elaine's for recipes, the publicist at the hotel told us that Chef Boyce really understands how to get full flavor from vegetables. This recipe is a testimony to that claim.

20 Candy-striped or red beets, about 2 pounds	2 cups verjus (see page 108)
20 golden beets, about 2 pounds	salt (optional)
4 cloves garlic, peeled	freshly ground pepper
4 shallots, peeled	1 to 2 tablespoons sugar
4 sprigs fresh thyme	12 sheets gelatin

Scrub the beets, trimming the tops to about ½ inch. Do not peel. Place in a pot with the garlic, shallots, and thyme. Cover with water and bring to a boil over high heat. Reduce the heat and simmer 3 to 10 minutes, depending on the size of the beets, until tender. Remove from the stove and cool in the cooking liquid. Peel the beets and cut in half. Set aside to air dry.

Heat the verjus and season with salt (if using), pepper, and 1 tablespoon of the sugar. Taste the mixture; it should be slightly sweet. If necessary, add the second tablespoon of sugar.

Bloom the gelatin sheets in cold water until pliable and whisk the softened sheets into the hot verjus until the gelatin is dissolved.

Line a terrine mold or baking dish with plastic wrap, allowing the wrap to hang over the sides for easier unmolding. Pour enough of the verjus-gelatin mixture into the terrine until it is about 1 inch high. Arrange the beets in layers, alternating the colors, until the beets come within ¼ inch of the top. Carefully pour the remaining verjus mixture over the terrine until the beets are fully submerged. Refrigerate until the terrine is set, 2 to 4 hours. Invert the mold onto a serving plate and unmold, discarding the plastic wrap. Slice and serve.

MAKES 8 SERVINGS

Joslin Choices: 2 carbohydrate (1 bread/starch, 1 fruit)

Per Serving: 146 calories (2% calories from fat), 0 total fat (0 saturated fat), 6 g protein, 33 g carbohydrate, 4 g dietary fiber, 0 cholesterol, 183 mg sodium, 761 mg potassium

Spicy Broccoli Rabe

Alice Waters, CHEZ PANISSE
BERKELEY, CALIFORNIA

This is an adaptation of Chef Waters's recipe that first appeared in her *Chez Panisse Café Cookbook* (HarperCollins). We have eaten this vegetable several times when dining at this very popular restaurant and wanted to share it with you. Broccoli rabe is not particularly popular here in the United States, which we think is a shame. When properly prepared, it is terrific. Try it; maybe you will like it as we do!

This preparation makes any vegetable a star. If you cannot find broccoli rabe, make this with regular broccoli, green beans, cauliflower, zucchini, or asparagus.

At the restaurant, they vary this by adding pounded anchovy and/or chopped olives to the cooked broccoli rabe. Serve at room temperature as part of an antipasto platter.

3 bunches broccoli rabe
1½ tablespoons extra-virgin olive oil
salt (optional)

3 large cloves garlic, finely chopped
generous pinch crushed red pepper flakes
red wine vinegar

Wash the broccoli rabe and coarsely chop the leaves and stems. Heat a large sauté pan and coat the bottom of the pan with ½ tablespoon of the olive oil. Add the broccoli rabe and season with salt (if using). Cook over high heat, tossing frequently, until the rabe starts to brown a little. Reduce the heat, add a splash of water, and cook until tender, stirring frequently. When the rabe is cooked, remove it from the pan and set aside.

While the pan is still hot, drizzle in the remaining 1 tablespoon olive oil; add the garlic and red pepper flakes. Warm briefly. Add the cooked rabe, a splash of red wine vinegar, and toss. Taste and correct the seasoning. Serve hot or at room temperature.

MAKES 4 SERVINGS

Joslin Choices: 1 low-fat protein, 1 carbohydrate (bread/starch)

Per Serving: 109 calories (35% calories from fat), 5 g total fat (1 g saturated fat), 8 g protein, 13 g carbohydrate, 0 dietary fiber, 0 cholesterol, 61 mg sodium, 13 mg potassium

Candlelight Dinner

Lasagne of French Mushrooms and Lovage with Fava Coulis *(page 141)*

Spicy Broccoli Rabe *(page 254)*

Soup of Apricot Jus with Fresh Fruit *(page 282)*

Joslin Choices: 2 medium-fat protein, 4 carbohydrate (2 bread/starch, 2 fruit), 2 fat, 577 calories (30% calories from fat)

Ragout of Caramelized Pearl Onions and Brussels Sprouts

Jimmy Schmidt, RATTLESNAKE
DETROIT, MICHIGAN

Jimmy Schmidt's Rattlesnake was not named "Zagat Survey's America's Top Restaurant" in 2000 and 2001 without good reason. Here he proves why. His ragout of pearl onions and Brussels sprouts will make the most finicky of eaters ask for seconds.

A vegetable like this will transform plain broiled chicken or fish into a wonderful meal.

2 tablespoons unsalted butter
2 cups pearl onions, peeled
sea salt (optional)
freshly ground pepper
2 cups Riesling wine
1 pound medium Brussels sprouts, trimmed of
    loose outer leaves, base trimmed and an
    X cut in the bottom of each sprout

½ cup snipped fresh chives
¼ cup freshly grated Parmesan cheese, preferably
    Parmigiano-Reggiano

In a large nonstick skillet, heat the butter over medium heat. Add the onions and cook until browned and tender, about 10 minutes. Season with salt (if using) and pepper. Add the wine, cooking until reduced and just coating the onions, about 5 minutes.

Meanwhile, in a medium pot of lightly salted boiling water, cook the Brussels sprouts until al dente, tender yet firm to the bite, about 4 to 5 minutes. Drain in a colander, then transfer to the onion skillet. Season with pepper. Cook until the sauce is reduced and coats the Brussels sprouts, about 3 minutes.

Add half of the chives and the Parmesan cheese, tossing to combine. Transfer to a warm serving dish and top with the remaining chives. Serve at once.

MAKES 6 SERVINGS

Joslin Choices: 1 carbohydrate (bread/starch), 1 fat

Per Serving: 176 calories (26% calories from fat), 5 g total fat (3 g saturated fat), 4 g protein, 17 g carbohydrate, 2 g dietary fiber, 14 mg cholesterol, 73 mg sodium, 316 mg potassium

Hawaiian Pineapple Fried Rice

Christian Jorgensen, TROPICA AT THE WESTIN MAUI
LAHAINA, MAUI, HAWAII

When Fran had this at Tropica, it was served in a white box used for Chinese take-out. When we asked Chef Jorgensen for the recipe, he said he was not sure he wanted to give the recipe, as it is a house specialty. We are glad he reconsidered. It's one that delights our guests back here on the Mainland.

½ teaspoon dark sesame oil

3 strips lean center-cut bacon, cooked very crisp, drained on paper towels, and crumbled

1 4-ounce cooked chicken breast half

1 medium red onion, finely chopped

1 medium carrot, finely chopped

1 small red bell pepper, seeded and finely chopped

1 small green bell pepper, seeded and finely chopped

1 small yellow bell pepper, seeded and finely chopped

5 cups cooked jasmine rice

2 tablespoons reduced-sodium soy sauce

2 tablespoons oyster sauce

1 tablespoon Sambal Oelek (see page 144)

½ cup diced fresh pineapple

¼ cup chopped macadamia nuts

salt (optional)

freshly ground white pepper to taste

Heat a wok over medium-high heat. Add the sesame oil. When just about smoking, add the bacon and chicken and stir-fry until the chicken is lightly browned. Add the onion, carrot, and bell peppers, and stir-fry for about 30 seconds. Add the cooked rice and continue to stir-fry, being sure to break up any lumps.

Add the soy sauce, oyster sauce, and Sambal Oelek. Continue to stir-fry, adding the pineapple, macadamia nuts, salt (if using), and white pepper. Transfer to individual serving bowls and serve hot.

MAKES 12 SERVINGS

Joslin Choices: 2 carbohydrate (bread/starch)

Per Serving: 167 calories (18% calories from fat), 3 g total fat (1 g saturated fat), 6 g protein, 28 g carbohydrate, 2 g dietary fiber, 9 mg cholesterol, 158 mg sodium, 123 mg potassium

Cumin Crackers

Todd Davies, BERTRAND @ MISTER A'S

SAN DIEGO, CALIFORNIA

Eating at Bertrand @ Mister A's is a pleasure. The restaurant is located high on top of the Financial Center, and serves some of the most elegant food that this city has to offer. Chef Davies came to San Diego via Philadelphia and New York. He calls his style "modern American cuisine with French and Mediterranean influences." You will call it delicious. These savory crackers are frequently served alongside an appetizer, soup, or salad. Be careful! They are addictive.

vegetable cooking spray

1 tablespoon ground cumin

½ teaspoon fine sea salt

1½ cups unbleached all-purpose flour

½ cup semolina flour (see Note below)

¾ to 1 cup warm water

1 teaspoon kosher salt

2 teaspoons sesame seeds

Preheat the oven to 500°F. Lightly coat a baking sheet with cooking spray.

Mix the cumin, sea salt, and the two flours in a food processor. Drizzle water through the feed tube in a steady stream until a ball is formed. Remove from the food processor and knead for 1 minute. Remove the dough and place on a lightly floured surface. The dough should not be sticky. If it is, knead in a little more flour by hand.

Cover and let rest for 30 minutes at room temperature. Using a rolling pin, roll the dough into a thin rectangle. Roll thinly on a lightly floured surface. Sprinkle with the kosher salt and sesame seeds. Using a small biscuit or cookie cutter, about 1½ inches in diameter, cut out bite-size crackers. Transfer the crackers to the prepared baking sheet. Mist the crackers with water and bake for 3 minutes, until crisp and lightly browned. Thinner crackers will cook much more quickly than thicker ones. (The crackers can be baked 1 day ahead, cooled, and stored overnight in an airtight container or frozen for up to 2 months. Re-crisp them in a 350°F oven for a minute or two.)

Serve warm or at room temperature.

MAKES 48 CRACKERS

Joslin Choices: 1 carbohydrate (bread/starch)

Per 3-Cracker Serving: 60 calories (5% calories from fat), 0 fat (0 saturated fat), 2 g protein, 12 g carbohydrate, 1 g dietary fiber, 0 cholesterol, 191 mg sodium, 11 mg potassium

Note: Semolina flour is available at larger supermarkets, natural food stores, and by mail order; see Sources (page 296).

Yellow Tomato Focaccia

Carole Peck, GOOD NEWS CAFÉ
WOODBURY, CONNECTICUT

Chef and owner Carole Peck is a rising star among women chefs and a frequent guest chef at the James Beard House in Manhattan. Carole places a basket of a variety of interesting breads on every table at her eclectic northwest Connecticut restaurant. Frequently there are slabs of this fabulous Italian hearth bread.

2 ¼-ounce envelopes (2 scant tablespoons)
   active dry yeast
1 teaspoon sugar
2 cups warm water at 110°F
5 cups unbleached all-purpose flour
2 cups peeled, seeded, and chopped yellow
   tomatoes (see Note below)

3 tablespoons extra-virgin olive oil
1 tablespoon chopped fresh rosemary or
   1 teaspoon crushed dried rosemary
2 teaspoons kosher salt

Put the yeast and sugar in a large bowl. Add the warm water and mix well. Let sit for 5 minutes. Stir in 1 cup of the flour and continue to add the flour until the dough forms a sticky ball.

Transfer the dough to a lightly floured work surface. Knead for about 7 minutes, using the remaining flour, as needed, to prevent the dough from sticking, until the dough is firm and elastic. Place the dough in a lightly oiled bowl, cover with plastic wrap, and let rise in a warm place until doubled in size (or overnight in the refrigerator).

Punch down the dough and knead in the tomatoes. Brush a 10½ x 15 x ½-inch rimmed baking sheet with 1 tablespoon of the olive oil. Using your fingers spread the dough in the baking sheet until it completely covers the bottom evenly. Take your time; the dough will be stiff. When the pan is fully covered, brush the dough with the remaining 2 tablespoons olive oil and sprinkle with the rosemary and salt. Let the dough rise in a warm place about 1½ hours, until doubled in size.

Preheat the oven to 400°F. Bake the dough for 20 to 25 minutes, until golden in color. Let cool, then cut into 3 x 2-inch pieces.

MAKES 1 LOAF, 24 SERVINGS

Joslin Choices: 1 carbohydrate (bread/starch)

Per Serving: 102 calories (16% calories from fat), 2 g total fat (0 saturated fat), 3 g protein, 18 g carbohydrate, 1 g dietary fiber, 0 cholesterol, 160 mg sodium, 42 mg potassium

Note: If yellow tomatoes are not in season, substitute red plum (Roma) tomatoes, seeded and chopped.

Rosemary Focaccia

Kevin Thomas Ascolese, SALVE!
DALLAS, TEXAS

The word "focaccia" is derived from the Latin word "focus," meaning "hearth." This delightful peasant-style bread evolved from the unleavened hearth cake eaten during the Middle Ages that was made by patting the dough into a flat round and cooking it directly on a hot stone or under a mound of hot ashes. Nowadays focaccia, whose true home is the area around Genoa, has become something of an Italian national dish. Whether soft or crisp, thick or thin, the dough is typically flavored with local herbs and olive oil as in Chef Ascolese's recipe, which uses lots of fresh rosemary, an herb that grows wild throughout Italy.

4 cups unbleached all-purpose flour
1 teaspoon salt
2 tablespoons chopped fresh rosemary
3 tablespoons chopped scallions

1¾ cups warm water
1 7-gram package dry yeast or ½-ounce fresh yeast
5 tablespoons olive oil
1 teaspoon kosher salt

In a large mixing bowl, combine the flour, salt, rosemary, and scallions. Mix well. Put the water into another bowl and whisk in the yeast, then 3 tablespoons of the olive oil. Pour into the flour mixture and stir until the flour is evenly moistened, then beat vigorously for 1 minute. Place the dough in a clean large bowl and cover with plastic wrap. Set in a warm, draft-free place to rise until doubled in size, about 1 hour.

Spread 1 tablespoon of the olive oil in a 14-inch cast-iron skillet. Scrape the dough out of the bowl and into the skillet, patting and pressing the dough to fill the pan completely. With your fingertips, poke holes in the dough at 2-inch intervals. Drizzle the remaining 1 tablespoon olive oil on top of the dough. Sprinkle with the coarse salt.

Preheat the oven to 450°F. Set a rack in the lower third of the oven.

Bake until golden brown, about 25 minutes. Check the bottom about halfway through the baking time by lifting the side of the focaccia with a spatula. If it's already browned, reduce the oven temperature to 400°F. When the focaccia sounds hollow when thumped with a finger, remove the focaccia from the oven.

Slide the focaccia out of the pan to a rack to cool. Cut into 16 pieces to serve. Serve warm or at room temperature.

MAKES 16 SERVINGS

Joslin Choices: 1½ carbohydrate (bread/starch), ½ fat

Per Serving: 139 calories (28% calories from fat), 4 g total fat (1 g saturated fat), 3 g protein, 21 g carbohydrate, 1 g dietary fiber, 0 cholesterol, 264 mg sodium, 13 mg potassium

Dinner for the Children

Spaghetti à la Crudaiola *(page 145)*

Rosemary Focaccia *(page 261)*

Frozen Yogurt

Joslin Choices: 4 carbohydrate (bread/starch), 1 fat, 391 calories (22% calories from fat)

Note: Items not referring to a specific recipe are not included in the nutritional analysis. Consult the Joslin Food Choices (page 287) for that information.

Fire-Roasted Salsa

Liz Baron, BLUE MESA GRILL

ADDISON, DALLAS, FORT WORTH, AND PLANO, TEXAS

This terrific salsa gets its rich color and smoky flavor from the ingredients being roasted on a mesquite grill. At home, we use soaked mesquite wood chips over the heated coals of our grill with excellent results. Serve this salsa with Liz's recipe for Crispy Chicken Flautas (page 77). Kept refrigerated, the salsa will stay fresh for up to 2 days. This is so good, you may find yourself eating more than a ¼-cup serving. If you do, ½ cup of this smoky-flavored salsa has only 6 grams of carbohydrate or 1 vegetable choice.

7 medium tomatoes, cored

4 scallions, trimmed, leaving 3 inches green

⅓ bunch cilantro

1 tablespoon canola oil

4 serrano peppers, stemmed but not seeded

2 teaspoons garlic puree

2 tablespoons fresh lime juice

1 teaspoon salt

¼ teaspoon ground white pepper

¼ teaspoon crushed dried oregano

⅓ cup water

Light a mesquite grill. When it is hot, place the tomatoes and scallions over the hot coals, not high flames. Pile the cilantro on top so that it does not touch the grill. Grill the vegetables about 7 minutes, until they are blistered.

Heat the oil in a sauté pan. Add the peppers and sauté until soft.

Discard the cilantro stems. Place the serranos, tomatoes, onions, and cilantro leaves in a food processor. Pulse until just coarsely ground. Transfer to a bowl and add the garlic puree, lime juice, salt, white pepper, oregano, and water. Mix well. Transfer to a serving bowl.

MAKES ABOUT 4 CUPS

Joslin Choices: free food

Per ¼-Cup Serving: 21 calories (40% calories from fat), 1 g total fat (0 saturated fat), 1 g protein, 3 g carbohydrate, 1 g dietary fiber, 0 cholesterol, 151 mg sodium, 136 mg potassium

Fruit and Light Desserts

Apple Strudel with Fresh Berry Sauce

Paul Ramsey, PINEHURST

PINEHURST VILLAGE, NORTH CAROLINA

Chef Ramsey of Pinehurst shares his recipe for an elegant strudel with berry sauce. You can use any fresh berries in season for the sauce that can serve as a topping for other desserts also.

4 medium Granny Smith apples, peeled, cored, quartered, and thinly sliced

¼ cup golden raisins

2 tablespoons light brown sugar

1¼ teaspoons ground cinnamon

⅛ teaspoon ground nutmeg

3 filo sheets

1 tablespoon clarified butter

⅓ cup fresh Berry Sauce (recipe follows)

1 tablespoon confectioners' sugar (optional)

Preheat the oven to 375°F.

Combine the apples, raisins, brown sugar, cinnamon, and nutmeg in a baking dish. Bake until the fruit is tender, about 15 to 20 minutes. Remove from the oven and allow the mixture to cool. Increase the oven temperature to 450°F.

Lay the 3 sheets of filo in a stack on a large nonstick baking sheet. Mound the fruit mixture in a row running along one of the short sides of the filo, leaving about 1½ inches empty around the apples on the sides. Fold the close short side over the apples and fold in the long sides. Roll the filo and filling over onto itself to form a strudel roll. Place the roll seam side on the baking sheet. Brush the top of the strudel with the butter. Score the strudel with a sharp knife to mark the 6 portions.

Bake to a golden brown, about 10 to 15 minutes. Allow to cool for 10 minutes, then cut into portions. Decorate 6 dessert plates with the berry sauce and top with the pieces of strudel. Dust with a sifting of the confectioners' sugar (if using) and serve.

MAKES 6 SERVINGS

Joslin Choices: 2 carbohydrate (fruit)

Per Serving: 140 calories (15% calories from fat), 3 g total fat (1 g saturated fat), 1 g protein, 29 g carbohydrate, 3 g dietary fiber, 5 mg cholesterol, 51 mg sodium, 187 mg potassium

Fresh Berry Sauce

½ cup fresh berries (raspberries, blueberries, or sliced strawberries)
1 tablespoon honey

2 teaspoons Kirschwasser (cherry brandy, optional)
2 tablespoons white wine

Combine all the ingredients in a blender. Puree until smooth. Push through a fine sieve to remove the seeds. Use as directed.

Roasted Peaches and Blueberries with Vanilla Cake

Waldy Malouf, BEACON

NEW YORK CITY AND STAMFORD, CONNECTICUT

This is a beautiful cake, worthy of your finest cake pedestal for very special occasions. We thank this talented chef for recognizing that people with special dietary needs love desserts—and what a scrumptious dessert this is!

6 large ripe peaches, pitted and sliced
6 cups blueberries
1 cup sugar
juice of 1 large lemon
¼ vanilla bean
6 tablespoons unsalted butter, cut in small pieces
2 large eggs

1 teaspoon vanilla extract
1 cup all-purpose flour
1½ teaspoons baking powder
½ teaspoon salt
½ cup milk
mint sprigs for garnish

Preheat the oven to 500°F.

Place the peaches, blueberries, ½ cup of the sugar, and the lemon juice in a large bowl; toss to coat well. Reserve 2 cups of the fruit; pour the remainder into a 9 x 13-inch baking dish. Cover the reserved fruit and refrigerate.

Scrape the seeds from the vanilla bean and reserve. Bury the empty pod in the fruit in the baking dish and arrange 2 tablespoons of the butter pieces on top. Bake for 30 minutes, stirring after about 15 minutes. Let cool on a rack; discard the vanilla pod.

Lower the oven temperature to 350°F. Grease and flour an 8-inch round cake pan.

In the bowl of an electric mixer fitted with the paddle attachment, cream the remaining ½ cup sugar and 4 tablespoons butter until very smooth. Beat in the eggs, vanilla extract, and reserved vanilla seeds. In a small bowl, combine the flour, baking powder, and salt. On low speed, add the flour mixture to the batter in three stages, alternating with the milk. Pour the batter into the prepared pan and bake for 25 minutes, until a tester inserted into the middle comes out clean. Let cool, then remove the cake from the pan.

With a long serrated knife, carefully slice the cake horizontally into 3 layers. Line a clean 8-inch cake pan with plastic wrap, leaving plenty of wrap overhanging. Place the bottom layer of the cake in the pan, cut side up. Using a slotted spoon, layer half the cooled fruit over the cake. Top with the middle layer of cake, and spoon on the remaining fruit; reserve the fruit juices. Cover with the top cake layer, cut side down. Press down gently on the cake and cover with the overhanging plastic wrap. Chill the cake for at least 8 hours, preferably overnight.

When ready to serve, turn the cake out onto a cutting board and discard the plastic wrap. Slice into 16 wedges and set each wedge on a dessert plate. Garnish each slice with a generous drizzle of the reserved fruit juices and some of the reserved raw fruit, and top with the mint sprigs.

MAKES 16 SERVINGS

Joslin Choices: 2 carbohydrate (1 bread/starch, 1 fruit), 1 fat

Per Serving: 191 calories (25% calories from fat), 5 g total fat (3 g saturated fat), 3 g protein, 34 g carbohydrate, 3 g dietary fiber, 39 mg cholesterol, 134 mg sodium, 201 mg potassium

Birthday Dinner

Clear Tomato Soup with Crab and Avocado (page 51)

Honeyed Alaskan Black Cod over Portobello Mushrooms and Sautéed Spinach (page 85)

Roasted Peaches and Blueberries with Vanilla Cake (page 266)

Joslin Choices: 3½ low-fat protein, 4 carbohydrate (3 bread/starch, 1 fruit), 1 fat, 530 calories (24% calories from fat)

Spiced Caramel Pears

Bonnie Stern, CANADA AM

TORONTO

When we picked up the phone to call Bonnie Stern, we knew we would be talking to a legend, but we did not know that we would also be speaking to a generous, personable, talented woman who willingly shares her expertise. She is the owner of the respected Bonnie Stern School of Cooking in Toronto and is the author of eight cookbooks, all of which have been national best-sellers. She writes a weekly column for the *Toronto Star,* contributes regularly to *Canadian Living* magazine, and produces a column for the James Beard Foundation Calendar and Newsletter.

Pears are a wonderful fruit that are often overlooked. Make sure your pears are fully ripe before cooking. Bonnie Stern calls for small pears here; if the ones you purchase are large, serve one-half per person.

6 pears, firm but ripe (preferably Bartlett or Bosc)
⅓ cup sugar
1 large lemon, thinly sliced
1 cinnamon stick, broken into 3 or 4 pieces

4 whole cloves
1 whole star anise
¼ cup port wine or orange juice
8 sprigs fresh mint

Cut the pears in half lengthwise. Scoop out the cores—a melon baller works well. You do not have to peel them.

Sprinkle the sugar over the bottom of a large skillet that will hold the pears all in one layer. Place on high heat and when the sugar starts to melt and brown, add the pears, cut side down, in a single layer. Arrange the lemon slices over the top and around the pears and scatter the spices over also.

Cook until the sugar browns well but be careful not to burn. Add the port or orange juice. Reduce the heat. Cook gently for 10 minutes. Cover the pan and remove from the heat. Let the pears rest, covered, for 30 minutes.

TO SERVE: Place 2 pear halves with cut side up on each of 6 plates. Drizzle the pears and plates with the syrup. Arrange a lemon slice on each pear and garnish each plate with the mint.

MAKES 6 SERVINGS

Joslin Choices: 1 carbohydrate (fruit)

Per Serving: 95 calories (5% calories from fat), 1 g total fat (0 saturated fat), 1 g protein, 24 g carbohydrate, 4 g dietary fiber, 0 cholesterol, 7 mg sodium, 272 mg potassium

Chocolate Grand Marnier Soufflé with Raspberry Coulis

Michel Bouchon, THE BALCONY

FORT WORTH, TEXAS

When Fran's husband ordered this dessert at the restaurant where Michel is not only the chef but also the owner, Fran thought that she would just have to look, but not taste. To her delight, when Michel arrived at the table to talk about being in this cookbook, he divulged that the recipe had been developed for a member of his family who has diabetes.

RASPBERRY COULIS:
¾ cup fresh raspberries

2 teaspoons butter
¼ cup plus 2 teaspoons sugar

1 tablespoon water
4 large egg whites, at room temperature
2 tablespoons good-quality cocoa powder
1 tablespoon Grand Marnier

TO MAKE THE RASPBERRY COULIS: In a food processor or a blender, puree the raspberries. Strain the mixture through a fine sieve to remove the seeds. Set aside.

Preheat the oven to 375°F. Lightly grease 4 1-cup individual soufflé dishes with the 2 teaspoons butter, including the rims. Sprinkle with the 2 teaspoons sugar. Set on a baking sheet.

Over medium heat, cook the ¼ cup sugar and the water until the mixture becomes thick and the bubbles are very small, but not golden-colored. Brush down any sugar crystals that form on the side of the pan with a wet pastry brush. Be careful; the mixture will be very hot.

Meanwhile, in a mixer, beat the egg whites until stiff. With the mixer set on low speed, pour the hot sugar mixture slowly on the beaten egg whites. Add the cocoa and mix well together. Add the Grand Marnier. Divide the soufflé mixture among the prepared dishes and tap the bottom of each dish with your hand to release any air bubbles. Bake for 12 minutes.

Immediately set the soufflés on 4 large dessert plates. At the table, insert a spoon into the center of each soufflé and spoon in a heaping tablespoon of the reserved Raspberry Coulis in the center. Serve at once.

MAKES 4 SERVINGS

Joslin Choices: ½ low-fat protein, 1½ carbohydrate (fruit)

Per Serving: 121 calories (17% calories from fat), 2 g total fat (1 g saturated fat), 4 g protein, 21 g carbohydrate, 2 g dietary fiber, 5 mg cholesterol, 56 mg sodium, 125 mg potassium

Baking with Sugar Substitutes

The main artificial sweeteners on the market today are aspartame, acesulfame K, saccharin, and sucralose. We frequently use sugar substitutes for all or part of the sugar requirements when baking and have tried every brand in the store. The newest, Splenda, is actually made from modified sugar molecules and has no calories. The manufacturer advertises that it can be used 1-to-1, that is 1 tablespoon of sugar substitute for each tablespoon of sugar in a recipe. We have found many substitutes to be quite sweet and frequently reduce the amount by up to one-quarter of the sugar called for. Older sugar substitutes tend to work well in recipes but not in cakes. If you are making a cake and using Splenda 1-to-1, add 1 teaspoon baking soda and ½ cup dry milk for every cup of the sugar substitute to make the cake more tender.

Le Soufflé Leger à la Pomme et Citron Vert
(Light Apple and Lime Soufflé)

Michel Guérard, LES PRÉS D'EUGÉNIE

EUGÉNIE-LES-BAINS, FRANCE

Chef Michel Guérard is known throughout Europe for his skills. When we asked him for a dessert that would fit our guidelines, he sent us this soufflé, which marries apples and limes to make a dessert that is truly French. He has taken classic techniques and made a dessert that we will enjoy over and over. *Merci,* Chef Guérard.

4 teaspoons softened butter
2 cups plus 2 tablespoons water
1½ ounces non-nutritive sweetener
2 5-ounce apples

zest and juice of 1 lime
2 large egg yolks
10 large egg whites
⅓ ounce non-nutritive sweetener

Preheat the oven to 400°F. Coat the insides (the dishes should be at least 1¾ inches high) of each of 4 individual soufflé dishes with 1 teaspoon of the butter.

In a pot, bring the 2 cups water and 1½ ounces non-nutritive sweetener to a boil. Stir until the sweetener is dissolved and the mixture forms a syrup. Remove from the heat and let cool.

Cut the apples in 4 pieces (do not peel or seed). Put in a pot with the remaining 2 tablespoons water. Cover and cook over low heat until the apples are cooked through, 10 to 12 minutes. Drain well and grind in a food processor or pass through a sieve. Cool.

Julienne the lime zest and blanch 3 times with boiling water. Place the zest in a bowl and cover with the syrup to preserve it.

Add the lime juice and egg yolks to the cooled apples. Remove the zest from the syrup and finely mince. Add the minced zest to the apple mixture. Discard the syrup. (Soufflés can be prepared to this point and refrigerated until time to bake if desired.)

Place the egg whites in a copper bowl or a mixing bowl and beat until they hold soft peaks. Add the ⅓ ounce non-nutritive sweetener. Gently mix one-quarter of the egg whites into the apple mixture, then carefully fold in the remaining egg whites. Pour into the prepared soufflé dishes and, with your thumb, wipe around the edge of the dishes in order to help the soufflés rise better.

Bake until lightly browned and puffed, about 7 minutes. Serve at once.

MAKES 4 SERVINGS

Joslin Choices: 1 medium-fat protein, 1 carbohydrate (fruit)

Per Serving: 152 calories (36% calories from fat), 6 g total fat (3 g saturated fat), 10 g protein, 16 g carbohydrate, 3 g dietary fiber, 117 mg cholesterol, 420 mg sodium, 221 mg potassium

Warm Mango Soufflé with Coconut Sauce

Kenny Kong, WESTIN PLAZA
SINGAPORE

Chef Kong is the executive pastry chef at this fine hotel located at the crossroads of Singapore's business, cultural, and shopping districts. What a wonderful way to enjoy this delectable fruit! Another time try the sauce on baked apples or fresh berries.

1 teaspoon unsalted butter
2 large firm, ripe mangoes
1 tablespoon finely ground white cornmeal
grated zest and juice of 1 large lemon
3 large egg whites
2 tablespoons light brown sugar

COCONUT SAUCE:
1/3 cup light coconut milk
1/3 cup skim milk
2 tablespoons sugar
1 tablespoon finely ground white cornmeal

Preheat the oven to 350°F. Lightly butter 6 1-cup soufflé dishes. Set on a baking sheet.

Peel and cut the flesh off 1 of the mangoes, discarding the seed. Puree the flesh in a food processor or a blender. Combine with the cornmeal in a small saucepan. Bring to a boil and add the lemon zest and juice. Remove from the heat and set aside. Peel and dice the flesh of the remaining mango, discarding the seed. Set aside.

Using an electric mixer on high speed, whip the egg whites with the brown sugar until the mixture forms stiff peaks. Gently fold into the puree mixture, then fold in the diced mango. Spoon the mixture into the prepared soufflé dishes and bake for 17 minutes until puffed and lightly browned.

While the soufflé is baking, in a small saucepan over medium heat, whisk together the coconut milk, skim milk, sugar, and cornmeal. Cook, stirring, until heated and slightly thickened. Remove from the heat.

TO SERVE: Place each soufflé dish on a dessert plate lined with a folded linen napkin. Transfer the Coconut Sauce to a serving dish. At the table, ladle 1 tablespoon of the sauce into the center of each soufflé.

MAKES 6 SERVINGS

Joslin Choices: 1 1/2 carbohydrate (fruit)

Per Serving: 106 calories (12% calories from fat), 2 g total fat (1 g saturated fat), 3 g protein, 23 g carbohydrate, 2 g dietary fiber, 0 cholesterol, 47 mg sodium, 189 mg potassium

Chai Rice Pudding

Bonnie Stern, CANADA AM
TORONTO

Chai refers to the mixture of aromatic spices used in this treat from Canada. Bonnie Stern writes, "This stovetop method of cooking rice pudding results in a very creamy rich texture, even though it is not really rich at all. On my stove, on medium-low heat, it takes 45 to 50 minutes to thicken, but the cooking time varies greatly on different stoves. But rest assured—it looks like a lot of milk at first, but I promise the pudding will thicken eventually."

½ cup short-grain rice
1 cup boiling water
1 teaspoon cornstarch
⅓ cup sugar
5 cups 2% low-fat milk
1 cinnamon stick, broken in half

10 white cardamom pods, bruised slightly
1 tablespoon grated lemon zest
¼ teaspoon grated nutmeg
1 teaspoon pure vanilla extract
1 teaspoon ground cinnamon

Place the rice and water in a saucepan. Bring to a boil, lower the heat, and cook gently, covered, for 10 minutes or until rice absorbs the water.

Meanwhile, combine the cornstarch with the sugar in a small bowl. Whisk in 1 cup of the milk and add the cornstarch-sugar mixture to the cooked rice along with the remaining milk.

Slowly bring to a boil. Add the cinnamon stick, cardamom pods, lemon zest, and nutmeg. Lower the heat and cook gently, covered, on medium-low or low heat, 45 minutes to 1 hour or longer, until the rice is creamy and the pudding has thickened. Add the vanilla. Try to remove the cinnamon sticks and cardamom pods or alert your guests that the whole spices are not to be eaten.

Divide among 8 ramekins or dessert bowls. Sprinkle each serving with a little cinnamon. Serve warm or cold.

MAKES 8 SERVINGS

Joslin Choices: 2 carbohydrate (bread/starch)

Per Serving: 159 calories (17% calories from fat), 3 g total fat (2 g saturated fat), 6 g protein, 27 g carbohydrate, 1 g dietary fiber, 11 mg cholesterol, 77 mg sodium, 256 mg potassium

Banana Pot Stickers with Mango Lime Sorbet and Roasted Pineapple

Michael Herschman, MOJO CAFÉ
CLEVELAND, OHIO

This is a popular dessert at this busy café where you might think you were dining in Greenwich Village in Manhattan if you did not get a glimpse of downtown Cleveland.

This is a dessert for special occasions. We thank Chef Herschman for offering such an elegant dessert recipe. You will have pot stickers and sorbet left over to enjoy at another meal.

POT STICKERS:
4 ripe bananas
2 tablespoons light brown sugar
¾ cup shredded unsweetened coconut
1 1-pound package 3-inch wonton wrappers

MANGO LIME SORBET:
4 large ripe mangoes, pitted, peeled, and chopped
finely chopped zest and juice of 2 large limes
4 cups cool water
2 cups granulated sugar
1 tablespoon vodka

ROASTED PINEAPPLE:
1 large ripe pineapple
2 cups fresh orange juice
½ cup granulated sugar
1 vanilla bean, split and scraped
2 tablespoons unsalted butter

1 tablespoon unsalted butter
1 cup fresh orange juice
¼ cup granulated sugar

In a mixing bowl, combine the bananas, brown sugar, and coconut. Using an electric mixer set on medium speed, beat until smooth.

On a flat surface, lay out 1 wonton wrapper. Using a pastry brush, moisten the edges with water. Place 1 heaping teaspoon of the banana mixture in the center of the wonton wrapper. Fold 1 corner to the opposite corner and press to seal the edges. Pleat the side folds of the pot stickers by pinching and twisting halfway.

Repeat, filling the remaining wonton wrappers. Store under a moist towel or refrigerate in a sealed container for up to 1 day.

TO PREPARE THE MANGO LIME SORBET: In a food processor or a blender, puree the mangoes, lime zest, and lime juice. Set aside.

In a medium saucepan, combine the water and sugar. Stir over medium heat until the sugar is dissolved. Remove from the stove and let cool.

Combine the mango mixture and the water-sugar mixture. Force through a fine sieve. Stir in the vodka. Chill the mixture, then freeze, following the directions on an ice cream/sorbet machine, or place in the freezer, stirring to break up the ice crystals every 20 minutes until the mixture freezes. Makes about 1½ quarts. (Any unused sorbet can be frozen in an airtight freezer container for up to 2 months.)

TO PREPARE THE ROASTED PINEAPPLE: Cut the top and bottom off the pineapple just before the curve of the fruit. Quarter and core lengthwise. Peel the quarters. Place the peeled quarters in a roasting pan.

Preheat the oven to 400°F.

Combine the orange juice, sugar, scrapings of the vanilla bean, and butter. Pour over the pineapple. Cover with foil and roast for about 1 hour until very caramelized. Remove from the oven and cool. Slice the pineapple into ¼-inch crosswise pieces. Set aside. (Any pineapple not used may be refrigerated in a sealed container to be used within 2 days.)

TO FINISH THE POT STICKERS: Melt the 1 tablespoon unsalted butter in a large nonreactive sauté pan over medium heat. Add 24 pot stickers, 3 per person, to the pan. When the bottom of the pot stickers begins to turn golden, add the 1 cup fresh orange juice and ¼ cup granulated sugar. Cover and turn the heat down to simmer the pot stickers for about 3 minutes, or until tender.

TO ASSEMBLE: Place a ¼-cup scoop of sorbet in the center of each of 8 large plates. Fan out 3 pot stickers on the side of each plate. Fan 3 slices of Roasted Pineapple over the pot stickers and spoon 2 tablespoons of the orange juice mixture in the sauté pan over all. Serve at once.

MAKES 8 SERVINGS

Joslin Choices: 4 carbohydrates (1 bread/starch, 3 fruit), 1 fat

Per Serving: 354 calories (13% calories from fat), 5 g total fat (3 g saturated fat), 3 g protein, 68 g carbohydrate, 3 g dietary fiber, 11 mg cholesterol, 145 mg sodium, 386 mg potassium

Joslin Choices (¼ cup sorbet only): 1 carbohydrate (fruit)

Per Serving: 54 calories (1% calories from fat), 0 total fat (0 saturated fat), 0 protein, 14 g carbohydrate, 0 dietary fiber, 0 cholesterol, 1 mg sodium, 31 mg potassium

Fresh Fruit Sorbet

Bill Wavrin, RANCHO LA PUERTA
TECATE, MEXICO

A haven for the body and soul, Rancho La Puerta is a favorite of Bonnie and her spa friends and our literary agent Loretta Fidel. Mostly vegetarian, the meals are prepared under the auspices of Chef Bill Wavrin. They are as beautiful to the eye as they are tasteful and satisfying to a discriminating palate.

    This is sure to be a crowd pleaser at your house when the temperature's soaring. It is so refreshing to see that healthy food tastes delicious!

1 large ripe banana, peeled and cut into several pieces

1 cup ripe strawberries, stemmed and quartered
1 cup fresh orange juice

Place all the ingredients in a food processor or a blender. Process until smooth. Transfer the mixture to a plastic freezer container and freeze, stirring to break up the ice crystals every 20 minutes until the mixture freezes firm.

TO SERVE: Scoop out into 4 dessert dishes and serve frozen.

MAKES 4 SERVINGS

Joslin Choices: 1 carbohydrate (fruit)

Per Serving: 72 calories (0% calories from fat), 0 total fat (0 saturated fat), 1 g protein, 17 g carbohydrate, 2 g dietary fiber, 0 cholesterol, 1 mg sodium, 328 mg potassium

Intense Lime Sorbet with Summer Berry Compote

Michael Leviton, LUMIÈRE
WEST NEWTON, MASSACHUSETTS

When *Food & Wine* went looking for the 10 best new chefs in the United States for the year 2000, they found chefs from Boston to Newport Beach, California. None is more applauded for his restaurant and French-influenced dishes than Michael Leviton. He and his wife Jill, who runs the front of the restaurant with precision and attention to every detail, make a meal at Lumière memorable. His philosophy for great food is ". . . simplicity, purity, and cooking in harmony with the seasons—if you pay attention to all those things, it's going to be difficult to screw up." Early in his career, this creative perfectionist trained with the best in New York at Le Bernardin, and with Daniel Boulud at Le Cirque. He also trained at Joyce Goldstein's acclaimed Square One and Ernie's in San Francisco.

INTENSE LIME SORBET:
½ cup water
1 cup sugar
1½ cups fresh lime juice

SUMMER BERRY COMPOTE:
2 tablespoons water
2 tablespoons sugar

2 cups fresh berries, any combination of
    strawberries, blueberries, blackberries, and
    raspberries
½ teaspoon fresh lemon juice

TO MAKE THE SORBET: Prepare a simple sugar syrup by combining the water and sugar in a saucepan. Simmer, stirring constantly, until the sugar dissolves. Cook and refrigerate in a closed jar until ready to use.

Combine the lime juice and simple sugar syrup. Freeze in an ice cream maker according to the manufacturer's directions or place in the freezer, stirring to break up the ice crystals every 20 minutes until the mixture freezes.

WHILE THE SORBET IS FREEZING, MAKE THE COMPOTE: In a medium sauté pan, heat the water and sugar until the sugar dissolves. Add the berries and lemon juice. Gently continue to heat until the berries are just warm. Remove from the heat and let cool.

TO SERVE: Divide the compote among 4 dessert plates. Top each with a ¼-cup scoop of the sorbet. Serve immediately. Freeze the remaining sorbet for another use.

MAKES 4 SERVINGS

Joslin Choices: 2½ carbohydrate (fruit)

Per Serving: 141 calories (2% calories from fat), 0 total fat (0 saturated fat), 1 g protein, 37 g carbohydrate, 2 g dietary fiber, 0 cholesterol, 3 mg sodium, 127 mg potassium

Joslin Choices (¼ cup sorbet only): 1½ carbohydrate (fruit)

Per Serving: 87 calories (0% calories from fat), 0 total fat (0 saturated fat), 0 protein, 23 g carbohydrate, 0 dietary fiber, 0 cholesterol, 1 mg sodium, 41 mg potassium

The Boss Comes to Dinner

Grilled Portobello Mushrooms over Mesclun with
  Fresh Herb Vinaigrette (page 72) •

Cumin Crackers (page 258) •

Rouget de Roche and Grilled Fresh Market Vegetables with
  Anchovy Sauce (page 206) •

Intense Lime Sorbet with Summer Berry Compote (page 278) •

Joslin Choices: 4 very-low-fat protein, 5½ carbohydrate (3 bread/starch, 2½ fruit), 2 vegetable, 2 fat, 700 calories (20% calories from fat) •

Raspberry Soufflés with Fresh Raspberry Sorbet

Carol McGavin, FROMAGERIE
RUMSON, NEW JERSEY

As we spoke to chefs, we found many had a great interest in learning more about how to cook for people with diabetes. Not only did Chef McGavin want to prepare a fantastic dessert, but she was willing to do research with the manufacturer of a newly marketed sugar substitute. Who is this talented and gracious woman? She was educated at Peter Krump's New York Cooking School. Before becoming executive chef at Fromagerie, she was the pastry sous-chef. She has won 25 ribbons in Culinary Arts and Baking in New Jersey and was the recipient of a James Beard Foundation scholarship in Pastry Arts.

Ranked one of the top restaurants in New Jersey, Fromagerie has been cited in *Gourmet* for its excellence. This French country inn–style restaurant has a long history of fine dining. It has hosted a James Beard Foundation benefit featuring the best-known chefs in America. Its menu is French in style but also features more contemporary cuisine.

These are soufflés you can make 6 hours ahead and put in the oven while your guests are finishing their main course.

FRESH RASPBERRY SORBET:
4 cups raspberry puree, seeds removed
Splenda to taste (optional)
4 to 6 ice cubes

SOUFFLÉS:
butter-flavored cooking spray
½ cup Splenda plus more for sprinkling
1 cup unsweetened raspberry puree, seeds removed

3 tablespoons Chambord (raspberry-flavored liqueur)
1 cup plus 1 tablespoon egg whites, at room temperature
2 tablespoons dried meringue powder (see Note below)
juice of ¼ large lemon
¼ cup light corn syrup
1 cup fresh raspberries, quartered
confectioners' sugar for dusting (optional)

TO MAKE THE SORBET: Place the puree in a blender. If the raspberries are not sweet, add Splenda to taste. Add the ice cubes and blend well. Freeze in an ice cream machine, following the manufacturer's directions, or place in the freezer, stirring to break up the ice crystals every 20 minutes until the mixture freezes firm. Keep frozen until ready to serve.

Spray 6 individual 8-ounce soufflé dishes with the cooking spray, including the rims, and lightly dust with Splenda, knocking out any excess. Set the dishes on a baking sheet.

TO MAKE THE SOUFFLÉS: In a large metal bowl, combine the raspberry puree and the Chambord. Place the bowl over a pan of simmering water and heat until warm and bright red. Keep warm.

In the bowl of an electric mixer fitted with a whisk attachment, combine the egg whites, meringue powder, and lemon juice. Whisk on medium speed until foamy and frothy.

In a heavy small saucepan, place the remaining ½ cup Splenda and the corn syrup over medium heat. Add a little water until the mixture forms a "wet sand"–like mixture, brushing down any sugar crystals on the sides of the pan with a wet pastry brush. Be careful; the mixture will be very hot. With the mixer set on medium speed, carefully pour the Splenda mixture into the egg whites in a direct slow stream between the whisk and the side of the bowl. When all of the Splenda mixture is added, increase the mixer speed to high and whisk until the mixture forms a meringue the consistency of shaving cream. Do not overwhip.

Remove the bowl of puree from the stove and place on a smooth work surface on top of a damp kitchen towel to keep the bowl from moving. Add one-third of the meringue mixture to the puree and, using a balloon whisk, gently fold in the mixture until no streaks of red are visible. Using a rubber spatula, fold half the remaining meringue into this mixture. Finally, fold in the rest of the meringue, then carefully fold in the raspberries.

Using a large pastry bag fitted with no tip (or a large self-sealing plastic bag, snipped at one corner), pipe the soufflé mixture into the prepared bowls, peaking them on top. (At this point, the soufflés may be made ahead and refrigerated up to 6 hours.)

Preheat the oven to 375°F. Place the soufflés in the oven for about 7 minutes, until puffed and firm to the touch. Remove the soufflés and place on individual plates. With a serrated knife, make a slight slit in the top of each soufflé and top with a ¼-cup scoop of the sorbet. Lightly dust with confectioners' sugar (if using) and serve immediately. Return any leftover sorbet to the freezer for another use within 1 month.

MAKES 6 SERVINGS

Joslin Choices: 1 very-low-fat protein, 2 carbohydrate (2 fruit)

Per Serving: 146 calories (3% calories from fat), 1 g total fat (0 saturated fat), 7 g protein, 29 g carbohydrate, 3 g dietary fiber, 0 cholesterol, 131 mg sodium, 231 mg potassium

Note: Dried meringue powder is available at cake decorating supply stores.

Soup of Apricot Jus with Fresh Fruit

Anselmo Ruiz, AMBRIA
CHICAGO

This classic and stylish restaurant has been rated one of the five best in Chicago. Chef Ruiz is Chef du Cuisine at Ambria and knows how to work magic in the kitchen. Although the restaurant has an elegant art nouveau dining room, the menu is planted firmly in the present. The restaurant received a 4-star rating from *Chicago* magazine, the *Chicago Tribune,* and the *Mobile Travel Guide,* as well as being celebrated in *Gourmet.*

1 quart water
¾ cup sugar
3 whole vanilla beans, split
3 whole star anise
2 pounds ripe apricots, pitted and peeled

6 cups fresh fruit—diced strawberries, whole raspberries, whole blueberries, or diced melon (cantaloupe, honeydew, Crenshaw, or watermelon), or a combination of any or all

Combine the water and sugar. Add the vanilla beans and star anise and stir over medium-high heat until the sugar dissolves and the mixture becomes a syrup. Remove from the heat and cool.

TO MAKE THE APRICOT JUS: In a food processor or a blender, puree the apricots. Strain through a fine sieve into the cooled syrup. Chill until ready to serve.

Place ½ cup of the fruit in each of 12 dessert dishes. Pour the apricot just over the diced fresh fruit. Serve cold.

MAKES 12 SERVINGS

Joslin Choices: 2 carbohydrate (fruit)

Per Serving: 196 calories (3% calories from fat), 1 g total fat (0 saturated fat), 2 g protein, 33 g carbohydrate, 4 g dietary fiber, 0 cholesterol, 9 mg sodium, 427 mg potassium

Zabaglione and Fresh Fruit

Terry Conlan, LAKE AUSTIN SPA AND RESORT
AUSTIN, TEXAS

Chef Conlan's excellent talent gives us this classic Italian dessert. Your guests will never know that they are eating the chef's fantastic spa cuisine.

3 cups evaporated skim milk
½ cup fat-free sweetened condensed milk
2 large eggs
½ cup egg substitute
2 teaspoons pure vanilla extract

2 tablespoons Marsala wine
4 cups sliced fresh strawberries or sliced peeled fresh peaches
½ ounce semisweet chocolate, grated

In the top of a double boiler over boiling water, combine and scald the milks. Gradually whisk some of the hot milk mixture into a bowl containing the eggs and egg substitute, then whisk all back into the milk mixture. Continue cooking, stirring, over simmering water until the mixture is thickened. Cool over ice, stirring. Whisk in the vanilla and Marsala.

Spoon alternate layers of the egg mixture and the fruit into 12 clear-stemmed glasses. Chill. Serve cold with a sprinkling of chocolate over each serving.

MAKES 12 SERVINGS

Joslin Choices: 1½ carbohydrate (½ fruit, 1 low-fat milk)

Per Serving: 136 calories (12% calories from fat), 2 g total fat (1 g saturated fat), 9 g protein, 20 g carbohydrate, 1 g dietary fiber, 39 mg cholesterol, 117 mg sodium, 404 mg potassium

Appendix 1:
Joslin Diabetes Center and Its Affiliates

Massachusetts

AYER
Joslin Clinic at
Deaconess-Nashoba Hospital
200 Groton Road
Ayer, MA 01432
978-784-9534

BOSTON
Joslin Clinic
1 Joslin Place
Boston, MA 02215
617-732-2400
joslin.org

NEEDHAM
Joslin Clinic at
Deaconess-Glover Hospital
148 Chestnut Street
Needham, MA 02192
781-453-5231

SPRINGFIELD
Joslin Diabetes Center
Affiliate at Mercy Hospital
299 Carew Street
Springfield, MA 01104
877-JOSLIN-8
413-748-7000

Connecticut

MYSTIC
Joslin Diabetes Center
Affiliate at Lawrence and
 Memorial Hospital
14 Clara Drive, Suite 4
Mystic, CT 06355
860-245-0565

NEW BRITAIN
Joslin Diabetes Center
Affiliate at New Britain
 General Hospital
100 Grand Street
New Britain, CT 06050
888-4-JOSLIN
860-224-5672

NEW LONDON
Joslin Diabetes Center
Affiliate at Lawrence and
 Memorial Hospital
50 Faire Harbor Place, Suite 2E
New London, CT 06320
877-JOSLIN-1
860-444-4737

TORRINGTON
Joslin Diabetes Center
Affiliate at Charlotte
 Hungerford Hospital
780 Litchfield Street
Torrington, CT 06790
860-489-0661

Florida

CLEARWATER
Joslin Diabetes Center
Affiliate at Morton Plant
 Hospital
455 Pinellas Street
Clearwater, FL 33756
727-461-8300

SAFETY HARBOR
Joslin Diabetes Center
Affiliate at Mease Countryside
 Hospital
3231 McMullen Booth Road
Safety Harbor, FL 34695
727-725-6283

Indiana

NEW ALBANY
Joslin Diabetes Center
Affiliate at Floyd Memorial
 Hospital & Health Services
1850 State Street
New Albany, IN 47150
888-77-FMHHS
812-949-5700

Maryland

BALTIMORE
Joslin Diabetes Center
Affiliate at University of
 Maryland Medical System
22 South Greene Street
Suite N6W100
Baltimore, MD 21201-1595
410-328-6584
888-JOSLIN-8

GLEN BURNIE
Joslin Diabetes Center
Affiliate at North Arundel
 Hospital
301 Hospital Drive
Glen Burnie, MD 21042
410-787-4940

New Jersey

LAKEWOOD
Joslin Diabetes Center
Education Affiliate at Kimball
 Medical Center
600 River Avenue
Lakewood, NJ 08701
732-886-4748

LIVINGSTON
Joslin Diabetes Center
Affiliate at Saint Barnabas
 Ambulatory Care Center
200 South Orange Avenue
Livingston, NJ 07039
973-322-7200

TOMS RIVER
Joslin Diabetes Center
Education Affiliate at
 Community Medical Center
368 Lakehurst Road, Suite 305
Toms River, NJ 08753
732-349-5757

New York

ELMIRA
Joslin Diabetes Center
Affiliate at Arnot Health
 HCFW
600 Fitch Street
Suites 202–203
Elmira, NY 14905
607-737-8107

SYRACUSE
Joslin Diabetes Center
Affiliate at SUNY Upstate
 Medical University
90 Presidential Plaza
Syracuse, NY 13202
315-464-5726

VALHALLA
Joslin Diabetes Center
Affiliate at Westchester
 Medical Center
Cedar Wood Hall
Lower Level CG 29B
Valhalla, NY 10595
866-456-7546

YORKTOWN HEIGHTS
Joslin Diabetes Center
Affiliate at Hudson Valley
 Hospital Center
225 Veterans Road
Suite 201
Yorktown Heights, NY 10598
888-HVHC-JOSLIN
(888-484-2567)
914-962-1320

Pennsylvania

MONROEVILLE
Joslin Diabetes Center
Affiliate at Forbes Regional
 Hospital
Forbes Lifestyle Center
Professional Office Building 2
2580 Haymaker Road
Suite 403
Monroeville, PA 15146
412-858-4474

PITTSBURGH
Joslin Diabetes Center
Affiliate at Western
 Pennsylvania Hospital
5140 Liberty Avenue
Pittsburgh, PA 15224
412-578-1724

South Carolina

FLORENCE
Joslin Diabetes Center
Affiliate at McLeod Regional
 Medical Center
121 South Evander Street
Florence, SC 29506
888-777-6965

Tennessee

CHATTANOOGA
Joslin Diabetes Center
Affiliate at Memorial Hospital
2525 de Sales Avenue
Chattanooga, TN 37404-3322
423-495-7970

Washington

SEATTLE
Joslin Diabetes Center
Education Affiliate at Swedish
  Medical Center
910 Boylston Avenue
Seattle, WA 98104-0999
888-JOSLIN-1
206-215-2440

West Virginia

JOSLIN DIABETES CENTER
Affiliate at St. Mary's Hospital
2900 First Avenue
Huntington, WV 25702
304-526-8363

Appendix 2:
Joslin Diabetes Center's Food List for Meal Planning

The exchange categories that follow are different from those of a few years ago because of a new understanding about how food is metabolized. Today, exchanges are grouped into Carbohydrate (bread/ starch, fruit, milk, and vegetables—when consumed in sufficient quantities), Protein, and Fat. This new method for exchanges allows for more individualized meal planning with your health care team, taking into account your lifestyle, food likes and dislikes, medical conditions, and goals.

Brand-name items and prepared foods are not included in the following list. If you wish to obtain a complete list, *Menu Planning—Simple!* is available from Joslin. Write to Publications, Joslin Diabetes Center, 1 Joslin Place, Boston, MA 02215, or call 617-732-2695 for ordering information.

Carbohydrate List

A carbohydrate serving (approximately 15 grams) may include a food choice from the fruit, milk, and starch categories. Vegetables are also carbohydrate but contain fewer grams of carbohydrate (5 grams) per serving, so if you are using carbohydrate counting as your meal-planning option, be sure to note the difference.

CARBOHYDRATE CHOICES

One choice provides:
Calories: 80
Protein: 3 g
Carbohydrate: 15 g
Fat: trace

Best choices: Whole-grain breads and cereals, dried beans, and peas. (In general, 1 bread choice equals 1 oz. of bread.)

BREADS

ITEM	PORTION
White, whole-wheat, rye, etc.	1 slice (1 oz.)
Raisin, unfrosted.	1 slice (1 oz.)
Italian and French.	1 slice (1 oz.)
"Light"	
(1 slice equals 40 calories)	2 slices
Pita	
Pocket, 6-in. diameter	½ pocket
Mini size.	1 pocket
Bagel	½ small (1 oz.)
English muffin	½ small
Rolls	
Kaiser or bulkie, hard.	½ small
Dinner, plain	1 small
Frankfurter.	½ medium
Hamburger.	½ medium
Bread crumbs	3 Tbsp.
Croutons.	3 Tbsp.
Taco shells, small	2 (+ 1 Fat)
Tortilla, corn, 6-in. diameter	1
Tortilla, flour, 7-in. diameter	1 (+ 1 Fat)

CEREALS

ITEM	PORTION
Cooked cereals	½ cup
Bran, concentrated	⅓ cup

STARCHY VEGETABLES

ITEM	PORTION
Corn	½ cup
Corn on the cob	1 small
Lima beans	½ cup
Mixed vegetables, with corn or peas	⅔ cup
Parsnips	½ cup
Peas, green, canned or frozen	⅔ cup
Plantain, cooked	⅓ cup
Potato, white	
Baked	½ medium or 1 small (3 oz.)
Mashed	½ cup
Sweet potato	
Mashed	⅓ cup
Baked	½ small or ½ cup (2 oz.)
Pumpkin	¾ cup
Winter squash, acorn or butternut	¾ cup

PASTA (COOKED)

ITEM	PORTION
Macaroni, noodles, spaghetti	½ cup

LEGUMES

ITEM	PORTION
Beans, peas, lentils (cooked)	½ cup

GRAINS

ITEM	PORTION
Barley, cooked	⅓ cup
Bulgur, cooked	⅓ cup
Cornmeal	2½ Tbsp.
Cornstarch	2 Tbsp.
Couscous, cooked	⅓ cup

ITEM	PORTION
Flour	3 Tbsp.
Kasha, cooked	⅓ cup
Millet, dry	3 Tbsp.
Rice, cooked	⅓ cup
Wheat germ	¼ cup = 1 carb + 1 low-fat protein

CRACKERS

Best choices: Lower-sodium products, i.e., saltines with unsalted tops.

ITEM	PORTION
Gingersnaps	3
Graham crackers, 2½-in. squares	3
Granola bar, low-fat plain	1
Matzoh or matzoh with bran	1 (¾ oz.)
Melba toast rectangles	5
Melba toast rounds	10
Popcorn: popped, no fat added	3 cups
*Pretzels	7 regular or 12 mini
*Saltines	6
*Snack chips:	
Baked potato or tortilla chips	15 small or 8 large (¾ oz.)
Social tea	4

FRUIT CHOICES

One choice provides:
Calories 60
Protein: 0
Carbohydrates: 15 g
Fat: 0

Best choices: Fresh whole fruit.
Be sure: To choose fresh, frozen, or canned fruit packed in its own juice or water with no added sugar.

ITEM	PORTION
Apple, 2-in. diameter	1 small
Apple, dried	4 rings

High in sodium.

ITEM	PORTION
Applesauce, unsweetened	½ cup
Apricots	
Fresh	4 medium
Canned	4 halves
Dried	7 halves
Banana, 9-in. length, peeled	½
Banana flakes or chips	3 Tbsp.
Blackberries	¾ cup
Blueberries	¾ cup
Boysenberries	1 cup
Canned fruit, unless otherwise stated	½ cup
Cantaloupe, 5-in. diameter	
Sectioned	⅓ melon
Cubed	1 cup
Casaba, 7-in. diameter	
Sectioned	⅙ melon
Cubed	1⅓ cups
Cherries	
Sweet fresh	12
Dried (no sugar added)	2 Tbsp.
Cranberries, dried (no sugar added)	2 Tbsp.
Currants	2 Tbsp.
Dates	3
Figs	
Fresh	2 small
Dried	1 small
Granadillas (passionfruit)	4
Grapefruit, 4-in. diameter	½
Grapes	15 small
Guavas	1½ small
Honeydew melon, 6½-in. diameter	
Sectioned	⅛ melon
Cubed	1 cup
Kiwi (3 oz.)	1 large
Kumquats	5 medium
Loquats, fresh	12
Lychees, fresh or dried	10
Mango	½ small
Sliced	½ cup
Nectarine, 2½-in. diameter	1 small
Orange, 3-in. diameter	1 small

ITEM	PORTION
Papaya, 3½-in. diameter	
Sectioned	½
Cubed	1 cup
Peach, 2½-in. diameter	1 small
Pear	1 small
Persimmon	
Native	2
Japanese, 2½-in. diameter	½
Pineapple	
Fresh, diced	¾ cup
Canned, packed in juice	⅓ cup
Plantain, cooked	⅓ cup
Plums, 2-in. diameter	2 small
Pomegranate, 3½-in. diameter	½
Prunes, dried, medium	3
Raisins	2 Tbsp.
Raspberries	1 cup
Rhubarb, fresh, diced	3 cups
Strawberries, whole	1⅓ cups
Tangerines, 2½-in. diameter	2 small
Watermelon, diced	1¼ cups

FRUIT JUICE

Be sure to monitor your blood glucose: Fruit juice may elevate blood glucose rapidly, especially when consumed on an empty stomach or with a small amount of food such as a snack. Limit your intake of juice to no more than 1 meal each day or to times when you are engaging in vigorous activity or treating a low blood sugar.

ITEM	PORTION
Apple juice, unsweetened	4 oz.
Cranapple, unsweetened	3 oz.
Cranberry, low-calorie	9 oz.
Cranberry, unsweetened	4 oz.
Grapefruit juice, unsweetened	5 oz.
Grape juice, unsweetened	3 oz.
Lemon juice	8 oz.
Orange juice, unsweetened	4 oz.
Pineapple juice, unsweetened	4 oz.
Prune juice, unsweetened	3 oz.

VEGETABLE CHOICES

One choice provides:
Calories: 25
Protein: 2 g
Carbohydrate: 5 g
Fat: 0

Best choices: Fresh or raw vegetables: dark green, leafy, or orange.
Be sure: To choose at least 2 vegetables each day.

We encourage: Steaming with a minimum amount of water. Portion listed is for cooked serving unless noted otherwise.

ITEM	PORTION
Artichoke	½
Asparagus	1 cup
Bamboo shoots	1 cup
Bean sprouts	½ cup
Beet greens	½ cup
Beets	½ cup
Broccoli	½ cup
Brussels sprouts	½ cup
Cabbage	1 cup
Carrots	½ cup
Cauliflower	1 cup
Celery	1 cup
Collard greens	1 cup
Eggplant	½ cup
Fennel leaf	1 cup
Green beans	1 cup
Green pepper	1 cup
Jicama, raw	½ cup
Kale	½ cup
Kohlrabi	½ cup
Leeks	½ cup
Mushrooms, fresh	1 cup
Mustard greens	1 cup
Okra	½ cup
Onion	½ cup
Pea pods, Chinese (snow peas)	½ cup
Radishes	1 cup
Red pepper	1 cup
Rutabagas	½ cup

ITEM	PORTION
*Sauerkraut	½ cup
Spinach	½ cup
Squash	
Spaghetti	½ cup
Summer	1 cup
Zucchini	1 cup
Swiss chard	1 cup
Tomato (ripe)	1 medium
*Tomato, canned	½ cup
Tomato juice or V8 juice	½ cup
*Tomato paste	1½ Tbsp.
Tomato sauce, canned	⅓ cup
Turnip greens	1 cup
Turnips	½ cup
Vegetables, mixed	½ cup
Water chestnuts	6 whole or ¼ cup
Wax beans	½ cup

Because of their low-carbohydrate and low-calorie content, the following *raw* vegetables may be used liberally.

Alfalfa sprouts	Lettuce, all types
Celery	Mushrooms
Chicory	Parsley
Chinese cabbage	*Pickles (unsweetened)
Cucumber	Pimento
Endive	Spinach
Escarole	Watercress

MILK CHOICES

Best choices: Nonfat or low-fat
Be sure: You take calcium supplements if you use less than 2 cups per day for adults, 3–4 cups per day for children.

* *These vegetables are high in sodium (salt). Low-sodium vegetables, juices, and sauces should be purchased if you are following a sodium-restricted diet. Fresh and frozen vegetables are lower in sodium than canned vegetables, unless the canned product states "low sodium."*

NONFAT SELECTIONS

One choice provides:
Calories: 90
Protein: 8 g
Carbohydrate: 12 g
Fat: 0

ITEM	PORTION
Canned, evaporated skim milk	½ cup
Nonfat buttermilk	1 cup
Nonfat milk (skim)	1 cup
½% milk.	1 cup
Nonfat plain yogurt.	¾ cup
Nonfat yogurt made with Aspartame	6–8 oz.
Powdered, nonfat milk, dry.	⅓ cup
*Sugar-free hot cocoa mix plus 6 oz. water	1 cup

LOW-FAT SELECTIONS

One choice provides:
Calories: 105
Protein: 8 g
Carbohydrate: 12 g
Fat: 3 g

ITEM	PORTION
1% buttermilk	1 cup
1% milk	1 cup
Yogurt, plain, unflavored.	¾ cup

MEDIUM- AND HIGH-FAT SELECTIONS

One choice provides:
Calories: 120–150
Protein: 8 g
Carbohydrate: 12 g
Fat: 5–8 g

---

* Most cocoa mixes do not provide the same amount of calcium as 1 cup of milk. Mixes that do provide the same amount should indicate on the label that the product contains 30% Daily Value for calcium.

The following milk items should be used sparingly due to their high saturated fat and cholesterol content.

ITEM	PORTION
2% milk	1 cup
Whole milk	1 cup

OTHER CARBOHYDRATES

DESSERTS

ITEM	PORTION	FOOD GROUP	GRAMS CARB	CAL
Angel food cake	½₂ of cake. .	2 carbs . . .	30 g . . .	160
Brownie, unfrosted. . .	2" square	2 carbs . . .	25 g . . .	205
		+ 1 fat		
Cake, frosted	2 oz.	3 carbs . . .	40 g . . .	285
		+ 1 fat		
Cake, unfrosted	2 oz.	2 carbs . . .	35 g . . .	205
		+ 1 fat		
Frozen yogurt				
Low-fat	½ cup	1 carb	17 g . . .	125
		+ 1 fat		
Fat-free	½ cup	1 carb	22 g . . .	80
Fat-free, no sugar added	½ cup	1 carb	18 g . . .	80
Ice cream:				
Regular	½ cup	1 carb	17 g . . .	170
		+ 2 fat		
Low-fat or fat-free	½ cup	1 carb	22 g . . .	80
No sugar added. . .	½ cup	1 carb	15 g . . .	125
		+ 1 fat		
Fat-free, no sugar added	½ cup	1 carb	19 g . . .	80
Pudding:				
Sugar-free	½ cup	1 carb	14 g . . .	80
Regular	½ cup	2 carbs . . .	29 g . . .	160

MISCELLANEOUS

ITEM	PORTION	FOOD GROUP	GRAMS CARB	CAL
Jam/jelly, honey, regular	1 Tbsp.	1 carb	13 g	80
Spaghetti sauce	½ cup	1 carb + 0–1 fat	10 g	125
Sugar	1 Tbsp.	1 carb	12 g	46
Syrup:				
Light	2 Tbsp.	1 carb	13 g	80
Regular	2 Tbsp.	2 carbs	27 g	160
Yogurt, fruited, regular	1 cup	3 carbs	45 g	240

"Free" Foods List

Be sure: The following foods contain very few calories and may be used freely in your meal plan. Items marked with an asterisk (*) are high in sodium; you should check with your health care provider or dietitian before using these products.

GENERAL

*Bouillon, broth, or
  consommé
Chewing gum, sugar-free
Cocoa powder
Coffee, tea
Cranberries
  (unsweetened)
Extracts
Gelatin mixes, sugar-free
Herbs, seasonings, spices
Lemon/lime juice
Lemon/lime/orange rind

Noncaloric diet soft
  drinks, unsweetened
  seltzer waters
*Pickles (unsweetened)
Postum (limit to
  3 cups daily)
*Soy sauce, steak sauce
*Hot pepper sauce, taco
  sauce
Unprocessed bran
  (1 Tbsp.)
Vinegar

Many fat-free choices contain one or more types of sugar. The amount of sweetener is small; however, the portion used should be no more than the amount listed on this page or no more than 20 *calories per serving,* approximately 3 times per day. Always read the labels carefully, and consult your health care provider or dietitian if you plan to use these items regularly.

Protein List

Best choices: Very-low-fat or low-fat selections.
Be sure: To trim off visible fat. Bake, broil, or steam selections with no added fat. Weigh your portion after cooking.
We encourage: Portions to be the accompaniment rather than the main course.

VERY-LOW-FAT SELECTIONS

One choice provides:
Calories: 35–45
Protein: 7 g
Carbohydrate: 0
Fat: 0–1 g

ITEM	PORTION
Beef:	
96% fat-free ground beef	1 oz.
*Cheese products, fat-free	1 slice; 3 Tbsp
*Cottage cheese, fat-free or 1%	¼ cup
*Ricotta, 100% fat-free	1 oz.
Dried beans, cooked	½ cup = 1 protein + 1 carb
Egg substitute, plain (less than 40 calories per serving)	¼ cup
Egg whites	2
Fish and seafood: fresh or frozen cod, flounder, haddock. halibut, trout, tuna (packed in water); clams, crab, lobster, scallops, shrimp, imitation crabmeat	1 oz.
Poultry: chicken, turkey, or Cornish hen—white meat only and skinless	1 oz.
Game: venison, buffalo, ostrich	1 oz.
Ground turkey, 93–99% fat-free only	1 oz.
*Hot dogs, 97% fat-free	1 oz.

* High in sodium.

ITEM	PORTION
*Luncheon meats:	
95% fat-free pastrami, ham, turkey ham,	
turkey bologna	1 oz.
*Turkey sausage, 97% fat-free	1 oz.

LOW-FAT SELECTIONS

One choice provides:
Calories: 55
Protein: 7 g
Carbohydrate: 0
Fat: 2–3 g

ITEM	PORTION
Beef:	
ground beef, 90% fat-free	1 oz.
USDA Select or Choice grades of flank,	
round, sirloin, T-bone, tenderloin cuts	1 oz.
*Cheeses:	
Cottage cheese, 4.5% fat	¼ cup
Mozzarella, light	1 oz.
Slices	1 oz.
Fish:	
herring, uncreamed or *smoked	1 oz.
Oysters, salmon, sardines (packed in tomato	
or mustard sauce*)	1 oz.
Ground turkey or chicken, lean only	1 oz.
*Hot dogs, 90% fat-free	1
*Luncheon meats, 90% fat-free	1 oz.
Pork: lean only, center loin, fresh ham, loin chop,	
tenderloin	1 oz.
Poultry:	
Chicken or turkey, dark meat, no skin, or white meat	
with skin	1 oz.
Tofu	3 oz.
*Turkey sausage, 90% fat-free	1 oz.
Veal: lean, trimmed only, loin chop, round	1 oz.

MEDIUM-FAT SELECTIONS

One choice provides:
Calories: 75
Protein: 7 g
Carbohydrate: 0
Fat: 4–5 g

ITEM	PORTION
Beef: chipped, chuck, flank steak; hamburger	
(90% fat-free), rib eye, rump, sirloin,	
tenderloin top and bottom round	1 oz.
*Cheese:	
part-skim mozzarella, part-skim ricotta,	
farmer, Neufchâtel, reduced-fat cheddar,	
reduced-fat Monterey Jack, reduced-fat	
Swiss	1 oz.
*Parmesan, Romano	3 Tbsp.
†Egg	1
Egg substitute with 60–80 calories	
per ¼ cup	¼ cup
Lamb, except for breast	1 oz.
*Luncheon meat, "light" (turkey bologna,	
turkey pastrami)	1 oz.
Peanut butter	1 Tbsp. = 1 protein + 1 fat
Pork, except for deviled ham, ground pork,	
and spare ribs	1 oz.
Turkey bacon	2 slices
Turkey franks, "light"	1 = 1½ protein
Veal, except for breast	1 oz.

High in sodium.
† Egg yolks are high in cholesterol. Limit consumption to 3 or 4 per week.

High in sodium.

HIGH-FAT SELECTIONS

One choice provides:
Calories: 100
Protein: 7 g
Carbohydrate: 0
Fat: 6–8 g

Be sure: Because of their high saturated fat and cholesterol content, the meat choices listed below should be used sparingly

ITEM	PORTION
Beef:	
brisket, club and rib steak, *corned beef, regular hamburger with 20% fat, rib roast, short ribs	1 oz.
Cheese, regular:	
*blue, Brie, Cheddar, Colby, *feta, Monterey Jack, muenster, provolone, Swiss, *pasteurized process	1 oz.
Fish, fried	1 oz.
Hot dog, regular, beef or pork	1 oz. = 1 protein + 1 fat
Lamb: breast	1 oz.
*Luncheon meats, regular: bologna, bratwurst, braunschweiger, knockwurst, liverwurst, pastrami, Polish sausage, salami	1 oz.
Organ meats:	
liver, heart, kidney	1 oz.
Pork:	
*deviled ham, ground pork, spareribs, *sausage (patty or link)	1 oz.
Poultry:	
capon, duck, goose	1 oz.
Veal: breast	1 oz.

High in sodium.

Fat List

One choice provides:
Calories: 45
Protein: 0
Carbohydrate: 0
Fat: 5 g

Best choices: Monounsaturated fats. However, limit total amount of all types of fat.
Be sure: When using low-calorie version of fat choices, use amounts equal to 45 calories for 1 serving.

MONOUNSATURATED FATS

ITEM	PORTION
Avocado, 4-in. diameter	⅛
Oils: canola, olive, peanut	1 tsp.
*Olives:	
Black	9 large
Green	10 large
Nondairy creamer:	
Liquid	2 Tbsp.
Reduced-fat liquid	5 Tbsp.
Nuts (unsalted):	
almonds	6
Brazil	2
cashews	6
filberts (hazelnuts)	5
macadamia	3
mixed	6
peanuts, Spanish	20
peanuts, Virginia	10
pecans	4 halves
pignolia (pine nuts)	1 Tbsp.
pistachio	12
Sesame seeds	1 Tbsp.
Tahini	2 tsp.

High in sodium.

POLYUNSATURATED FATS

ITEM	PORTION
Margarine: stick, tub, or squeeze	1 tsp.
Reduced-fat	1 Tbsp.
Mayonnaise	1 tsp.
Reduced-fat	1 Tbsp.
Nuts: walnuts (unsalted)	4 halves
Oils: corn, cottonseed, safflower, soy, sunflower	1 tsp.
Salad dressings, regular:	
*French, 1,000 Island	1 Tbsp.
*Italian	2 tsp.
Creamy types	2 tsp.
Salad dressings, reduced-calorie:	
*Italian	2 Tbsp.
*Ranch	1 Tbsp.
Red wine vinegar and oil	2 Tbsp.
*Seeds: pumpkin, sunflower (unsalted)	1 Tbsp.

High in sodium.

SATURATED FATS

ITEM	PORTION
*Bacon, cooked	1 strip
Butter:	
Stick	1 tsp.
Whipped	2 tsp.
Reduced-fat	1 Tbsp.
Chitterlings	2 Tbsp. (½ oz.)
Coconut, shredded	2 Tbsp.
Coffee whitener, liquid	2 Tbsp.
Coffee whitener, powder	4 Tbsp.
Cream:	
Half and half	2 Tbsp.
Heavy	1 Tbsp.
Light	1½ Tbsp.
Whipped	1 Tbsp.
Whipped, pressurized	⅓ cup
Cream cheese:	
Regular	1 Tbsp.
Reduced-fat	2 Tbsp.
Oils: coconut or palm	1 tsp.
*Salt pork	¼ oz.
Shortening or lard	1 tsp.
Sour cream:	
Regular	2 Tbsp.
Reduced-fat	3 Tbsp.

High in sodium.

Appendix 3:
Sources

If you are unable to locate some of the ingredients used in the recipes in this book, you can order them through the mail-order and Internet sources listed below. This list is provided as a service and is not an endorsement of these companies by Joslin Diabetes Center or the authors.

D'Artagnan
399-419 St. Paul Avenue
Jersey City, NY 07306
(800) 327-8246

most fowl, wild game, smoked game

Dean and Deluca
Mail Order Department
560 Broadway
New York, NY 10012
(800)-221-7714
www.deananddeluca.com

grains, beans, dried chiles, canned chipotle peppers, specialty foods

Frieda's Finest
(714) 826-6100
www.friedas.com

vegetables by mail including banana leaves, jicama, and chayote plus a good selection of fresh chiles

Hog Wild Specialties
www.hogwild.ab.ca

wild boar

Oakville Grocery
(800) 973-6324
www.stores.yahoo.com/oakvillegrocery

verjus, specialty oils and vinegars

Pendery's
(800) 533-1870
www.penderys.com

dried chiles and spices

Appendix 4:
Metric Conversion Table

Liquid Measurements

¼ teaspoon = 1.25 milliliters
½ teaspoon = 2.5 milliliters
1 teaspoon = 5 milliliters
1 tablespoon = 15 milliliters
2 tablespoons = 30 milliliters
¼ cup = 60 milliliters
⅓ cup = 80 milliliters
½ cup = 120 milliliters
⅔ cup = 160 milliliters
¾ cup = 180 milliliters
1 cup = 240 milliliters
1 pint (2 cups) = 480 milliliters
1 quart (4 cups) = 960 milliliters (.96 liters)

Equivalents for Dry Measurements

AMOUNT	FINE POWDER (FLOUR)	GRAIN (RICE)
1 cup	140 grams	150 grams
¾ cup	105 grams	113 grams
⅔ cup	93 grams	100 grams
½ cup	70 grams	75 grams
⅓ cup	47 grams	50 grams
¼ cup	35 grams	38 grams
⅛ cup	18 grams	19 grams

AMOUNT	GRANULAR (SUGAR)	SOLIDS (BUTTER)
1 cup	190 grams	200 grams
¾ cup	143 grams	150 grams
⅔ cup	125 grams	133 grams
½ cup	95 grams	100 grams
⅓ cup	63 grams	67 grams
¼ cup	48 grams	50 grams
⅛ cup	24 grams	15 grams

Oven Temperatures

	FAHRENHEIT	CELSIUS	GAS MARK
Freeze water	32°F	0°C	
Room temperature	68°F	20°C	
Boil water	212°F	100°C	
Bake	325°F	160°C	3
	350°F	180°C	4
	375°F	190°C	5
	400°F	200°C	6
	425°F	220°C	7
	450°F	230°C	8

Equivalents for Weights

1 ounce = 30 grams
4 ounces = 120 grams
8 ounces = 240 grams
12 ounces = ⅔ pound = 360 grams
16 ounces = 1 pound = 480 grams

Equivalents for Length

1 inch = 2.5 centimeters
6 inches = ½ foot = 15 centimeters
12 inches = 1 foot = 30 centimeters
36 inches = 3 feet = 1 yard = 90 centimeters
40 inches = 100 centimeters = 1 meter

Index

(Page numbers in *italics* refer to the photo insert.)